DARKNESS OVER GERMANY

DARKNESS OVER GERMANY

A Warning from History

E. Amy Buller

Foreword by Professor Kurt Barling

Afterword by Edmund Newell

Interlink Books

An imprint of Interlink Publishing Group, Inc.
Northampton, Massachusetts

This edition first published 2018 by

INTERLINK BOOKS
An imprint of Interlink Publishing Group, Inc.
46 Crosby Street, Northampton, MA 01060
www.interlinkbooks.com

Published simultaneously in Great Britain by Arcadia Books.
Originally published by Longmans, Green and Co. 1943
Republished with permission
© Erica Jephson and Maureen O'Neil 2017
Kurt Barling's Foreword © Elisabeth Sandmann Verlag, Munich 2015

Photo credits: Cumberland Lodge © (photo of Cumberland Lodge);
By kind permission of Maureen O'Neil and Erica Jephson (photos of Amy
Buller in her office, Amy Buller at Eastbourne 1917, and Amy Buller with
Fr Talbot); All other photos © Archiv Elisabeth Sandmann Verlag.

ISBN 978-1-62371-996-8

Library of Congress Cataloging-in-Publication Data available

Typeset in Jenson by MacGuru Ltd

Printed and bound in the United States of America

CONTENTS

Foreword   vii
Preface   xxxvii

Prologue   1

PART I
1. The Dilemma of a German Teacher   5
2. A Catholic Priest Faces Conflict   17
3. German Officer on Counteracting Nazi Teaching   24
4. German Officer and Alternatives to Hitler   30
5. German Officer after Munich   38
6. Nazi Labour Front   45
7. German Women Oppose Nazi Education – I   52
8. German Women Oppose Nazi Education – II   55
9. German Foreign Office Proper   67
10. Von Ribbentrop's Nazi Foreign Office   83
11. Dilemma of a Civil Servant and Young German
    Airman   95
12. The Courage of Children who Opposed Nazis   106
13. In the Early Days – A Study in Contrasts   116
14. Tribute to Ambassador   122

PART II
1. The Tragedy of the Unemployed Student   127
2. A Professor Meets the SS at Midnight   136
3. The Professor Discusses Nazi Philosophy and
   Students – I   142

4. The Professor Discusses Nazi Philosophy and
   Students – II   150
5. Austrian Priest and Nazi Heresies   155
6. Two Sides of the Same Story – Hitler Jugend and
   Lutheran Pastors   162
7. Swiss Barrister and Nazi Mythology in Western
   Civilization   174
8. A Traitor to Himself   183
9. Religious Foundations of Nazi Speeches   194

PART III
1. Nuremberg   203
2. Hitler   214

Epilogue   229

Afterword   239
Notes to Foreword   249

FOREWORD

On June 5, 2016, shortly after the publication of the first German translation of this book (translated as *Finsternis in Deutschland*), myself, my publisher Elisabeth Sandmann, and the Director of Cumberland Lodge, Dr. Edmund Newell, were invited to present a copy of this new German edition to Her Majesty Queen Elizabeth II at Windsor.

The Queen took on the role of patron of Cumberland Lodge from her mother, who had been instrumental in the creation of this educational foundation by Amy Buller in the splendour of Windsor Great Park. The vision was to make it a place for young people and experts to come together to discuss and learn about the challenges facing the world. The King (George VI) and Queen (known later as the Queen Mother) had gifted the use of this former royal residence to Buller's foundation in 1947.

I think most people recognise that during her long reign Queen Elizabeth II has encountered more fascinating and important people than probably anyone else on the planet. It was clear from our exchange that Amy Buller made a very great impression on her during the many years Her Majesty and her family knew Buller. Over 40 years after Buller's death, I submit that is not an insignificant fact in understanding the power, intensity and purposefulness of Buller's character.

In 2017 Cumberland Lodge celebrated its seventieth anniversary. It continues to pursue Buller's vision sharing expertise and youth and hold a special conference exploring the challenges of extremism that we continue to face in our times. The anniversary coincided with the first new English edition of the book since its original publication in 1944.

Launching the book at St. Paul's Cathedral, Dr. Rowan Williams, the former Archbishop of Canterbury, chose to highlight the spread of populism, nationalism and extremism in current times and the lessons we might learn from the experiences of German people in the 1930s, as recounted in *Darkness over Germany*. He described Buller's work, underpinned by her Christian faith, as "*a really remarkable book by a very remarkable woman*".

Williams explored the spiritual vacuum that had emerged in the inter-war period in Germany and the risks to a generation growing up in that environment and seeking a mythical "problem-solver" to meet their needs. Williams sought to draw parallels with our current vexed and polarising political discourse, identifying the consequences of the collapse of consensual politics, and lamented a renewed unwillingness to argue, negotiate and compromise to reach a political settlement. He warned that talk of a crisis tends to produce a crisis, and that political optimism is often the most effective way of defeating intolerance.

The Queen, accompanied by the Duke of Edinburgh, was presented with a copy of the new English edition in a small ceremony at Cumberland Lodge in July 2017, pleased to learn that the message of '*learning how to disagree well*' presented by Buller in her book still resonated with modern readers. Now this American edition brings Buller's arguments to a new audience in tumultuous times.

The journey of reigniting this book began for me in 2014. I personally knew the ethos and culture of the Lodge; I had first visited the place as a PhD student at the London School of Economics (LSE) in 1984, which involved stimulating discussions long into the night, lubricated by intelligent company and red wine. I have travelled a long way with this work since late 2014 when I was asked to give a lecture at Cumberland Lodge. Never did I imagine then that Queen Elizabeth would take a personal interest in the book. It gives me immense pride and satisfaction to know that Buller's work can once again be considered as a means to explore the world we want to live in, rather than the one that we must inevitably exist in.

Now considered an expert, I could not pass up the opportunity to address a group of young LSE undergraduates.[1] I took the opportunity of my visit to discuss the origins of Cumberland Lodge with its programme director and he reacquainted me with Amy Buller's story. We searched for a rather weary copy of her book and I read the introduction with an open mind and a keen spirit.

I was born in 1961, when the Second World War was still part of the dominant British narrative of national survival and rebirth. Recovery from that conflict was still shaping the global political economy and stirring passions across Europe, as the Cold War teetered on the brink of a new hot one with the building of the Berlin Wall.

As a young boy I had a very close relationship with my English grandfather and a more distant one with my German one. Like all young children, and perhaps boys in particular, I was keen to know what each had done during the war. This was still difficult territory to navigate in my early years.

In England the public talk of the war was always filled with a mixture of pride and nostalgia with occasional overtones of regret. But it was never the regret of a loser, rather that of personal loss and economic devastation. My mother's father had served in the British Royal Navy and although he didn't like talking about his war experiences very much, when he did it was with a sense of quiet satisfaction that his duty had been done and he was part of the generation that defeated Nazism. He never hated Germans and one of his heroes incidentally was another German, Karl Marx.

With my German family it was altogether different. Asking what they did in the war was always more challenging. First of all there was a language barrier, so I had to rely on my father's interpretation of his father's war to find out if and how much his family had supported the National Socialists. How on earth did the Nazis take control? What did our family do to stop it? Or even more grievous was the silence that so many young Germans faced when so many of my generation asked, why did you take part? The responses were often a mixture of self-justification, confusion, excuses and suppressed guilt.

In my family's case my grandfather did get involved. This information was not kept secret, as in some families, neither was it boasted about – just stated as fact. Unemployment was high, politics was rotten, Germans wanted certainty and hope. My father's father joined the Party and eventually put on a soldier's uniform and fought on the Eastern Front. He is long departed but the question of 'guilt by association' still remains as part of the DNA of the German lived experience.

In America and Europe many of those who fought Germany nevertheless sought to forgive Germans after the conflict was over. The war has left many modern Germans with a sense of regret and shame over what was done in their names but which their forebears failed to heed or avert. My family and father were perhaps overwhelmed by the propaganda of Goebbels, the hope the pageantry and pomp appeared to offer, the appeal of patriotism wrapped up in a sense of encirclement, a togetherness against a hostile world, and something else that is becoming familiar today – the blatant twisting of the truth for no better reason than to secure opportunistic advantage.

For me Buller's account is a sobering reminder of the dangers inherent in any populist movement. It warns too that we can never assume that any of us are immune to the kind of political naivety or self-deception that my father was honest enough to admit to and was plagued by his whole adult life.

These questions have ruminated in the German part of my psyche for nearly fifty years. Every now and then in my subconscious search for clearer explanations of this past, a new discovery shines a fresh light on this uncertain memory which continues to shape modern Germany and Europe. I, like many Germans, am always searching for credible reasons for such an incredible catastrophe of Germany's own making. One of the great strengths of modern Germany is that it continues to confront that past. Many recognize that the deep legacy of living through Nazism is not yet over.

Buller's book held up a mirror to the context of my own lecture addressing modern Islamist terrorism. In the original edition in 1943, A. D. Lindsay's foreword to *Darkness over Germany* neatly summed up how I felt this text might still resonate with the challenges we face today – extremism and a descent into madness. In 1943 he wrote,

It was in about 1934 when she told me that she had again been in Germany and had been seeing a good deal of men and women who were bitterly opposed to the Nazis. Many had told her of their isolation and how much they would like to meet men and women from England but added, 'You will not be allowed to talk to us unless you allow the Nazis to talk to you first'.[2]

I scoured Internet sites for out-of-print books and fortunately found one dropping through my letterbox within the week. In it I felt I heard voices from the wilderness, intimate voices from a distant world that spoke to me of betrayal and broken-heartedness but also of blindness and idealism leading to Europe's greatest twentieth-century catastrophe.

Would these voices be heard in the same way in Germany, I wondered? My German publisher, Elisabeth Sandmann, wondered too.

To get a better understanding of the context of Buller's writing, it was important to explore the Buller archive housed at St. Antony's College, Oxford. This gives an insight into the Anglo-German world in which Buller shaped her ideas. Using these original sources to inform my interpretation of the book, I believe that Buller's work makes a unique contribution to long-standing questions about how ordinary Germans dealt with the darkness of fascism as it descended on Germany.

The archive is a reflection of her persistence and strong networks both within the UK intelligentsia and German intellectual circles. She was certainly considerably more than what one rather dismissive academic said of her: some schoolteacher who did a few exchanges to Germany. In the voices of ordinary Germans (captured by an Englishwoman), *Darkness over Germany* is a testament to the failure to prevent a catastrophe. It is not an exhaustive book but it is insightful and may put a fresh spin on a familiar story for readers.

I certainly believe those reading these voices can be reconnected to a more nuanced narrative of the past; not to absolve any sense of guilt but to give a voice to those who did not have the courage to fight and instead remained resolutely silent. Buller recognised that the creeping totalitarianism of the Nazi regime left many Germans feeling alone.[3] How might that memory resonate with many people across the world today?

The book's enduring message

We live in troubled times and we are looking for answers in a world of uncertainty. Sometimes there are clues from the past that can guide us. Lord David Ramsbotham, Buller's godson, has argued that she believed that identifying national strengths and weaknesses, with regard to the protection and projection of core values we wish to maintain, must involve constructive dialogue between generations.

The book comes at a time when Germany has been reassessing its grim past to understand it more deeply and frame a modern German identity. In Europe we stand at another historic juncture. Refugees from conflicts in the Middle East have reached Europe in unprecedented numbers, adding to the fears of 'Islamisation' stoked by political movements like *Pegida*. Politicians and activists often descend into cliché, half-truths and modern myths underpinned by a deep intolerance to 'foreigners' not seen in Germany for a generation.

But it also comes at a time when political discourse has shifted towards the narratives of nationalism and populism. An age when emotion can trump reason in political debate, where politicians can claim that expert opinion is hindering the political decisions that need to be made. An age in which politicians spend a lot of time shaping a political discourse that suggests they have simple answers to complex problems.

The election of President Trump has had a dramatic effect on American political discourse. The turbulence over a modern presidential term has rarely been higher. The re-emergence of a populist political culture may have many causes, but it is certainly a force that Liberals cannot ignore. In Britain they misjudged the referendum vote, which has charted a path to Brexit from the European Union. In France politicians of the Nationalist Front National are making sizeable gains in the popularity stakes. For so long an outsider party, it is now very much shaping political debate as a credible force.

In Turkey the president and his supporters have made opposition more difficult and have silenced opponents, including many journalists, with imprisonment. These are no longer tolerant times and the divisions in politics are less susceptible to the compromise and consensus of the recent past. In fact the polarisation of political debate and therefore the style of uncompromising governance is very much de rigueur.

Amy Buller – theological beginnings

But let's return to the life and times of the author of *Darkness over Germany*.

Ernestine Amy Buller was born in 1891 in London. Great Britain was still at the heart of an empire on which the sun never set. Amy and her older sister moved to South Africa as children and she only returned to England in 1911, aged twenty. Her fascination with Germany began as soon as she returned to Europe, where she travelled around the country and learned about its culture and history between 1912 and the outbreak of the Great War in 1914. By then she had returned to London and enrolled at Birkbeck College where she became one of a handful of women to graduate in 1917. This was a world long before women's liberation and feminism, in which women were mostly seen and not heard in polite circles. In the corridors of power and influence, men called the shots. Women had still not been given the vote in elections!

Buller was raised in a religious home, in the Baptist tradition. She converted to Anglo-Catholicism whilst undertaking her studies at Birkbeck. This was to have a significant impact on her involvement in the great debates of the times and particularly helped shape the networks she would build among Britain's senior clergy for the rest of her life. Not long after the end of the Great War she joined the staff of the Student Christian Movement[4] and it was through the SCM that she met powerful mentors like William Temple, who would later become the Archbishop of Canterbury.[5] It proved a vibrant forum for the debates that emerged out of that catastrophic conflict.

The surge of interest in politics, ethics, philosophy and religion amongst students was fuelled by the trauma and tumult engulfing Europe. The younger generations who had fought the Great War were keen to build new alliances and find ways to make it truly the war to end all wars. In that climate the fashion for 'fellowship groups' thrived, providing forums in which men and women could come together to discuss the major issues of the times.

The SCM was not only a forum for debate but also for activism. In the years immediately following the war it enabled Buller to gain firsthand knowledge of Czechoslovakia and other parts of Europe like Denmark and France as they underwent radical political change. It is easy to forget that this was a time of tumultuous upheaval and revolution in Europe too. Revolution in Russia sparked a refugee crisis that the Church responded to, and Germany also had become a violent political battleground.[6] Buller was involved in organizing debates and it was this valuable experience with the SCM that shaped her honest and collaborative approach to public discourse for the rest of her working life.

Buller quickly gained a reputation as a woman of clear convictions and deep faith, and the SCM fostered the diplomatic talents she would so effectively deploy in years to come. She also displayed an idealistic streak which ten years hence encouraged her to try and replicate the fellowship approach in her Anglo-German discussion groups. The philosophy was simple – that people should not just meet, but if possible live and work together for a few days to deepen their understanding of their differences in human terms, not simply through rational academic debate.

Buller was not from a monied family and so she soon decided she needed paid work. Despite being invited to study theology at Oxford University, she turned down the life of a theologian. Instead, the qualities she had displayed as part of the collective leadership of the SCM stood her in good stead for the vacant role of warden at Liverpool University's women's-only residential hall. The position

gave her an academic berth that was to begin her lifelong association with university education, although it was not to become a life
of scholarship. By the time she arrived in Liverpool, Buller nevertheless had experience, administrative confidence and a reputation
as a principled fighter.

Darkness over Germany is not a traditional academic book and I'm
sure it was never intended to be. I think instead Buller wanted to
adopt a more accessible journalistic and impressionistic style, so that
it became a book informed by her German experiences and widely
read rather than a piece of academic research read by a handful of
professors. As we shall see later, it attracted unusual readers.

Buller's German mission?

As Germany experienced its own revolutionary and counter-revo-
lutionary struggles after the armistice in 1918, it became clear to the
British establishment that radicalism in France, along with revolution in Russia[7] and a defeated Germany could eventually spill
across the English Channel. Britain had an Empire to preserve, a
monarchy to protect and a determination not to be dragged into
the European tumult.

After the signing of the Treaty of Versailles in 1919, Buller was
one of many intellectuals drawn into these discussions, principally
through her roles within the SCM. She was beginning to nurture a
strong personal network of powerful churchmen and intellectuals.

When the Nazi Revolution began in the early 1930s, Buller's
facility with the German language and her knowledge of German
culture made her a natural person to undertake the delicate work
of finding out what was really happening in Germany with Adolf
Hitler's appointment as chancellor.[8] It is quite possible that her
principal mentor Archbishop Temple, who from the outset supported her development of what became known as the Anglo-German discussion groups, was in fact the instigator of them. Temple
gave his patronage to the venture and was an active sponsor of
Buller's new mission, writing in support of her efforts to establish

links with the German Foreign Office from 1935 onwards.

Part of the support for this German engagement came from a sensibility within the English establishment that Versailles[9] had been an unjust treaty and was partly responsible for the popular support for Nazism. Buller found herself in the company of Lord Philip Lothian[10] and other Liberal-minded Establishment figures and academics like the vice-chancellor of Oxford University, A. D. Lindsay.

Buller herself continued with her frequent trips, and in a letter to the German ambassador to London, Baron Leopold von Hoesch, in July 1935, she first outlined the desire to take a group of educationalists to Germany. She clearly had sufficient interest from fellow Britons to suggest that assembling a group of serious intellectuals to go to Berlin would be easy. As she later explained in a briefing to the first travelling party, the purpose of the German engagement was straightforward.

> The object is one of friendly enquiry by a group of people who are deeply concerned to further understanding between England and Germany, and who hope that a small contribution to that understanding may be made by asking for an opportunity to be given for them to listen to exponents of the main trends of thought under National Socialism.[11]

1935 was the beginning in earnest of her mission to set up these Anglo-German discussion groups. They were structured and organized in line with the practice at SCM conferences, and although not religious in character Buller always insisted in correspondence with her German counterparts that the groups should be independent of the State and free from political interference. Buller could only really guarantee this on the British side, and it must have been obvious from the start that Nazi officials would never allow her to dictate who the participants on the German side would be. They were, after all, in the midst of a Nazi revolution.

With the full support of Ambassador Hoesch, Buller was able to organize a full study conference in Berlin in September 1935 under the patronage of A. D. Lindsay and Archbishop Temple.[12] The group that finally assembled in the lavish surroundings at the Kaiserhof Hotel in Berlin consisted of dozens of eminent Nazi thinkers, educators and diplomats alongside a high-powered delegation of British intellectuals.[13]

Buller ensured that topics as wide-ranging as political economy, political philosophy, the nature of the State, the civil service, education and the role of women were on the varied agenda.

Among those attending this first *Studienwoche* was the chief Nazi ideologue Reichsleiter Alfred Rosenberg. It seems the Nazi Party leadership was particularly keen to impress the English in its search for allies. Rosenberg tried hard in his keynote speech to paint a picture in which the Nazi movement could justify its reasoning for a clear break with the past. It played to the sensibilities that Germany had suffered great hardship and needed a complete realignment across German society after the failures of the Great War.

> It is quite clear that the German revolution is in many things a declaration of war to lives and customs that were valid before the Great War. To us it seems natural that after the great and fateful event of the World War, the people could not go back to their homes and simply take up their old lives as if nothing had happened.[14]

Rosenberg's speech must have tried to set the tone of the event. But other evidence demonstrates even at this point the convivial gathering could not disguise the rampant anti-Semitism that had become rife in Nazi circles. It undoubtedly caused some of the English delegation to wonder why the Nazis were so successful and what the consequences for Europe might be. It's perhaps no accident that this first, largely successful visit took place just a week before the notorious Nuremberg Laws were passed in 1935, which began to strip Jews of their inalienable rights, possessions and standing in German society.

Buller and her sponsors used the success of the Kaiserhof visit to press on quickly for a second. The plans developed to hold further events either in Berlin or London. Buller herself even talked of visiting the Nuremberg Party Congress in 1935, to further the informal talks with the Nazi leadership to pursue this aim.

Already there were those amongst the British group who were suspicious of how their event was being potentially manipulated and even bugged by the Gestapo.[15] Despite these reservations the English recognized the Anglo-German forum might become a useful way to explore just how much opposition and criticism the Nazis would entertain. It might help gauge if the party itself would end up as an absolute dictatorship.

Despite the political climate in Britain becoming considerably more hostile to the Nazi regime, Buller along with Lord Lothian had established in their own minds a rationale for their continued efforts. The openness of the forum was dealt a major blow with the death of Ambassador Hoesch[16] in late 1935 and the arrival of von Ribbentrop as the Nazi Ambassador to St. James.[17] Nevertheless the intensity of the planning for these reciprocal visits grew.

In meetings and correspondence with Ambassador von Ribbentrop, Buller continued to follow the rules of diplomatic contact. Sometimes the ingratiating tone of her letters makes a modern reader's toes curl, but in truth it was the only way she could guarantee the Anglo-German discussion groups' continued acceptability to the Nazi leadership. The next successful visit took place in 1936 directly after the Berlin Olympics. It was carefully planned, much larger and included a wider range of high-profile academics. But from 1937 organizing visits to Germany started to get much harder. Buller was conscious that public discussion of the venture, particularly in the British press, might compromise the support of Nazis like von Ribbentrop who were quite clearly in it for the propaganda gains. Without his patronage her Anglo-German venture was increasingly a dead duck, and she must have realized that she would have less and less control over any agenda on visits to Germany.

Very few of our German friends knew until they arrived in the room who we were and what our purpose was and I was unable to let my British group know anything except three names before they actually arrived in Berlin, which showed their trustfulness that this thing was worth doing. But I have been strongly urged this time to see that both the German and British groups are better informed before our actual meetings take place.[18]

By 1937 Buller realised that she was walking a propaganda tightrope. On the one hand, it was hard to avoid the realization that the Nazi organizers were manipulating the group's agenda. On the other hand, Buller was also well aware that she needed to avoid negative publicity of the events in the British press, which was ratcheting up its hostile commentary on the Nazis. It may well have been that as a woman and outsider Buller had to fight to be heard, but it possibly made it difficult for her to listen too.

As well as these organized formal visits Buller continued making other regular, informal visits to friends in Germany, and she would have sensed the deterioration in the ability of Germans to voice their criticism openly. Nonetheless, she persisted with the venture and was supported by some of the German career diplomats with whom she exchanged copious correspondence. Perhaps they believed that the venture might continue to exercise a moderating influence on relations between the two countries as the Nazi leadership became more strident in its philosophy and actions.

Antipathy from the press meant that allegations of appeasement of such an overtly militaristic dictatorship began to circulate. Of course, appeasement became the British government's official diplomatic position, but there was a very strong backlash led by Winston Churchill, which prompted several prominent supporters of the Anglo-German discussion groups to openly criticize continuing with the venture.

Buller stuck to her plans doggedly, even after the Austrian Anschluss in 1938. She had retained the support of a number of the people associated with the British side of the venture, including Archbishop Temple and – albeit with increasing reluctance – Lord Lothian. But times were becoming fraught with the growing international militancy of the Nazi regime. For Buller in England it must have become frustratingly difficult to maintain any officially sanctioned conversations with the Nazi regime.

Her principal political patron, Lord Lothian,[19] eventually pulled out of the conference planned for Easter 1938, arguing that 'It would be a profound mistake for one who had been publicly so identified with the German case as myself to go to Berlin at this moment'.

The conference never took place and instead it was organized for several prominent Nazi officials to visit Oxford, Lord Lothian's country mansion Blickling Hall and London, where they met members of the Labour Party. Reports from the time suggest these events were used to continue the attempts to persuade the Nazis of the dim view the English took of their treatment of the Jews and other persecuted minorities, as well as the increased suppression of freedom.[20] By now of course the Nazi leadership were not for turning.

There is plenty of evidence Buller was hostile to the Nazis outlook, but felt it imperative to continue to work with their leadership to foster a manageable relationship between Germany and England. With hindsight it was a forlorn hope and some have suggested it displayed a lack of political nous or even outright naivety on her part.

But Buller was not alone in her generation in trying to seek desperate alternatives to war, as the British government's policy of appeasement turned out to be. There is sufficient evidence that she persisted because of her belief that greater fellowship could avert a fresh conflict between Germany and England.

In a letter to the director of Hamburg University, Dr. Adolf Rein,[21] in which she is plainly trying to resurrect a new meeting in Germany for Easter 1939 after the failures of 1938, Buller demonstrates that hope is ebbing to avert conflict between the two countries she so clearly loved.

> Before our frontiers close against one another and all our efforts and longing for a better understanding between our nations get lost once more in a deadly struggle … I would make a plea that through all of the tragic suffering that is ahead, we and you should keep alight our profound conviction, built on a knowledge of one

another's countries and personal friendship, that war between Germany and England is an unmitigated tragedy and that when the time comes those of us who are still alive will undaunted try once more to build bridges out of a terrible wreckage.[22]

Against the backdrop of Neville Chamberlain's failed Munich agreement and the German invasion of Czechoslovakia in March 1939,[23] it is hard to see why else Buller would have persisted with such desperate attempts to organize an event in Berlin for Easter 1939. With hindsight it's hard not to feel that her continuing associations with the Nazi high command must have increasingly cast Buller in an unfavourable light in England.

Her idealism was being overwhelmed by *realpolitik*. Buller may even have been slightly obsessed with the religious foundation of Nazism to the point where she willfully suppressed the immediate sense of political disaster that was looming over Europe.

The last small Nazi delegation to visit London, as part of these Anglo-German discussions, arrived in March 1939 and included the head of the German Women's organization Fuhrerin Gertrud Scholtz-Klink.[24] Scholtz-Klink's quasi-religious speech captures the way in which leading Nazis had subverted the interests of Germany and the Germans to the will of Adolf Hitler.

The foundation of every state is the family, as created by nature; the stronger and healthier it is, the stronger is the State too. This makes it axiomatic that the relationship between man and wife forms the foundation of a nation and cannot only be self-centered ... but that there must stand above them a third, greater aim of duty: the nation into which they have both been placed ... After many periods of splendor in the course of centuries Germany has now been through fourteen years when, instead of ideals rooted in the community and realized in the nation, a Marxist-Bolshevist philosophy entirely foreign to us preached an outlook based on utter individualism and so brought a proud people conscious of its own character to slow decay ... Our leader Adolf Hitler saved us from this fate; he has helped us to recover the good in ourselves and to see every German as a brother. In a national renaissance such as this there is no difference of the sexes, for neither men nor women alone could tread this path since in true communities the sexes always tend to supplement each other … Risen in the community which will testify to future generations how all Germans found the way back to their proper selves thanks to their greatest son, Adolf Hitler.

Scholtz's speech in London is a strong illustration of how confident and righteous the Nazis believed their ultimately deeply flawed cause to be. Whilst it is hard to see Buller signing up to such a vision for women, these were strange and idealistic times. In London it was clear the Nazis had cemented their hold on German society and they firmly believed theirs was a civilizing mission.

As late as July 1939 Buller was still involved in protracted correspondence with the German Embassy in London, enquiring whether her official invitation to the Reichsparteitag in Nuremberg could be assured. Incredibly she received a response wishing her 'happy holidays' just days before the Nazis invaded Poland and war was declared between the two countries.

In modern-day parlance Buller had persisted in talking to the extremists until it was no longer credible after war was declared on 3 September 1939. But as we shall see, in the midst of the conflict she insisted on pursuing her mission to present the importance of understanding the ideas that had radicalized German youth in particular, so that the Allied governments could consider alternative strategies to deal with the enemy once it was militarily defeated.

Liverpool calling – Buller's mission transformed

At the outbreak of war, Buller was back with her students at Liverpool University. Whilst the 'phoney war'[25] persisted, between the invasion of Poland and the Battle for France in 1940, there was little she could do with her knowledge of Germany other than regale her students with stories of her friends whose lives had been affected by Nazism. But as the bombing of British cities escalated beyond the London Blitz after September 1940, and the war showed every sign of spreading as Germany launched offensive after offensive in Russia, Scandinavia, Africa, the Middle East and Southern Europe, Buller began to turn her attention to the need to figure out how to deal with Germany and the Germans who survived once the war was over.

The war had almost certainly turned a corner in the minds of the British by the time she was writing *Darkness over Germany*. Until mid-1942 the darkness had threatened to envelop Britain too. Whilst the British had the support of the United States in aid, it was not until after the attack on Pearl Harbor in December 1941 that the Americans entered the war as a combatant nation.

The British press was quick to capture the mood change and reported a series of events on the battlefield that conveyed encouraging progress on the fight against Nazism. In January 1942 Adolf Hitler announced that Germany had entered a phase of total war that made it clear to the Allies as a whole, and German sympathizers in particular, that a negotiated settlement was no longer possible with Hitler in charge. Only the total capitulation of Germany would end the war.

There was also a public mood shift amongst the Allies in June 1942, in the aftermath of the assassination of Reinhard Heydrich in occupied Czechoslovakia. On the orders of Hitler the Nazis set about exterminating the Czech village of Lidice in retaliation, when it was discovered that it was the home of Heydrich's assassins. When this was eventually reported in the allied press, what started as a Nazi propaganda exercise in terror turned into a propaganda victory for the Allies. After Lidice, no one could doubt the need to utterly defeat Nazism. [26]

In a 1942 lecture by Buller she recognizes that the Germany she knew was being pulled inexorably towards the edge of the abyss. It seems to have re-galvanized her efforts to influence the debate in the circles of power she still had access to, on how to shape British relations with Germany when the war was finally over.

Hitler's recent speech means the end of any real law and order in Germany and henceforth Himmler's men may take sudden action against anyone, and both among civilian and army people any suspect may be arrested. Dr. 't Hooft says there is a real danger that considerable numbers drawn from just the elements of German life with which we would wish to negotiate and see back in control may get wiped out if Hitler does decide to hit out on the home front as savagely as some anticipate once he knows the end is approaching.[27]

It is worth comparing this report of events in Europe with the words in the prologue to *Darkness over Germany*, which Buller had already started work on in 1942. It illustrates the strength of her conviction and explains how her initial mission to prevent war needed refocusing on a post-war mission to win the peace.

I record these stories to emphasize the need for youth and those who plan the training of youth to consider carefully the full significance of the tragedy of a whole generation of German youth who, having no faith, made Nazism their religion.[28]

Buller was no fool and recognized that good government needed strong debate even at a time of war, as she pointed out in the same lecture outlining the purpose of her book.

The object of this book is to raise questions which are significant and which I believe need careful consideration by more than Cabinets. Rather to stimulate thought and discussion than to suggest answers but while holding primely that the task, in fact the only task at the moment is to win the war. I am convinced that includes understanding what happened in Germany. It is not a soft plea for soft terms but rather a settlement which will punish the guilty and that must necessarily involve not only punishing some guilty men but I think it is essential for the German youth to witness the march in of troops from all the occupied allied lands for a time at least.[29]

Her lectures and her book are perhaps examples of how Buller felt she could best challenge the views of her most strident male critics, like Lord Vansittart. Her work drew on the character and determination shepherded during her SCM days in the 1920s. She would have needed such fortitude in abundance arguing against the prevailing wisdom of dealing ruthlessly and punitively with Germany and the Germans.

> The kind of thing people like Vansitard [sic] encourage seems to me not only to be a gift to the Nazis for whipping up the last ounce of strength but they do indicate not a vision of reconstruction in Europe but a nightmare of further conflict and deepened destruction.[30]

Buller wrote a book to remind her audience of the humanity at stake. And however much her faith was being challenged, it was that faith that probably sustained her in this thankless mission. She didn't share what she described as a British war aim of 'killing the Germans rather than understanding them'. She wanted a corrective to that simplistic discourse.

More than seventy years since its publication, it is this human aspect that stands the test of time. The authenticity and richness of the voices of the Germans that Buller knew personally, and whose opinions she relayed empathically in her book, reflect her profound understanding of what has been referred to latterly as the German trauma.[31]

Buller herself always believed once the war was underway that she was seen in some quarters as somewhat of an apologist for Germany, although her public lectures, as we have already seen, voice a more nuanced perspective.

In a letter to one of her friends she confided that she thought Lord Vansittart had placed her on some kind of blacklist at the beginning of the war, which had prevented her from being allowed by MI5 to lecture troops. She put this down to her trips to Germany to talk with Nazis in the 1930s as well as the publication of *Darkness over Germany*.[32] Eventually, her friends in high places helped ensure this mistaken view did not prevail and prevent her from taking part in German reconstruction.

It is important to remember that this book was published in England when censorship was rigorous and sympathy for the plight of Germans was at an all-time low. There were few English people as well placed as Buller was in 1943, plugged in both to the Establishment in England and with a wide exposure to leading Nazis up until 1939. This dual knowledge allowed her to offer a unique view of Germany at the time. Buller's book remains a strong indication of her strength of character and the powerful sponsors who helped get her insights heard.

Although the voices presented in this book are mediated by Buller and often impressionistic, they still make compulsive reading because they are allowed to stand largely on their own without contextualizing commentary. Many of the interviews were anonymized in case the Gestapo got hold of the names and retaliated against the individuals.[33]

For those hostile to any contact with official Germany after the Munich Agreement in 1938, it would have been easy to characterize Buller as an appeaser.[34] But Buller's was a view shared at the heart of the Establishment. It is a view often overlooked in the history of the period, and although difficult to quantify, it may well have had an effect on the magnanimity with which Churchill and others approached the eventual task of reconstruction. As we shall see presently, by early 1944 Buller's book and ideas managed to reach the very top of the Establishment.

What were Buller's politics?

We have no firm answers as to why the book was last published in 1945. Perhaps it was a narrative the British occupation authorities didn't want explored? Perhaps Germany in 1945 was not a place where it could be told?

In some ways Buller's book should be judged on simple merits.

It is a book written and published in Britain in the middle of a war that was not yet won, by a woman with strong links to the British Establishment that was deeply empathetic to Germans.

From the outset of this German venture there were those who harboured serious doubts about Buller's attitude to the Nazis. For some she seemed too sympathetic to the idealism in the National Socialist (NS) movement. Her empathy for the impact of change on the lives of ordinary Germans seems to have been her real motivation, and through the latter 1930s her correspondence reveals her hostility to what she called the Nazi 'gangsters' at the commanding heights of the regime. It is improbable that such a devout woman would have deliberately reported her interviews inaccurately.

But to really appreciate Buller's reach and informal influence you need to understand who was listening to her. There is one particular twist in her post-war emergence as a grande dame of the Higher Education establishment in Britain that reveals her back-channel influence. It is the story of how Buller came to establish her own educational foundation, St. Catherine's, at Cumberland Lodge in Windsor Great Park. It became (and remains) linked with LSE and other institutions that employed the great public intellectuals in 1940s and 1950s Britain.

Shortly after the book was published, one of Buller's clergy friends Edward Woods, as the Bishop of Lichfield, had the rather quaint and intriguing duty of drawing up appropriate reading material for the Queen of England, Queen Elizabeth, married to George VI.[35] He put *Darkness over Germany* on the list. We are not privy to what the Queen immediately thought, but she was sufficiently interested to ask to meet Buller herself.

The meeting took place at Buckingham Palace in March 1944, just before the Nazi wonder weapons began to rain down on London, and Buller used the occasion to plant the seed that her ambition was to build a college. If her nerves got the better of her during her Royal meeting they had recovered sufficiently in her letter to the Queen after her visit. As she writes, Buller appears a little overwhelmed by the interest shown by the Queen, who clearly warmed to her ideas and indicated in person her continued support.

> May I be allowed to say how deeply honoured I am to have been granted an audience by Your Majesty and how profoundly inspiring it is to know of your sympathy and understanding of the problems of the younger generation on whom so much responsibility for rebuilding the world must rest.[36]

At the end of the war Buller continued her lecturing to troops (by now the reservations of MI5 had been overcome) and to German prisoners of war based in camps around the United Kingdom. At the same time she was bending the ear of every person of influence, standing and deep pockets she knew, to secure her ambition of setting up the college.

Queen Elizabeth appears to have continued to take an interest in the developments. Buller meanwhile was pursuing an endless number of fruitless leads.

Fortunately for Buller, her assistant, Elizabeth Elphinstone, was also associated with the royal household. It seems just when Buller had run out of hope of ever getting the right support for the foundation, Queen Elizabeth's active interest led to discussion with King George VI, and ultimately to the bequest of the former royal residence to start Cumberland Lodge.

The royal couple remained involved in the college long after it was founded. This whole saga offers a window onto another view England took of Germany, one that has not been without controversy in Britain from then until now. It runs counter to the simple popular narrative that Germany of the Third Reich equals universal bad and Britain equals a just cause.[37]

Buller's more nuanced view was easily overlooked in the period when the British government and military were determined to fight on to an unconditional surrender against a corrupt, brutal and almost messianic Nazi regime. Of course, it is indisputable that by 1944 the Nazis were in the midst of committing unspeakable crimes against humanity.

Perhaps in today's world Amy Buller would have become a politician. After all, her book was a not-so-subtle manifesto of what ought to be done at the end of the war. Not an easy position to take, argue and maintain in a world where men made all the decisions about governance and war.

We shouldn't overlook the historical reality of women in public discourse at the time. Women had only just been given the vote in Britain and there were few prominent women in public life and even fewer close to the circles of power and influence. In Britain, women were virtually non-existent in the University Academy, in politics and in the church hierarchy. This makes Buller's contemporaneous view of Nazi Germany all the more fascinating precisely because she was involved in all these circles. Perhaps she identified that the most natural place for a woman to freely express and disseminate her views was in the permanence of the written word.

In some ways the book reveals Buller at war with her own conscience. Living through a second world war had a profound impact on Buller's own sense of faith (not unlike many devout Christians) and she was prone to question just how much faith in Christianity had been undermined by both these twentieth-century wars. The book is as much about a loss of faith in Christianity as it is about the rise of the Nazis and their false gods. Buller's biographer wrote,

> She saw the falsehoods of the Nazi idols, but while she realized the need for a true God, she seemed to admit to herself that men were not going to agree together on that God. She came to believe therefore, as many said of her, 'in the search'.[38]

Buller certainly was not a hostage to political ideology. She understood the Hitler myth as a way of Germans expunging the humiliation of the Versailles Treaty and the pain that had resulted from the destitution visited on Germany as a consequence. As this rather curt observation notes, 'It has been well said when men are drowning they will not be very particular about the type of rope that picks them up'.[39]

But no book like this, soaked as it is in the ethos of the times, should be taken at face value. The 1930s were an intense political period, emerging from the Great War and a Great Depression. It is easy to forget that people in those times approached the politics of 'communism' and 'fascism' through a different lens.

Immediately following the Great War it was liberal democracy that had a crisis of legitimacy and certainly many people, including in Britain, were attracted to one or the other, communism or fascism. Those within the establishment in Britain saw the rise of communism as an existential threat and fascism as a potential bulwark against it, if not in Britain at least in continental Europe. In Britain a prominent Labour politician, Oswald Moseley, founded the British Union of Fascists, which for a time attracted large numbers of supporters in their Blackshirts.[40]

It is worth noting here the original distributor of *Darkness Over Germany*, the Right Book Club. This organization was set up by a number of those on the Right as an antidote to Victor Gollancz's Left Book Club which had so successfully published cheap versions of political tracts from the Left to arm workers with evidence. There is no suggestion here that Buller was influenced by this political debate, but even if Buller herself wasn't overtly political, not in any case a political activist, her book cannot be said to be devoid of a political meaning. The Right Book Club will have surely weighed this up.

What did the book achieve?

One of the difficulties with assessing this book is that so little came after it by way of Buller's own writings. This makes it hard to place it in a context of a scholarly canon of Buller's work. Nor is it a scientific piece of work that subsequent historians could labour over and test her footnotes and sources. This has perhaps subsequently made it far easier to be dismissive of the book's contribution to understanding 1930s Germany and its people.

Unlike Sebastian Haffner[41] in his 1940 book *Germany: Jekyll and Hyde*, Buller did not dwell on Hitler himself; she was certainly no expert on the dictator and devotes just a few pages to him. She limits her observations to suggesting Hitler was the beneficiary of the German people's anxiety and a deep malaise arising from the parlous state of the Germany economy. Buller certainly didn't believe Hitler was the instigator of that need for change. *Darkness over Germany* demonstrates Buller was much keener on trying to explain the sensibilities of the ordinary people she had befriended and encountered and how they had become seduced or trapped by the Hitler Myth.

It is not a new observation that many Germans were full of gloom at the outbreak of war, unlike the fervent patriotism in 1914. But read today, Buller's book presents us with authentic voices from that pre-war period of German optimism that was already tinged with fear and foreboding. This puts in a different light the more positive support that grew after the war began and Hitler's armies achieved repeated blitzkrieg victories – particularly after the fall of Paris in June 1940 – when more and more Germans did warm to the Nazi military successes. By then resistance by individuals was futile or fatal.

Darkness over Germany is also not concerned with the conceptual condition of the nation-state, but rather the state of mind of young Germans in particular and how in the future they could be made less vulnerable to extremism. Buller wanted to foster the idea that an absence of critical thinking in Germany had allowed academics to become easy bedfellows with political determinists and extremists. She makes the case that the universities need to be the bulwark of civilization, underpinning its values and defending an open society. This is in fact the philosophy she used to underpin the educational foundation she created at Cumberland Lodge in 1947 and which still projects this ethos today.

Ultimately, Buller's thesis in the book is that it would be foolhardy to fight a war without considering the peace; Britain and her allies couldn't simply identify an enemy without considering how they would properly engage with them once they were defeated. It is a warning from history of how we must pay close attention to populists and even extremists in order to work out how we are to deal effectively with the narratives of fear they often peddle.

Why now?

Edmund Burke, the Anglo-Irish statesman, author and philosopher, who despite sitting in the House of Commons supported the patriots against an over-bearing King George III, recognized the righteousness of the American revolution. He quite famously wrote, "those who don't know history are doomed to repeat it."

After nearly seven decades of relative peace and the prevalence of liberal democracy in most Western states, Europe is in danger of abandoning the political vision of the founders of the European Coal and Steel Community. That cooperation agreement resulted from a need to restore equilibrium after a passionate and deadly struggle which left millions dead. In America, too, the benefits of post-war stability are giving way to a clamour for greatness without a clear idea of what that is beyond the nostalgia it promotes.

In short, the culture that grew to support democracy is fraying at its edges as the attributes of democracy are whittled down to a simplistic proposition that it rests solely on majority decisions and the collective self-interest of a population. In this context, the language of debate becomes increasingly polarised and ever more tied to election cycles.

In a growing number of places, it seems this new spirit is connected with a nostalgia for so-called strong and characterful leadership. It plays to the tune of media celebrity and shares certain characteristics with earlier times when voters had dwindling confidence in a broad range of historic institutions which had once offered attractive and credible narratives of improving standards of living. These hopes were later dashed by failing economies and high unemployment, where workers became separated from meaningful activity and from a sense that as individuals they could make a blind bit of difference in their destiny. In short, it brought on disillusionment.

To be clear, this book is not about Nazi atrocities. It couldn't be; it came too early in our understanding of the Holocaust, even though it was abundantly clear that the SS, Wehrmacht and Gestapo were all up to their necks in atrocities by 1943.

What it *is* about, is living through and coping with turbulent times. There are examples of modern atrocities aplenty, and the rise of intolerance and national sentiment driven by emotion rather than reason is polluting political discourse almost everywhere. It is perhaps wise just now to look back to deepen our understanding of how easily it is to divide opinion and mobilize hostility against a particular group with an appeal to nationalism, despite that group not really being a significant cause of national troubles. That didn't and doesn't stop them being scapegoated as such.

Beyond this introduction, the book follows the layout of the original. It is not presented as an academic text and should hardly be judged by those exacting standards. It is a very personal book based on conversations Buller had with friends and contacts in Germany, as their nation was consumed by its intoxication with National Social-ism. Buller lends an ear to the voices of the Nazi faithful, the indif-ferent, the agnostics, the opportunists and those who knew their card was marked by a regime they detested. The voices Buller illuminates help to show this in a very raw and emotional way.

But make no mistake; of all the British overtures to understand the Nazi philosophy and the people who undertook to support and uphold it, Buller's Anglo-German discussion groups had a privileged view precisely because they had access to the movers and shakers in the Nazi movement. Buller also had access to the zeit-geist because of the numerous personal visits she made to people like schoolteachers, university directors, public servants, priests and ordinary men, women and children who celebrated or strug-gled against the impact of National Socialism on their private and public lives. Nazism succeeded because so many people saw the benefits and little of the harm of joining in.

So we hear from the teacher who worries about politics creeping into the classroom and the senior teaching staff who lament the loss of independence from the state and freedom from political interference. She explores the motives of the Catholic priest who is able to challenge the state with a simple urging of the Bavarian greeting of 'Gruss Gott' rather than 'Heil Hitler' but is blacklisted as a result by local Nazi bigwigs and even imprisoned briefly.

Buller explores the plight of women who want to protect their children and others who see no harm in the Nazi movement's approach to womanhood. She recognizes the fear of talking openly in company as the network of spies grew stronger, embedded in each apartment block in many communities.

Perhaps because she was a teacher Buller had a close affinity with the preoccupations of the student generation. In chapter one she explores the ethical dilemmas facing Walter and Wilhelm and although the context differs, their experiences parallel those of many young people now. In general there is the sense that their struggles have gone unheard by a generation that received the privileges of a generous state, and on an individual level they appear to feel betrayed by broken promises and are struggling to find a role in society.

It is something of a cliché to say that each generation feels it is misunderstood by its elders. Wilhelm felt that, whilst Buller was attempting to understand the attraction of the Nazis to the young, she couldn't quite get her head around it because she didn't understand what it was like to be unemployed with no sense of purpose or what the future might yield. Wilhelm was not alone.

Buller goes further and confronts Wilhelm, whom she had known from a young boy as a family friend. He had become an SS official and she recalls how conflicted he became when challenged about the crude politics of the Nazis. She says of his complaint that things always remain the same whomever is in power, 'I cannot think what you are doing to your mind, if you allow yourself to accept such stuff as that'. Buller recognized that a kind of schizophrenic mindset had overcome young people like Wilhelm, who felt unable to defend his stance openly and even admitted to the inner conflict it created.

Buller makes it perfectly clear to her English audience that even some loyal Nazis were deeply troubled when questioned about their dubious cause. In other words, they were not all tarred with the same fanatical brush.

Buller's commentary is minimal and the text is by no means exhaustive, but it is a window onto an alternative current of thought in England in the midst of the most brutal European war in history. The experience tested Buller to the limits of her own faith. It is rather ironic that dealing with the Nazis and Germany's descent into darkness may well have undermined her deep faith in the SCM and more importantly her Christian faith itself.[42]

Interpretations of history inclusive of oral testimony are much more widely accepted today. Historians are no longer revered in the same manner as they were when *Darkness over Germany* was published. It is now commonplace to write histories using a mixture of anecdote and eyewitness testimony, as well as trawling through academic archives. In that sense Buller can be seen as a populist writer ahead of her time.

For me, Buller's observations resonate in a modern world where once again the nature of faith and the lure of extremism has captured the hearts and minds of a generation. Since 9/11 we have seen this discourse focused on young Muslims, but in Europe we also see the rise of nationalist movements fueled by youthful anxiety. Germany in the 1920s was a land of opportunity arising out of a crushing defeat in the Great War. No one imagined a great civilization could be brought so low by rampant populism. But the arc of history does not necessarily point towards justice, even though we may live in hope that it does. The slaughter of European Jews gave the lie to such a romantic notion. *Nie wieder* (never again) was the mantra for a generation. It is a call

that needs greater amplification in our troubled times.

To a generation without faith, the Nazis gave a brutal philosophy and millions of lives have been sacrificed to free the world of this false answer to a real need, but let us not fail to understand that it was caused by a real need. We are now faced with the greater risk of bringing healing to the nations including our own. I am convinced this cannot be done without a faith in God adequate to the tremendous task of reconstruction.[43]

Buller was certainly not dismissed as a person of little or no import. In later life she created an educational foundation that endures to this day, in its original location on land owned by the Crown. In 1943 the vice-chancellor of Oxford University, A. D. Lindsay, wrote in his foreword to the book,

> If we are going to have the least chance of bringing young Germans back to sanity after Germany is beaten we had better understand what made them insane. That in itself is a reason why we should all read this remarkable book.[44]

Seventy years later, by publishing this book in German for the first time we are echoing these sentiments and giving them a modern legacy.

So, whilst it remains difficult to exactly assess the impact Buller's outlook might have had in Britain, it is fair to observe that the Allied victors approached peace and reconstruction with magnanimity that was a far cry from the punitive Versailles Treaty of 1919. Buller's desire to understand Germans as a way to win the peace can be seen as part of a powerful corrective to the prevailing wisdom in the midst of the Second World War.

Professor Kurt Barling,
London, 2017

PREFACE

All the material in this book is founded on fact. Some of the stories are true even to minute detail, in others I have changed details in order to complete the disguise as the need for this will be obvious. Names of places and of people have all been altered and some incidents have been deliberately telescoped and confused though they remain substantially true. Nearly all the people in the book are real, a very few are types chosen to emphasize some common point of view, and in some cases statements made by one person were in fact made by several people and vice versa.

My own connection with Germany has been intimate and covers a period of thirty years. During the whole of that period I have remained in close touch with many families in different parts of the country. It will be evident why I can say no more than that and it will be equally evident from the stories who were the groups and type of Germans with whom I have had intimate and continuous contact.

One very obvious omission is the labour movement. My contact with working-class people in Germany has only been casual and for that reason I have left out stories of their reaction to National Socialism because I have not lived among them enough to feel I had the right to try to interpret their point of view.

There is reference at times to conferences and discussions with Nazi leaders, most of whose names have not been disguised. Between the years 1934 and 1938 I took over to Germany on several occasions, small or larger groups of educationalists, theologians and economists in an attempt to study the fundamental doctrines of the Nazi philosophy. These conferences were private and would not have continued but for the encouragement given by non-Nazi friends who urged that there might yet be some value in visitors, who were unafraid and not personally involved, challenging the Nazis about their fundamental teaching. To the best of my knowledge these conferences were never exploited by the Nazis, though by 1937 it became obvious that von Ribbentrop, having discovered that he could not use these groups as he used many other parties visiting Germany, for propaganda purposes, was bitterly opposed to their continuance. The British members of these groups are not named and the impressions given of the meetings are personal.

Many books have been written which rightly pay high tribute to those in Germany who from the beginning refused all compromise with the Nazis, deliberate or otherwise. They paid the price of their decision by exile or death or in a concentration camp, and I would join in the tribute paid to them, but this book makes no attempt to deal with that courageous company of men and women.

Many more books and plays have been written about Nazi gangsters and German traitors. I do not wish to minimize the appalling charge of ruthless brutality, of pillage and murder. The men who do these things are Germans and their deeds are known throughout the world. But these stories are not about them.

Between these two groups there are the vast majority of the German people about whom widely different generalizations are made. Many of these are based on a false simplification.

The stories in this book are an attempt to let certain representatives of a limited but very important section of Germans speak for themselves. What they have to say is significant both because it throws light on how their enslavement came about and because they will have an important part to play in the rebuilding of Germany and in particular in the re-educating of the German youth.

I am well aware that our first task is to defeat the Nazis and as far as they are in control in Germany that means to defeat the Germans. But even in this, political warfare has its part to play and will only succeed if it refuses to accept any of the undue simplifications of the complex German situation behind the scenes. Secondly, as the end of the war draws nearer it becomes important that we should consider the German situation as a whole and above all decide who are the groups in that country with whom we can cooperate.

Military and economic control inside Germany may prove essential for a long time to come, but in some quarters in this country there are those who seem to suggest that for the Nazi control of men's minds and spirits we should substitute a United Nations control of the minds and spirits of the younger generation in Germany. It would be interesting to know by what machinery anything so fantastic could be attempted and whether the United Nations would then produce a new kind of Gauleiter and Gestapo to ensure that school and home and church were all faithful to the prescribed doctrine.

In any case there is conflict and confusion enough in this country about the training of our youth for the future and it seems unlikely that there will be a body of agreed doctrine among the United Nations which could be forced on Germany.

But to deplore any such suggestion does not mean I would underestimate the appalling need for true teaching in Germany.

If every Nazi were slain tomorrow we should be left with the deeper and more terrible phenomenon of a German youth in desperate need of a faith. That need must be met primarily by Germans themselves for it is obvious that in such a situation healing must come from within and most certainly it cannot be forced on a defeated nation by victorious invaders.

That these Germans will need and indeed seek the cooperation of other nations is clear, and it is surely also clear that we shall only be able to give that help and cooperation on two conditions. In the first place we must understand the full significance of the fact that a whole generation could so easily be led astray by false doctrine and become fanatical followers of such false prophets. This means a much more careful study of pre-Nazi conditions in Germany. Secondly, the United Nations must show signs that they in their several countries know how to meet the needs of their own youth.

I am indebted to many friends who for some years have urged me to write a book on some of the aspects of German life about which I have lectured. But in particular I am grateful to Rev. E. K. Talbot and Eric Fenn, without whose inspiration and help this book would hardly have been completed; to Francis and Frieda Scott, whose friendship gave me a beautiful home in which to write; to Dr Armstrong Gibbs and Dr Leonard Browne for their kindness in reading and correcting the manuscript; also to Dr Lindsay to whose wisdom and cooperation through many years I owe so much. Finally, to the women students of Liverpool University, whose courage in war and eager understanding of some of the problems of reconstruction indicate that given the chance, the youth of this country has a significant contribution to make to the winning of peace both at home and abroad.

E. Amy Buller
London, September 1943

To
Peter and Joan
of
Matson Ground

Left: Amy Buller

Below: Amy Buller in her office at Cumberland Lodge, now the Princess Helena Room

Left: Amy Buller, Eastbourne, September 1917

Below: Her Majesty Queen Elizabeth the Queen Mother unveiling a portrait of Amy Buller in the Drawing Room at Cumberland Lodge, 1971. Amy Buller is pictured standing on the far right

Amy Buller at Matson Ground with her mentor Fr Edward Talbot, Superior of the Community of the Resurrection, Mirfield

Cumberland Lodge in Windsor Great Park

Above: A street scene in Augsburg, Bavaria, where the main road is amply decorated with Nazi flags

Left: Amy Buller during her trip through Germany and Austria

Wehrmacht soldiers in front of the Brandenburg Gate, Berlin

One of the many typical Nazi parades with cheering viewers

Even the youngest ones were already misled by Nazi doctrine

In the Berchtesgarden area near Salzburg where Hitler
often stayed in his country house in Obersalzberg

Private picture taken in a decorated room where
propaganda speeches were taking place

Monument built by the Nazis for solemn vigil and in adoration
of the rebels who died during the so-called Hitler Putsch,
November 9th, 1923. Munich, near Odeonsplatz

WINTER 1940 – A UNIVERSITY HALL FOR WOMEN STUDENTS

Six women students who formed a fire-fighting team sat in an office on the ground floor of a hall for university students in a city in the north-west of England. They were dressed in slacks and woollen cardigans with brightly coloured jumpers and all wore steel helmets. It struck midnight as one of them rose to poke the fire while another poured out some fresh coffee and handed it round. After a heavy barrage the noise of the guns had died down but now the menacing throb of many engines could be heard and suddenly the harsh ugly rattle of machine-gun fire.

'I hate to hear them fighting,' said the captain of the fire team. 'It seems all wrong that we should sit round a fire and drink coffee while a life and death struggle goes on overhead.'

'I wonder,' said another student, 'whether all the Germans in the bombers are Nazis.'

'I expect so,' said a third, 'and anyhow they must agree with them or they wouldn't be fighting.'

'Oh, you can't know that,' said the captain. 'How could they help it? I have been in Germany and met many students who were not Nazis but I expect they are all fighting now.' Then turning to me she said, 'How is it that an entire nation let Hitler and his gang get control? Surely there must have been some way of stopping him before it was too late.'

'Before it was too late,' I said, 'that of course is the point. I think the majority of the German people undoubtedly did not wake up to the full implications of what was happening until it was impossible to organize resistance.'

'We're too tired to study any longer,' said the captain, and it may be ages before the "All Clear" goes. Do go on with the stories you were telling the fire team last week. I mean about the people you knew in Germany who did not leave their country but tried in many different ways to stand up against the Nazis – the people in the church and civil service, and some in the army as well as the students.'

The stories that follow were told to groups of students on fire duty during the long winter nights of 1940–1, while German bombers were overhead. They are being recorded in this book for two reasons. First in the hope that a wider circle of students and others may wish to hear of those silent men and women in Germany who were slow to realize what was happening, but since have all in their own ways waged ceaseless war against 'spiritual wickedness in high places'. They more than any others must build the new Germany out of the ruins of the Third Reich. Secondly I record these stories to emphasize the need for youth and those who plan the training of youth to consider carefully the full significance of the tragedy of a whole generation of German youth, who, having no faith, made Nazism their religion. Many were innocent, many more merely ignorant, some were traitors to themselves and all were led forth in the name of that 'religion' to carry war and desolation to the ends of the earth and finally to suffer complete destruction themselves.

PART I

CHAPTER I

THE DILEMMA OF A
GERMAN TEACHER

'Of course I agree with you that the Nazi teaching about race is what you in England call rot.' So said an intelligent teacher of geography as we sat on his balcony after dinner one summer evening overlooking his garden and the hills on the outskirts of a large town in Saxony. Franz Schuster was about thirty-five years old and would certainly have been appointed headmaster of a good school had not the Nazi revolution come just at the time he was applying for a headship.

'Well, what do you do about it in your school if you believe it is all rot? It must be difficult to carry on.'

Dr Schuster rose and looked over the balcony, saying, 'It would probably be all right to talk here but one never knows, so let's talk of other things till we go inside later.'

As darkness fell we entered the maisonette and closing all doors and windows, he drew across thick curtains, unconsciously anticipating nights of blackout in Europe. Then offering me a glass of good Saxon cherry brandy, he settled down with his own glass of beer, saying: 'I would like to tell you the kind of position I find myself in. It's a relief to talk to someone who is outside this struggle. We talk and talk among ourselves but even among one's friends one has to be careful, and I sometimes wonder if any one of us sees straight any more. But you lead such a different life, you have no fears and no conflict and you are perhaps in a better position to judge if I make the right decision.' Then lighting a cigarette he added, 'No, I'm wrong, of course you cannot exactly do that, because each of us has to make his own decision, and here in Germany even in identical circumstances people may find their consciences lead them along different roads. After all, it only matters that each of us should be true to himself whatever happens, but it is not easy to be sure what the true way is. Anyhow, it will help me to clear my mind if I may talk to you.'

'Go ahead,' I said.

'I will put it this way,' he continued. 'There are for me four possibilities for the future and I must add I am very lucky, because for most of my colleagues there are only two possibilities since they have no opportunities to go abroad, and having no money they cannot retire.

'First then I may decide that it is impossible to remain in this country where there is no longer any intellectual freedom and where education is being degraded by political interference. I can argue that all I believe about true education is now at stake and that it is quite impossible for me to allow political agents, often ignorant and stupid men, to interfere with my teaching of geography. Some of them don't seem to realize that any countries exist except Germany,' he added with a grunt of disgust.

'I have now an opportunity to go to America where I have been before. Shall I go? In many ways it would be a wonderful escape. My headmaster, who is new and young and a very keen Nazi – in fact he would not have this post if he were not a Party man – greatly hopes that I will leave. That is obvious, for he will get high praise if he can quickly obtain an all-Nazi staff. There is my first opportunity. To leave the country because I have both friends and an opening abroad.

'The second way is for me to attempt to escape this revolution in my country altogether, by resigning from the school, digging in my garden and writing books. I could even begin to prepare books on the teaching of geography and history, which will be much in demand when this disease of National Socialism is over. Perhaps I might even, in informal ways, help to challenge the Nazi teaching, since, if I leave the school, I should not be under authority.

'The third way is to stay in my school but to defy the headmaster and refuse to give Nazi lessons on race. This would soon end in an outburst – I might even try to do it in front of the whole school and denounce Hitler and all his works. That would mean prison, and of course, some of my colleagues are already there. Again the headmaster would be very happy, and you will understand what I mean when I say I doubt if my witness would have any value for the boys. A few might be influenced and later perhaps more, but at the moment this new young headmaster has made a great impression on the majority of the boys. His predecessor was a bit elderly and conventional and the boys feel now there is new life and action, and it is natural that they applaud this attack on scholarship, since it means they do not have to work so hard.

'By the way, a hateful thing happened in our school last week. Our classics master is quiet and reserved and physically neither strong nor active. He is simply nauseated by all this Nazi show, with its bombast and vulgarity and he hates the over-emphasis on physical education at the expense of decent learning. He tries to take no part in anything, but of course he has to be present at the endless Nazi ceremonies we now have at the school. Poor man, he stands there with a sort of bewildered look on his face, as though he cannot understand why he suddenly finds himself in a sort of madhouse! I could laugh when I look at him, if I did not know his unspeakable misery. He cannot go away or resign, for he has a wife who is an invalid and he has no money except what he earns, and he also helps his old mother, who has only a small pension because her husband was killed in the last war. Last week this classics master, stung into protest by a vulgar speech made by a Gauleiter who visited the school, apparently said something to his senior form about how serious it was to discredit scholarship for which Germany was renowned all over the world. That afternoon, after school, six young Nazis – his pupils, mind you – though most of them the stupidest boys in the form, seized him and ducked him in the river that runs through the school grounds. Of course, the headmaster "ticked the boys off", but only rather formally and they, as well as most of the school, knew perfectly well that the headmaster really admired the boys for doing it. The only really courageous protest came from the school caretaker. I wish you could have heard what he said to the boys, and they are a bit afraid of him because he is a big chap and was very angry.

'The discipline in the school is very bad now, for one of the things I notice more and more in many schools is that the boys who are models of discipline when they are in Nazi formation or doing exercises – they will make great sacrifices and show much endurance to reach really high standards of efficiency as young Nazis – are the same boys who in the rest of their school life show an appalling lack of discipline. It is a kind of reaction, I think, rather like an army kept under too strict control reacting later in violent excesses. It is difficult to tell you what I mean but if you lived in my school, or in one of the others with Nazi headmasters, you would realize that there is an element of hysteria in the extreme discipline and effort expended in Party organization. It is a very external kind of discipline through which few of the Hitler Jugend have learned any personal moral and spiritual restraint, rather the reverse.

'But, to return to my unfortunate colleague, his life is hell and he has no way out of it. Of course the headmaster knows that, and hopes he will break down and resign. There are in Germany today men in that position in the teaching profession who would really be happier in a prison cell, but few of them feel free even to make such a decision, because it would involve their dependants in terrible hardship. I see some schoolmasters in a dire dilemma over this, and of course not only masters but many other Germans who are in the civil service or the church. It is much easier for a man, say, in a bank or shop, as his job does not bring him into direct conflict with the Party so easily. It is one thing to suffer yourself, but it is much harder to involve your wife and young children in misery.

'My position is very different as I am free. Perhaps I should take this third choice, go to prison and let a young Nazi take my job in the school. But let me tell you what I have done so far, for this is the fourth possibility. I must add I am not happy and there is a constant strain. I remain on the staff and I pay lip service to all the Nazi school ceremonies and I do not show any open hostility, at least not enough to "get the sack" as you say, but quite enough to make my position precarious and at times most unpleasant. I am trying through the teaching of geography to do everything in my power to give the boys knowledge and I hope later on, judgement, so that when, as they grow older, the Nazi fever dies down and it again becomes possible to offer some opposition, they may be prepared. I never refer to the Party or its teaching directly, and the boys are, I think, mostly unaware that I am trying deliberately to undermine it. There are four or five masters who are non-Nazis left in our school now, and we all work on the same plan. If we leave, four Nazis will come in and there will be no honest teaching in the whole school. "Honest," did I say – are we being honest I sometimes wonder? It is very exhausting as well as dangerous to live under the strain of a deliberate compromise with evil, and unless we remain all the time sensitive to its perils we may so easily become dishonest with ourselves, and then we are no good to the boys or to anyone else.

'But if I went to America and left others to it, would that be honest, or are the only honest people those in prison cells? If only there could be some collective action among teachers. But we cannot meet in conference, we cannot have a newspaper. What do you think is honest – what would you do yourself?'

I was greatly relieved to be spared answering this question, for the door opened just then and a tall, fair and very handsome young woman entered the room.

'Oh, I meant to tell you,' said Dr Schuster. 'I invited my cousin to come to see you, as she loves England very much and was an exchange teacher in your country for a year. She hates the Nazis as much as I do, but she also, as you say, "sticks it out" and goes to all the Nazi Girls' Camps and everywhere she can with her pupils, because she says she will not leave them to these dreadful Nazi women. Isn't that right, Elizabeth?'

'Yes,' she said, 'I think it is important that we who oppose the Nazis should be cleverer than they are, and I am not giving in to them. It is difficult, but it can be done in lots of little ways. For instance, at all our summer camps we have fireside talks, which are often concerned with old German folklore. These Nazi women know only a very few stories, and they are the ones the Party suggests, and the teachers repeat them till the children get bored. I know a great many more stories and different ones.'

She laughed. 'Sometimes I say to the children: "Now I am going to make up some new German stories." I try to make my stories exciting, and they teach quite different things from the Nazi stories.'

'But don't the other Nazi teachers see what you are after?' I said.

'I have to be careful, of course, but so far I have been lucky. So many of the ardent Nazi women are of two kinds: either twisted, dissatisfied people or just very stupid people – at least this is true of the older women. There are, of course, many quite young women who have been caught up in the movement and have not yet realized haw dangerous it all is. But in my school the only ones who would be hostile to what I do are the older women, and I am fortunate because they are the very stupid sort.'

'But,' I continued, 'how do you teach history, which I think you said was your main subject? You do not believe the Nazi race theories and yet you must teach them.'

'I hope you will forgive me for saying so, but I got an idea from English schools how to do it!'

'Whatever do you mean?' I said.

'Well, I spent one year in an English school and I travelled to many others to listen to teaching and I sometimes listened to scripture lessons. Sometimes these lessons were most interesting and the children learnt a lot. At other times the teacher did not believe and was not herself interested, with the result that the lesson became formal. The children quick to grasp the true position learnt nothing whatever. I can assure you that many teachers in Germany today give purely formal Nazi lessons and the children all know perfectly well that it is "formal" and that the teacher is forced to give them those lessons. Nazi race theories can quite easily be made very dull, whereas I try to make my other lessons as interesting as possible. At times my Nazi lesson and my non-Nazi lesson don't fit too well and when the children ask questions I always answer "We do not discuss what the Führer tells us". That is a perfectly good Nazi reply! I think in the end we shall win and not the Führer or the Nazis.'

Elizabeth was quite excited now and continued, 'I have a friend who teaches biology, and she has a great deal of fun along the same lines, because the children find her biology lessons very thrilling and in the end they will realize that they all contradict the formal teaching. Of course, at times we get sick of the whole thing. After all, we only ask for freedom to teach decently and without distortion, but when I feel tired and think of giving it up, I remember that would mean handing my schoolchildren over to the Nazis.

'I hope my friends in England understand that there are many more than those in prison who try to fight Nazi teaching and, if only war doesn't come, I still think this fever in our land will pass.'

'You are wrong,' said her cousin. 'War will come. It will mean that you and I will be identified with the Nazis and perhaps lose for ever the friendship of those in England whose help we need. Anyhow, what's the good of talking, since many of us will be killed fighting against our friends, because if Germany goes to war, I, as a reserve officer, shall be called up, and I think, however sick one's country is, one fights for it all the same. You, Elizabeth, will be lucky because you will be left with your schoolchildren and there will be greater freedom because there will not be so many Nazi officials interfering with the schools, as, thank God, they will have to fight too, and perhaps they will learn some sense in the army where they will not be so important.'

'Tell me,' I said, 'does Hitler want war?'

'Does a madman want anything,' said Dr Schuster, 'except to go his own mad way and destroy everything in his path?'

As Franz said this the door opened and his mother entered with a tray of coffee and biscuits. Hearing her son's last remark she said with a grunt of disgust, 'Sounds as though you are talking of our great new German Führer!'

Then turning to me she said, 'I expect in England you think we are all mad, for certainly the way we behave looks like it. I sometimes think the Führer is a strange kind of personification of the madness and evil of the last war and all that it left behind in Germany. I know if we have another war Germany will be to blame, for I understand it is impossible for any country to come to terms with the Nazis. But forgive me if I say that many of us can never, never understand whose fault it was that real peace was not made between our countries when we had different rulers in Germany. Perhaps there was in Europe – I mean England and France also – too much poison left after the last war. Perhaps the generations that had been at war could never again become really sane and achieve true peace between the nations. I do not know. I, like my son and my niece, love England and I do not want to be unjust. I think that whereas near history will blame Germany alone if we have another war – and in a way that is right – when in future years, historians write of the period since the last war, they will write many criticisms of all the countries even though after 1933 they say Germany was the most to blame. I lie awake at night sometimes and think of all the horrors of the last war in which my brother was killed and my husband lost his health permanently. I think now of my son, for certainly if there is another war he will have to fight; it is impossible otherwise nothing is gained if he is shot as a deserter. But that he should fight under a Nazi flag is terrible to think about.'

'Yes, Mother,' said Franz, 'but I sometimes think perhaps war is the only way to get rid of the Nazis. It is true that, if we have a war, at any rate to begin with there will be a new unity in Germany – it is always so. But that will not last because you know there are many in the army who hate the Nazis, and the feeling between many army officers and the SS is very bitter. In the end it will be the army that will take control and turn the Nazis out.'

'Yes, that is possible,' replied his mother. 'But how many people like you who want to build a different Germany will be killed, and then we shall be left with only the younger generation who have been brought up as Nazis.'

'But, Auntie,' said Elizabeth, 'don't be too pessimistic, because if all the Nazis go to fight, many will also be killed and there will certainly not be so many left to go on with Nazi teaching in the schools or in the homes. And I think too,' she added, turning to me, 'that in the suffering and realism of war, much of the shoddy propaganda will not work so well. I am sure, whether there is a war or not, that in the girls' schools we shall in the end win against the Nazis' teaching. But,' she went on, 'we must be going for it is now nearly midnight and our English guest and I will find no trams soon.'

We went into the entrance hall and as Franz helped me on with my coat he added, 'Will you do me a favour in England?'

'Certainly if I can.'

'Will you ask some of the English teachers you know well what they would do in my place and Elizabeth's? I know it is difficult, if not impossible, for them to picture the kind of position we find ourselves in here, but will you tell them the four possibilities that I think exist for German teachers who are anti-Nazi? And then ask them which they would choose. Or if they have a fifth idea, what it is, and then when you come back to Germany tell me what they say.

'I want to visit England so much,' he continued, 'but now it is made impossible unless I consent with the carefully planned Nazi parties of schoolboys with Nazi Youth leaders. As you know, before they go abroad, they have to go through a sort of training conference, and they are all told what they must say in England or France, or wherever they go, and when they come back they have to go to another conference – it is almost like a kind of "cleansing" conference to take away from them any "wrong" ideas they may have learnt abroad.

'One of the cleverest things these Nazis do when they are

accused of being too nationalist is to reply "But we send more boys abroad than ever before". They do not add that they take care to send them in such a way that it is difficult for them to learn anything, and I sometimes wonder if they spread rather dangerous propaganda among the young people in the countries they visit. They are young, happy and enjoying themselves, and they know nothing about the bad side of National Socialism, so they are quite sincere. They are idealistic too, and I think they may give the boys in England false ideas about many things.'

'Franz,' called Elizabeth, who had gone ahead into the garden with her aunt, 'if you talk any longer we shall miss the last tram.'

'Goodbye. Come again soon,' he called as I joined his cousin.

We did miss the tram but it was a lovely night and, as Elizabeth's home was in the same direction as my hotel, we walked along together and she continued to talk of women teachers. 'But,' I questioned, 'isn't it true that in many girls' schools women teachers are being replaced by young Nazi men teachers? May I tell you of an experience of a friend of mine who is headmistress of a famous school in England?'

'Yes, do,' said Elizabeth.

'I met this English friend recently in Germany, where she is spending the summer, and she told me that she had just visited a large girls' school and had been horrified to find that instead of the scholarly and very sane headmistress greeting her, as she had done before, she was met by an ardent Nazi headmaster. With great enthusiasm and apparently without the slightest idea how repelled my friend was, he said, "Oh yes, in many girls' schools we now have headmasters and, whereas there used to be all women teachers in this school, I have now made many changes and by degrees I shall have nearly all young masters. Of course, I shall keep women for the cooking and sewing lessons and perhaps for a little art, but I think not for music, because our singing must be in the right atmosphere of the Nazi revolution. I have found too that masters are much better at teaching many subjects, especially history and biology."

"'I see," said my friend, with great courage. "History and biology are of course the two subjects you use, or if you will allow me to say so, misuse, in order to inculcate your propaganda on race."

"'Well, you see, it is so important," said the headmaster quite unperturbed, "we must use every means we can."

'The English headmistress seemed to think that it "was obvious", from these and many other conversations in German schools this summer, that women teachers, even those who are not deliberately hostile, are proving on the whole to be temperamentally far less suited for the incessant drumming in of propaganda than some of the raw young men being introduced into the schools, and that girls tended to get bored much more quickly than boys.'

'Yes, I know,' said Elizabeth, 'please do not misunderstand me and think I am being too optimistic. I do realize how terrible it all is, and I could talk all night about the bad and discouraging things. Sometimes I too see it as a losing battle and if it were a battle for my own generation then I think I would be tempted to give up, but when I get back to school and see the children I become angry again, and that helps me vow that I will not leave these children to the Nazis, and that I will fight in a way the Nazis will not discover. How I would love to visit England and breathe freely again, but as my cousin says, the Nazis make that too difficult, and now, if we have war, we shall be fighting against the people who stand for the things we want to get back in this country. I think my cousin is wrong – war will never help us, for as my aunt says, National Socialism is a sort of disease left over from the last war and all the terrible years that followed, and if we have another war, then there will still be more disease in every land. No, I cannot see any hope in war. But, if only it does not come, I think that in time we shall find a way to get back our freedom.'

As she spoke we reached the foot of the steps leading to the brilliantly lighted hotel and although it was midnight the sound of dance music in the lounge could be heard outside. In the light I saw how tired Elizabeth had become after our long discussions and so said, 'Although it is late, won't you come in and have a drink before you go home?'

'No, thank you, I dare not, for my mother will be anxious if I am too late,' she said, and then stopped speaking and stared at two SS guards who were coming down the hotel steps. They did not heed us as they were talking and laughing in a coarse unpleasant way, but I wish I could picture to you the look on Elizabeth's face, half of anger and half of pity. When they had passed she said quietly, 'One of those boys was at the university with me. He's got good brains and had the chance of being a fine person. It is terrible that he is now in the Gestapo – my aunt is right, it is madness. But I must go because my mother is alone tonight and once already the Gestapo has visited our house, and if I am too late she will think something has happened. Goodbye. Tell your friends in England I do not think that such nonsense, such madness, can last for ever in this country.'

As Elizabeth walked away into the darkness I entered the hotel lounge and ordered a cup of coffee before going to bed. A great many young Nazis were sitting in groups round their glasses of beer and, as I watched them, I felt bewildered. Some looked brutal enough, some stupid, some had twisted unhappy faces, but many looked happy and healthy and one or two very intelligent. All seemed alive and spoke as though they had a keen purpose in life, and as I sat and thought, the same question came back again and again. How and why did the great majority of the younger generation get caught up in a madness which meant that an excellent young teacher like Elizabeth must hurry home because her mother would be anxious lest harm had come to her, and that Franz was torn by a bitter conflict as to whether he could best serve his country by martyrdom, exile or all the dangers of a deliberate compromise.

CHAPTER II

A CATHOLIC PRIEST FACES CONFLICT

I was staying in a fascinating little Bavarian market town set in the midst of beautiful country with friends who were Christians and anti-Nazi but, at the moment, it is not of them I wish to speak, but of an experience that will long remain in my mind. It makes some of the easy talk in England and elsewhere about 'Why don't the Germans stand out against the Nazis?' seem ill-informed as applied to some Germans, at any rate. This is what happened. The local village priest in the Catholic Church there is an old friend of mine. He is an interesting and vivid personality and combines considerable classical scholarship and wide reading with a passionate concern about the social and economic order. Before the last war he was a Marxist and called himself an atheist, but after the war he became a Catholic and later a priest. None of his zeal for a new economic order has gone, and he keeps in touch with his socialist and communist friends. But for Dr Heim it must now be a Catholic social order and he enters into fierce conflict with his friends on the Christian values of personality and human freedom on which he believes socialism must rest, and contends that the methods used to achieve an ideal must remain true to the ideal itself. Finally, perhaps most fundamentally, he maintains that the social order here on earth only gains its full significance because man is a citizen of a spiritual as well as of an earthly realm, and that the earthly order will only remain free from corruption or stagnation as long as it is inspired by the things of the spirit and as men recognize this greater loyalty.

It is magnificent to hear him challenge the young communists and they him. He equals them in conviction, as they recognize, and, although the smaller-minded of them may feel much that he says to be irrelevant, or feel too fearful to look at it too closely, others, whose minds and spirits move in a wider sphere, are arrested by his conviction and wonder if there is something they have missed or are missing.

On that day in Bavaria, I rang up Dr Heim and asked if I might have a talk with him. To my surprise the friendly welcome in his voice had gone and he replied, almost curtly: 'If you meet me outside the coffee house in the Market Square in one hour's time I can see you for a little while. It is market day and there will be many people in the square, but stand still and I will find you. Goodbye.'

Puzzled, I turned to my friends and said, 'What is the matter with Dr Heim, I wonder? He has not by any chance become a Nazi, or anti-British, or anything else, has he? Or is it that it is Holy Week and he is too busy to be bothered with guests just now?'

My friends, who are Protestants and belong to a neighbouring Confessional Church, whose pastor has only recently been let out of prison, replied, 'It was not very wise for you to phone. We should have warned you. You see, he is always in danger because he is so courageous. He is a wonderful man and an inspiration to all non-Nazis in this district. When he was in prison he met some of our pastors and since then they have often met secretly for prayer. Though Dr Heim is an ardent Catholic, he never ceases to urge that all Christians must stand together against the forces of paganism. In fact, when he realized there would be trouble in a Lutheran Church meeting in this neighbourhood one evening, he remained near the church and, when the Gestapo rushed the meeting and tried to close it, Dr Heim went in after them and challenged their right to interfere. It rather startled the young SS men, because they were acting without authority, and they knew that Dr Heim had a big following in the town, which is largely Catholic. It must have been a strange sight and would have made a good picture. An elderly Lutheran pastor and a small humble congregation singing Luther's hymns, with a group of arrogant young Nazis shouting them down, and then this Catholic priest with flaming passion demanding of the Nazis what they wanted with their noise and their arms against a few old people saying their prayers. It was almost like a modern version of "Are ye come out as against a thief with swords and with staves to take Me?"'

'Was that why Dr Heim went to prison?' I asked.

'Well, that partly, but actually it was because he will never give the Hitler salute and has never let the words "Heil Hitler" pass his lips. And in the Catholic schools here he has got the children and all the young people in the church inspired with the zeal of crusaders so that they use the old German greeting of "Grüss Gott" to indicate their allegiance. Recently a Gauleiter visited this Catholic school and every time he shouted "Heil Hitler" the children shouted back "Grüss Gott".'

With that I left my friends and made for the coffee house in the Market Square. Presently I saw a small car stop on the other side. Dr Heim got out and mingled with the crowd. He was obviously well known and loved, and as he came nearer I saw a gallant smile on the face of many a sturdy old peasant farmer as well as on the faces of boys and girls as they used their password "Grüss Gott".

Some miles out of the town we left the car in a wood and climbed a hill. Here we were really free to talk as we looked across a lovely valley with fruit trees in full blossom, in the midst of which rose the spire of the church in which this priest taught his people: 'Come what may, your greeting and all it implies is, "Grüss Gott". For three hours we talked as he unfolded the struggle that lay within his story.

'I have now been forbidden to teach in the schools, though I can teach on Sunday in the church, but I expect that soon I shall not be allowed to preach. There arises, therefore, for me a terrible conflict, not, believe me, about the most courageous thing to do, but because we know now in the circumstances in which we find ourselves that it is imperative that we must show skill and strategy as well as courage if we are to meet the evil forces around us and not be defeated.

'Let me give you an example of what I mean, for I had rather a bitter experience last week. There was, in this province, a meeting of clergy and laymen to discuss a provincial Catholic paper. I felt we were not being nearly courageous enough and got up and said that if the Catholic paper under discussion were run by those who had faith and courage they would attack again and again the whole Nazi system as an evil which must be fought and overcome. The elderly owner of the paper replied and thanked me for the candour of my outburst with which he said he had great sympathy, but that when he had given me the story of what happened he hoped I'd tell him what was the courageous thing he should have done. He went on: "My paper has been suppressed on five occasions already and if it is suppressed again it will be permanently banned. Now, if we could get one edition out and circulated to all Catholics in this province and others beyond who read it, stating emphatically and fully our case against the Nazis and urging relentless opposition, I would think it worth doing, in fact, the only possible thing to do, even though it meant imprisonment or even death. I can only ask you, Dr Heim, to believe me when I say that.

"But the position is that there is now attached to my office a Nazi official who is always on the premises the night the paper is printed, and sees an advance copy so that the paper would never get farther than our office, and the attempt would mean a permanent ban." We have decided, not without great concern and difficulty, that we can help more by keeping in circulation a Catholic paper which takes care to state emphatically the Catholic faith, and hope thereby to strengthen the judgement of those who daily struggle to be faithful, and to prepare them for the day when other and greater opportunities for opposition arise. Will you tell me what we ought to have done, what is the right answer to our problem?"

'I rose,' said Dr Heim, 'and replied, "I do not know the right answer, but I apologize for charging you with cowardice!"'

We sat in silence for some minutes and then Dr Heim spoke again.

'We don't know the answer, that is the heart of the tragedy. This enslavement is such that we have been taken unawares. And, whereas it often seems easy enough to judge, it is only with agony that one makes any decision these days. You see, I cannot decide whether to insist on entering my school and preaching, thus giving the Nazis the excuse to arrest me, which is exactly what they want. I would fight them if we had arms, for it would be a more just war than I've ever known, but we are totally unarmed.

'If I accept their ban on teaching, other restrictions will follow, but so far I remain free to move among my people and visit them, and above all to give what help I can to the young who come for advice, as they in their turn face questions, every day of the week, that are as difficult as my own. In our present circumstances to compromise at all is a dangerous path, and particularly so for the people to whom the young look for guidance. Should I withdraw? Nothing would suit the Nazis better than to lock up as many Catholic priests as possible.

'Therefore, at present I have decided to remain free and to accept the negative restrictions, but to refuse outright to take any part at all in Party ways, plans or greetings. Later, I may decide I am wrong. I do not think we can be sure of the answer. I sometimes wonder what the martyrs of old would have done in these circumstances, for it does seem as though today individual martyrdom is not always the right way – and yet, how careful we need to be because we may be deceiving ourselves.

'Of course, our real guilt lies in our slowness and in letting these gangsters get the whole country in their grip sufficiently to paralyze all collective opposition. So many people were so relieved to see any kind of order emerge out of the uncertainty and chaos that they said "Certain things the Nazis are doing are good", and left it at that, without inquiring on what this new order was based or what was the spirit of the movement that was sweeping the land.'

'May I tell you,' I said, 'of some young Catholic students I met in

Vienna who puzzled me because they called themselves Catholic Nazis and who, it seemed, had formed a small fellowship in which each member had resolved to attend Mass every day for a year and to pray for the capture of the Nazi movement by the Catholic Church. When I asked them to explain what that meant, they said, "Well, you see, apart from any particular leaders or programme, there has been let loose though this movement a great dynamic energy, and we are convinced that this need not all develop along Nazi Party lines. We see this movement as a lusty pagan infant born in the midst of Europe, and we want it baptized into the church.'"

'Yes, I know that movement,' said Dr Heim, 'and many other young Catholics as well as some of the younger members of the Protestant German Christian group who are in the Party. It is tragic that there should be such confusion in the minds of those who should know better. Can you wonder that the Nazi movement has swept the younger generation off its feet, if so many young Christians can be so misled? They will find their error and pay bitterly for it, I fear. But I must not judge them harshly because you realize that I too, in another sense, am confused and bewildered about the right action, even though I have no illusions, for this movement is of the devil. Of course, we cannot escape the fact that not only did we not fight soon enough, but we must now realize that this could not have happened in Germany if there had not been a fundamental lack of the deepest sanity, which is belief in God. People have forgotten that this claim is final, and they are trying to find out whether they can fit God into another allegiance they have put in front of Him.

'Tell me about the young people in England now. I should like to visit them again and especially to meet students. Have they got a faith in something strong enough to hold against any onslaught? For there must be many false gods besides the Nazi idols at a time in history when there are signs of spiritual bankruptcy everywhere. Your country would have so much to give if it really understands the nature of this breakdown in Europe and realizes the Nazi fervour is religious but that their creed is the Devil's creed.

'By the way,' he added, 'I saw an English paper recently and I was interested in its criticism of Christians here, saying how lacking in courage we must all be not to stand up to the Nazis better. Tell them we welcome their criticism. In fact we share it, but tell them also that it's not so easy to judge sitting by an English fireside, or in one of your lovely gardens. The conflict here is much deeper than they know. Tell them we know we were blind fools not to have fought earlier and before we were in chains, but that they should look for the writing on the wall in Europe and America as well as Germany.

'Tell them, above all, that many of us are not sure what is the right action, but that we wrestle night and day to find it, and let them know that in this little town there are old men and women, as well as quite young children, whose hearts beat faster with both faith and fear as they retort with courage to the Nazi bully who salutes them in the street: "Grüss Gott."

'I must go back to church – it is Holy Week. Perhaps we may not meet again before the war, because there is, I believe, no hope of avoiding war with these men in power. But they will fall, and millions with them, and pray God that those who survive will have learned never again to allow the minds and spirits of men to be fettered.'

CHAPTER III

GERMAN OFFICER ON COUNTERACTING NAZI TEACHING

'Thank God we have played our trump card today.' So said a German officer of some standing as he found his wife and me drinking coffee under a tree in a garden on the outskirts of Berlin, late one afternoon in August in 1936.

It was a very hot day and taking off his cap and mopping his brow he turned to me and said, 'Tomorrow it will be announced publicly that our compulsory military training will be for two years instead of only for one year.'

'But why trump card?' I replied. 'Do you mean the army's trump card in its preparation for war?'

'Not at all,' he said. 'I mean our trump card against the Nazis.'

'Fritz, for goodness sake be careful what you say; remember we are in the garden and one never knows who listens over garden walls,' said his wife.

'You are right,' he replied, adding rather irritably: 'How sick I get of this need for caution. We cannot now have the most ordinary conversation without behaving as though we were gangsters plotting murder. However, it's quite true that what I want to tell you is better not heard by the Nazis, so let's go inside.'

As we moved towards the house Frau von Arnsberg said, 'You will stay to dinner, won't you? That will give you and my husband a chance for a good talk and also my nephew whom you have not seen for several years may come in late and he would be very glad to see you. He is also an officer and a bit of a Nazi, I fear.'

'Will you have a cigarette?' said Herr von Arnsberg. 'In England you have not yet decided it is unwomanly to smoke,' he added with a laugh. Then, as he lighted my cigarette he started talking seriously and was obviously anxious that I should understand his point of view. One of the interesting things about Germany was the passionate desire on all sides to be understood. This was particularly true of those who had deliberately come to terms of compromise with Hitler and their very insistence on the reasonableness and rightness of their position only indicated the conflict still in their own minds.

'You asked if the two years' military service is a preparation for war. No, not directly, though many of us agree that every year since the last war looks less like peace and it is important that Germany should be prepared for anything.'

'Anything the Nazis lead her into?' I asked.

'Yes, if you like, though it is not only the Nazis that make Europe restless. But we will not quarrel over that just now.

'In Germany,' he continued, 'it is very different from England for in your country it would not be true to say that the British army has played a significant part in the development of British character and ideas of citizenship. In Germany, on the other hand, the army has in the past played a most important role in building up certain standards – some good, some bad – and has given our young men certain ideals that have been good for German life.

'But let us talk of the present,' he said. 'At the moment the Nazi Party is trying to take over the whole education of our nation and it seems to make the teaching it gives in all the Party organizations more important than the teaching the young get either in the schools or the home, or even in the church.

'Now many of us are very concerned about much of this Nazi teaching which is false. So that by trump card I mean (and many other German officers would agree with me) we have found that if the German youth goes first into the Hitler Jugend and then the Labour Front, it takes more than one year to knock all the Nazi nonsense out of them when they come to us. Thank God, now we shall get them for two years and we shall have a better chance, because almost the entire young manhood of Germany passes through our ranks and in many ways we can do something to break down the pagan and stupid ideas they have learnt before they came to the army.'

We sat talking for some hours during which the nephew joined us.

It was obvious that these two represented, not perhaps a large, but a very significant group of German officers who really seemed to feel something akin to a sense of mission in their task as German officers in face of so much that was false in Nazi teaching.

'You see, we do not exactly enter into any controversy over Nazi teaching by attacking it, but we try to re-inculcate a belief in the Christian religion by positive teaching, or even more, by letting the men see how highly some of their officers estimate the church and what it stands for. Also we quite openly oppose much of the Nazi anti-Semitic teaching and indirectly we try to make them realize that universities and schools and places of learning should not be interfered with by Party agencies. So much of National Socialism is cheap and vulgar, even its teaching on discipline and simplicity which might be good is based on wrong assumptions. We do not think that up to now the Nazi teaching has gone very deep in many young men, and we believe that in some way we can re-educate the German youth during their military training.'

'Yes,' joined in the nephew, 'don't you see how much more thrilling our task as officers is, for now it is not only to make good soldiers, but to re-educate German citizens. Because,' he added, with the almost light-hearted confidence of many Germans not in the Party, 'much of the Nazi teaching will die quite soon. It's such nonsense. But in the meantime, I think German officers have a wonderful opportunity.'

There was silence for a few moments as we sat in the gathering twilight. Then Herr von Arnsberg, looking across at me with a face that had grown serious, said, 'I hope we do not give you false impressions, because we are deeply indebted to Hitler.'

He saw the look of surprise on my face.

'Let me explain. I, and many other officers, will now spend much of our time and thought in trying all sorts of ways to teach what is in direct opposition to most of the Nazi teaching. But that does not mean that, as German officers, we can ever forget the gratitude and allegiance we owe to Adolf Hitler. You see, the German army had fallen into disrepute, it scarcely existed, it was dishonoured and discredited and suffered every sort of indignity. Adolf Hitler has brought it back to the place of supreme importance in the life of our nation, and above all, to a place of honour. This we must never forget and we remain true in our allegiance to him, however much we may work against his teaching, when it means the wrong education of our youth.'

Then, as the last streak of light faded behind the pine trees beyond the French windows by which we had been sitting, Herr von Arnsberg added, speaking more to himself than to me: 'Yes, our oath is to Adolf Hitler who restored the German army. Would to God he had been a gentleman, a Christian and an officer. He is a decorator, a pagan and a civilian. But to him we are bound by military oath and by eternal gratitude.'

Darkness fell and Frau von Arnsberg came in to say that her husband's father, a retired general who was ill and lived a few doors down the road, would like her son to call in.

'I am sorry he is too ill to see you, because he would have given you a different picture from mine as he thinks we are making a mistake to compromise at all. He is what you would call a die-hard general of the old school, and he says the Nazis will bring disaster. I think it is because he is so worried that he becomes ill so often.'

When I was left alone with the young officer, he turned to me, perhaps realizing that I felt rather horrified by what his uncle had said about allegiance to Hitler and said, 'You do see my uncle is right, don't you. His generation suffered most deeply in the war and afterwards saw degradation at home, and whereas I as a young man should now be unemployed and unwanted, I owe it to Hitler that I have a marvellous job, made the more important by the very falseness of his own Party's teaching. It is all right for my great-uncle because his life is now nearly over, but for our generation it is wonderful that we have at last got employment and something important to do. After all I sometimes think that I would put up with almost anything if in my lifetime this feeling of defeat could be removed from the German army. I know much is bad in what the Nazis do, but it will not last, it is the sort of thing that happens in revolutions.'

A week later I was repeating this conversation to a German scholar who had retired and lived in Koblenz. He had given a great deal of time to studying the history of the German army. He was old and wise and very bitter about the Nazis. 'Ach,' he explained irritably, 'it is what you call a gratitude complex these officers have for Hitler. It is terrible now that Hindenburg has gone that the army is under oath to Hitler. These officers should see that they can only educate Germany if for some years the army takes control instead of the Nazis. But with the oath it is very difficult. Some day they will have to break that oath, because one day it will be realized that it is only the army that can take control in Germany and throw the Nazis out. I am sure we must have a period with a kind of army dictatorship until we can get a con-stitutional government again, for after Hitler there is bound to be chaos. The fact that the officers feel they must compromise because of their oath to Hitler only makes things more difficult. 'It is just the same with many people outside the army,' he contin-ued. 'If you look far enough you will see there is conflict in many aspects of German life today. Too many people are comforting themselves by saying "Down with Nazi teaching" at the same time as they say "Heil Hitler". They do not seem to see that it is an impossible position, for all the time they are strengthening Hitler, even if they hate his teaching.

'One of the difficulties is that what I call this thanksgiving complex is in the people as well as in the army. In spite of a certain reaction against the army after the last war, there is a very deep feeling in this country for the German army. There is in the Reich a deep desire that the army should again hold an honourable and powerful place. It is therefore true that many civilians talk about a sense of gratitude to the Führer for restoring the prestige of the army. Also you must remember that Nazi propaganda has worked up a great sense of insecurity because other countries round us had not disarmed and Blomberg, for instance, talks about "the people's birthright of defence". That is, of course, true, but it is all so confused. You will find in many military families like the one you know that they will say, "At least one feels some reassurance in the knowledge that Germany is again something to be reckoned with in Europe and is not just kicked about".

'Many of these things may be true, but it is very dangerous that the army should feel so bound up with Hitler, for though they do not think themselves Nazis, they will be in great difficulties. You will notice how in army circles they always talk of the Party as "they" and never include themselves, but that state of affairs can hardly last.

'Anyhow, Himmler and the SS are determined to try to Nazify the army, and there is always the possibility of serious trouble between the SS and the army, because,' he added with a bitter laugh, 'there is no one who has a thanksgiving complex for Himmler. Of course, if war comes, the Party will have sooner or later to learn that there is only one power in this land, and that is the army and not the SS or any other Nazi organization.'

CHAPTER IV

GERMAN OFFICER AND
ALTERNATIVES TO HITLER

'The only alternative to the Nazi Party now is a military dictator-ship for a few years to keep order in the country during a period of transition from the kind of slave organization the Nazis have set up to some saner form of government.'

So said Herr von Bretten, a German officer, in the year 1936.

'Do you mean that there is no other political group left in the country with a real programme and enough coherence to take control at any rate for a time?' I said. 'Have all the former parties suffered complete disintegration?'

'Well,' he replied, 'as you know, I do not often quote the Führer, but on one point he is right, namely, that there is only one Party ready to take over if the Nazis collapse, and that is the Commu-nist Party. You see, they have their rule-of-thumb programme and their outside connections, and they would not be concerned, as all other parties are, to relate their politics to existing condi-tions out of which they would hope to evolve something sane. The strength of the communists is that they know exactly what they want, and there is no doubt that one of the reasons Hitler has got such complete control is that many people were already frightened of communism and Hitler exploited their fear very cleverly. Of course, they never guessed, for who could, that the Nazis would do the very thing they most feared in communism, namely, sup-press the freedom in the church, the university and the press, and by their people's courts destroy the foundations of justice and law. Don't mistake me, there are many people in Germany who are very much afraid of communist economic ideas, but there are a great many more who are inclined to be socialists or at least are not afraid of economic changes, who nevertheless were appalled at the religious persecution and the control of the universities, and general lack of freedom in Russia.

'But there is another very important point in relation to what sort of group could take over from Hitler, and it is this. One of the reasons why the masses of the people are so enthusiastic for Hitler and his Party is because in some way they have found in National Socialism – well, what shall I say – a kind of salvation. They have put into this movement the sort of confidence a man has in his faith and not in his political party as a rule. So that we see something very much like religious power and drive that is really a sort of hysteria. This, I think, is partly due to the last war and all the unsettled, evil years since. If you asked some of these enthusiasts about the political and economic conceptions of National Socialism, they would know very little, because their trust is really in Hitler who is to them a miracle man.

'I do not say communism is the same as Nazism, but it is the only alternative with a kind of *Weltanschauung*, and would more easily interest the Nazi mentality because of that. The whole machinery of dictatorship, propaganda and Gestapo would much more easily be turned into a communist regime than into any other form of government. I am sure that it is most important that the fever in this country should die down and not just seek some other form of totalitarian expression.

'You know,' he said, 'what is true of some individuals in their own lives is sometimes true of a nation. When men find that the circumstances they have to face are hard and that they have to go down a long and difficult road, they will move away from real life where there is so much disappointment and frustration and live in a kind of fantasy where everything comes right. Germany is in that kind of fantasy, and Hitler is the magician who makes everything come right.

'But this kind of fantasy in the minds of so many will end in disillusionment and that, together with the fact that the Nazis are deliberately destroying all the machinery for a decent government, means that if the Nazis give up or are turned out, there will be the wildest chaos. And, if endless competing parties spring up, it is likely that some highly undesirable elements may again get control. It will be especially dangerous after this period of dictatorship, because, no doubt there are dictators other than Nazis who might like to take control.

'It is a grim thought,' he continued, 'but we are in such a mess now that it is difficult to get out without several more disasters. I see no hope of going from the Nazis straight on to anything resembling a form of government that would be good and permanent. There must be this transition stage during which there is a strong control, and it would be best that the control should be army control, because that is obviously not a permanent form of government. But it might give a sense of security while the masses get over their dream of "all being well" and realize they have a long hard road with no flattering magician to lead them. During this interim period the state must find some better means of governing than a dictatorship of gangsters.'

We went on talking for another hour, and then Herr von Bretten said, 'After all I have told you, you will realize how vital we feel it to be that the army should keep as free as possible of the Nazi machine. You probably know that Hitler wants to do one of two things. First he suggests that the SS should be armed as a separate army division. Most of us are deeply opposed to this. Hitler wants the SS to be a kind of private army for himself so that, if trouble came in Germany, he could fight to keep his control. You can see how dangerous that would be as it would be, as it were, a second army, a sort of Praetorian Guard, and that after all the Nazi bragging that Germany is more united than ever before.

'The alternative he wants if he cannot get this is to Nazify the army. He has some plan to insist that those who aspire to be army officers must go into the SS for a year first. Both these things we shall continue to oppose, and when I say "we", I mean all the different elements in the army. We have our fire-eaters, of course, and we have some in the army who want war because they want the chance to wipe out the defeat of 1918. I do not agree with either of these groups of officers, but we all agree that the Party, and in particular that loathsome fellow Himmler, shall not control the army. The German army belongs to the German Reich, and it must stand alone as the only armed force within the nation.'

I did not see this officer again for two full years after this conversation. In the meantime the grip of the Nazis over Germany had become a stranglehold, and among many people the belief in Hitler as a magician had increased, especially since the seizure of Austria. Also the whole international situation had become more dangerous and the German army had now grown very much stronger and bigger.

Herr von Bretten phoned me one morning after he heard I was in Germany two years later. 'I will fetch you at your hotel and we will have dinner at the Adlon, as my wife is away, but afterwards we will go home for coffee.' As we drove off he said, 'You will realize that at the Adlon we can only talk of England and of personal matters, but we can talk about German politics when we get back to the flat.'

I thought the colonel was looking tired and strained as so many officers looked in 1938, and he told me that his son, who had been transferred from his cavalry regiment to the German airforce had only had ten days' leave in three years. 'We work at an almost impossible rate just now,' he said.

After dinner I had just got into the taxi that was to take us back to the flat when another officer stopped Herr von Bretten and talked to him for a moment or two on the pavement outside the hotel. As I sat in the taxi with the driver holding the door open, a long procession of SA men passed down Unter den Linden. A look of suppressed irritation crossed the face of the sturdy taxi driver who must have been about sixty years old, and, realizing I was English, he put his head in the taxi and said with the dry humour and impatience of some of the German working class: 'No doubt you have seen several processions already in this country. I expect you'll see several more. So long as the SA has any shoe leather, they will go on marching.' Then shrugging his shoulders he added, 'Aber was Werden daraus?' ('What will come of it all?')

Back in the flat, the maid brought in coffee and then as she went away Herr von Bretten turned to me and said, 'The situation looks dangerous enough now. What do you think?'

Ignoring the question I said, 'Do you remember our conversation in 1936?' Herr von Bretten nodded. 'Then you know what I'm thinking. Why doesn't the army take over power in Germany now and throw the Nazis out? You are much stronger than when you talked to me two years ago, and the situation is, as you say, far more dangerous. You told me then that a temporary military dictatorship was the inevitable next step. Why delay? The Nazis will certainly land us in war if they go on as they are doing now.'

He remained silent for a moment and then said, 'Excuse me using your slang English, but what the hell could we do with Germany if we did take control now?'

Then getting up he crossed the room and detached his telephone, saying with a wry smile, 'It is always best to be as safe as possible. I do not understand how it is possible, but many of us have been warned it is better if we want to talk very privately to detach the telephone. You see,' he said earnestly, 'the answer to your question cannot be found in Germany any more and certainly not in the German army. The whole economic situation has become desperate, and the answer to the economic problem is not in one country alone, and must be solved outside as well as inside Germany.'

There then followed a terrific onslaught on the whole economic structure of Nazi Germany as something which must collapse unless some form of international economic cooperation comes in to save the situation. 'I know,' he went on, 'the Nazis talk of labour camps and no more unemployment. Labour camps may be good as temporary ambulance work, but they are no cure. There is less unemployment, but the employment is on war production. If the army took over now and did not continue this war production, there would be collapse again. What is the good of the army taking over a state that must go to war or collapse? It would only mean a communist rising, and all we should have done would be to have prepared the way for another equally and dangerous slave government. No, dear lady, if – and imagine it is impossible – France, England and America could come to some economic arrangement with this country so that health might be restored to all of us and war avoided, then, with a prospect of real recovery, the army could take over till a good political system was evolved out of the chaos these Nazis have created. But that is all a hopeless dream – just nonsense because, although every decent economist and business man in all our countries knows it is only common sense that we should work together to prevent war and collapse in Europe, the politicians will not allow it. No one, army or anyone else, can take over this country now with any hope of success, unless it were a party with whom the other countries would cooperate. And that being now impossible we just drift on – God knows whither.

'In any case,' he said, 'the rebuilding of our army has caused anxiety and tension abroad, and I think that probably many countries, including your own, would not be happy if the army took control and would think such action could only mean war. Also another great difficulty arises because the army officers are now all so terribly hard worked that they have no time for politics. I, for instance, am both interested and also very worried about the political side, but the business of training and equipping our rapidly expanding army uses up all my energy.

'No,' he said, 'if there were some other reasonable alternative, or even if some of the more moderate elements, who were in the Party at the start, could have taken control, then the army might back up such changes, but it cannot initiate them.

'I am depressed just now, partly because I am so tired. I sometimes think it is part of the Führer's policy to make officers so tired, or at least, so busy, that they will leave politics alone.'

'You certainly make me feel there is no way to escape war,' I said, 'but what then?'

'No,' he said, 'I do not think war is quite inevitable. I think it is a race against time. I feel certain that if we have time, this country – I mean groups within it, such as the church, the civil service, the professions and the labour group will somehow create real opposition. But they are only slowly recovering from bewilderment at the situation in which they find themselves. It is a race between the real Germany reasserting herself and finding a way, however difficult, out of this slavery and war.

'If it is war, then, whatever happens in the end, the army will take control, unless the war were to go very badly, and then I think there might be communist risings. I do not know. But I fancy the propaganda on which Nazi teaching depends so largely, at present spread in their endless organizations, such as the Labour Front and the Hitler Jugend, would tend to become less efficient, because there would be less time and fewer people to work at it.

'On the other hand, to begin with, war brings unity to a country and everyone, however anti-Nazi he is, will work his hardest to avoid another defeat like 1918. The army also will fight to win, and any success they may achieve will be used, anyhow at first, to strengthen the Nazis. But there is one thing I am glad to tell you: you remember Hitler's idea of forming a separate SS army. That at least has failed, so we can be sure that there will not be an armed force to try to keep the Nazis in power when at last we have a chance to throw them out. It would be dangerous to have an SS army in peace; in war it would be even more dangerous.'

I came away that night greatly depressed. There is a kind of helpless fatalism in many, even the best Germans, that is most puzzling. How is it, I kept thinking, that with so many anti-Nazi groups in the church, professions, civil service, etc., they can forge no instrument of opposition, but seem paralyzed? I know my friend was right that the stranglehold was there before anyone really realized what was happening, but somehow I cannot escape the thought that all this vast Nazi organization is not kept going by machinery alone. It derives its power from the immense energy and drive in it, and it seems so desperate that the life which keeps this machine going is evil and that these other groups do not seem yet to have got the kind of dynamic that could forge the instruments that would set them free. But I could only go on hoping that Herr von Bretten was right that it would come in time, and that these people were facing a new situation so that they had no parallel in history from which they could learn.

I became more and more convinced that in the early days of National Socialism these considerable groups outside the Party did not begin to realize the danger of the whole Hitler business until it was too late. To many of them the fact that they were losing all personal liberty, the freedom of the press, all chance of meeting in conferences to discuss things, never really came home until the mischief was done. When the truth did at length dawn on them they were at first paralyzed and quite uncertain as to their right course of action.

But I saw signs of growing alarm and resolution which I am convinced must have found expression in something more effective than individual martyrdom if war hadn't come to unify the nation. I remember so well Herr von Bretten's closing remark: 'The danger is, of course, if the Führer suspects any real setback or decline in power, the chances are he will make war to liquidate his home problems.'

CHAPTER V

GERMAN OFFICER AFTER MUNICH

It was shortly after Munich. A reservist of the German army who hated everything National Socialism stood for crossed the floor of the hotel lounge where we were to meet. With a face solemn, in the way only a German can look solemn, he dispensed with any greeting beyond a kiss of the hand and said, almost abruptly, 'Thank God we are not yet at war.' And then, 'Forgive me, but I have not asked, are you well, did you have a good journey? Will you have a cup of coffee?'

Herr von Liebstadt could scarcely wait for the coffee to be placed before us and the waiter to move away before he gave a quick glance round – so familiar a habit of those who knew they might be watched – and in a subdued voice began, 'Do you realize there will be war? A change in the economic situation and a change of control here are the only things to save it and they won't come in time. We talk now but we are going to fight. Do you also realize we shall both be fighting for precisely the same thing – the abolition of National Socialism?

'But I shall fight – we all, although outside the Party, will fight to the last drop of our blood to see that we get the chance to make the Peace Treaty and not France or England. I am convinced that even if the Nazi Party did not collapse during a war, a victorious German army would throw out these gangsters who destroy so much and poison the very blood of the younger generation. But you understand that for many of us, if we fight we shall fight, not only to defeat the Nazis, but to make sure that France and England do not decide our fate a second time. Our destiny is at stake.

'Forgive me, you know I love England, but you and France have had your chance of victory and of making peace. There is no peace in Europe and I think France is most to blame, but I also think that England has allowed herself to be led into an attitude which is not natural to her. I am convinced that the blockade, for instance, was not the kind of thing that England would have done in a sane moment. But I suppose the real difficulty is that no one is sane after terrible war. I do not suggest that Germany is not also to blame. Especially since Hitler came to power I think we have been impossible to deal with. But when history comes to be written, I do not think that the story of the years 1918–33 will show Germany alone to have been responsible for the failure to reach a settlement in Europe.

'If war comes, and you win again, you will certainly say that the Treaty of Versailles was not severe enough, and your terms will be much harsher and once again we shall have sown the seeds of yet another war.

'But if it is tragic, it is at least good to realize that if we fight now, there will be people like you and me on opposite sides who will fight and pray not only for victory, but for the knowledge of how to make a lasting peace.'

I could scarcely break into the torrent of his words, but finally managed to throw in the question, 'Do you think that Brest-Litovsk, and indeed the Treaty of 1870, look as though Germany knows how to make treaties that will lead to peace?'

'You are right. We do not, but I hope that all we have suffered since the last war, not only through defeat, but through the Nazis, may prove to have taught us something. At any rate, I shall fight as never before for my country – I say my country and not the Nazis – to be given a chance. It is our turn to try and I at least am prepared to die in the attempt to get the chance, so you must know that if war comes, we who hate the Nazis and love England will fight to win.'

Herr von Liebstadt sat silent for a few minutes and then added thoughtfully: 'It may sound a strange thing to say, but I hope I do not get killed in this war because I would hate to be buried under a Nazi flag! I should like to live to see the flag destroyed for ever.'

'Do you think this country wants war?' I said.

'Wants war? In God's name, no. Believe me,' he went on, 'I am convinced that one of the reasons Hitler has got so much power is because the people really believe he wants peace. And the extraordinary thing is that I think he does. That is why he gives them a feeling that he is sincere. But he entirely fails to see that he cannot get everything he wants without making war. It is appalling that he knows no languages and that he has no real contact with the saner and more knowledgeable older members of the Foreign Office, and that he takes all his advice from such swine as von Ribbentrop and people who have no understanding at all of international affairs.

'Of course,' he added, 'I think also it is true to say that there seems to be something in Hitler that makes for destruction, and the same thing is true of many of his younger followers. There is some kind of momentum in this movement that will carry it on to destruction and to war. I feel some of the young men I meet must find a way to some ultimate surrender of life, for Hitler is like a madman who calls peace as he hurls himself on to a sword.'

'I have heard that before,' I said. 'Several friends have said similar things and some of the young Nazis I have met have given me exactly the same kind of impression.'

'Mind you,' he added, 'I think this also means that if there is a war the first onslaught from this country will be terrific. The whole energy and dynamic of this movement will throw itself into battle and that combined with the working off of a sense of defeat by many of the older generation will be tremendous.

'There is also no doubt that at the outset war would unite this entire nation; that always happens in war. Goebbels and his gang will know how to frighten people into putting their all into winning the war for fear of defeat and another blockade, and all the other evils they remember so well. But, whereas the war effort will be united and hence tremendous, the war purpose in the nation will be very different. My sons, for instance, who were in the Party but are now violently anti-Nazi, will fight side by side with those who fight so that Hitler may live for ever – my sons hope he will perish very soon.'

'Why did your sons change so?' I asked. 'Well,' he said, 'a most terrible thing has happened to their cousin, my brother's only boy, who was a young army officer.'

'Do you mean young Georg? I remember him well as a schoolboy.'

'Yes. He was murdered by the Gestapo.'

'How could that be?' I said. 'Surely the army could prevent that.'

'His father is, as you know, a general and he has done a great deal towards the rapid expansion and training of the army, but his son Georg was very outspoken and at one time he denounced Himmler and the SS, and mocked their idea of a second army. He was sent to a concentration camp and of course it could not be denied that he had said these things which included things against Hitler. Some months ago Hitler sent for the general and told him how very pleased he was with all he had done for the army. He asked him if there was anything he would like as recognition for his services – I suppose he meant some honour or other. The general begged that his son might be forgiven for a hot-headed outburst which had got him into a concentration camp, and be allowed to return to the army. Hitler wrote a note ordering his release. He was let out of the camp on a Sunday, and two weeks later, as he was coming home one night late, he was murdered by two SS men. Someone saw them escape and recognized their uniform. That is Himmler's method. Since then the general has had a breakdown and retired, but you can imagine what my sons and other officers think about the SS and Himmler.'

'How impossible it seems,' I said, 'that officials of the state, for that is what the SS men are, are sent out to murder in cold blood.'

'That is what Hitler's government has brought us to,' he said.

'Would you mind if we talked about the German army,' I said, 'because, as you know, there are many in my country, and in fact in every country, who feel that much of the ruthlessness and brutality of the SS is in fact only another more chaotic form of what we call Prussianism, which has always been characteristic of Prussian militarism. For instance you will remember in 1912 when I first met you, there was all that trouble about what was called the Zabern affair, when young Lieutenant Forster, a typical Prussian, brutally cut down a civilian for no very good reason. But I also remember then how angry you were, as also were many other German officers who were not in sympathy with that type of Prussianism. It does seem as though there are such very different groups within the army.'

'Yes, that is undoubtedly so,' replied Herr von Liebstadt. 'Before I try to answer the question I must remind you that my mother was an Austrian and my father a Bavarian, so that you will know I have certain prejudices.'

Herr von Liebstadt remained silent for some time and then said, 'I think it is true to say that although officers like Lieutenant Forster still exist, the type is a great deal less common than before the last war. Most of that sort have had a pretty thin time since 1918. To say that is not to lessen the seriousness of your charge against Germany, because you see this most ruthless, brutal movement, Nazism, is not led by Prussians, in fact, exactly the reverse. Very few of the leaders are Prussians. Leaving for the time the undeniable militarism of Prussia, the thing that is much more serious is the tendency at moments of national crisis for a group in this country of an extremely brutal kind to get control. Even in the Nazi Party there were some stronger and saner elements in the early days, but by degrees it is the gangster element that has now assumed control. I cannot say why. It must have something to do with the lack of political education, which is one of my country's very serious shortcomings, and it is appalling that nowadays any kind of education which would encourage independent judgement is impossible.

'But I think,' he added, 'it is only fair to say that in many ways during these last few years the army has done much to restore order, and that they take a very different view from the Gestapo. For instance, I have heard stories of the difference in behaviour between the troops going into Austria and the SS. I agree the army did not take a strong enough line, because, in spite of individual acts of decency and courage by German officers in defending Jews who were being beaten up, nevertheless, it is on the whole true that although the army behaved differently itself, it did not have sufficient courage to interfere with what the Gestapo was doing.'

'You would agree perhaps with what an Austrian friend said to me,' I asked. 'The German army coming into Austria may not have lost its honour by anything that it did, but it lost much honour by being present at what the Gestapo did and not interfering.'

'Yes, I am afraid there is some truth in that.' And then he added a very interesting comment: 'You know,' he said, 'I saw something of English officers in the last war, and naturally a great many German officers, and there is to me one essential difference between them.

'The Englishman always remains a civilian at heart, even though he fights as a good soldier. He would always find it hard to take any action, even in a war, which by his moral standards as a civilian he would deplore. He may do it if necessity makes him, but he'll hate it as a military necessity.

'A German officer, on the other hand, seems to have no memory of his civilian standards and becomes completely the soldier and quite ruthless in carrying out efficiently military necessities. I can only express this by saying that a British officer might give a certain order by saying "Damn it all, you'd better blow up the place", obviously wishing he had not to do it, while the German would give the order with great satisfaction if he felt that it was the efficient thing to do in wartime, and his civilian feelings would play no part. I don't believe the British can be two such different people as the German officer at war and the same man in peace. I am talking of the general run of officers now and not of the brute.'

Again there was a long silence which Herr von Liebstadt broke by saying rather slowly and with great weariness, 'But we sit here and talk of these things too academically, and as we talk war draws nearer between our two nations who desire no war. Seldom does Hitler speak the truth, but when he said that if England and Germany became friends there could be peace for a hundred years, he spoke truly. But once again we are going to fight, and once again we are going to fix a terrible gulf between those of goodwill on both sides who want not war but peace.'

'I wonder what the ordinary man or woman could have done since the last war to see it did not happen again. How is it that with the world longing for peace – I mean the vast majority of decent people – and dreading war, nevertheless, nations can find no way, and after twenty years of trial the world will be soaked in blood again,' I said.

'I wonder too,' he said, and we remained silent for some time, and then with a sigh he added, as he got up, 'But it is late. I must go. The only hope is that when we fight again we shall remember these men of goodwill on both sides who, whatever happens, will hold on to the belief that among the enemy there are such men also. Goodbye.'

After Herr von Liebstadt left I decided to go for a short walk before going to bed. It was after 11 p.m., but as I crossed Wilhelmplatz where the Chancellery is I saw a huge crowd and joined them. They were waiting for Hitler who was expected back in Berlin that night. The crowd swayed backwards and forwards as they sang their Nazi songs, and under the lamp I caught sight of the faces of some of the SS men – sullen, brutal, fanatical. I thought of Herr von Liebstadt and how he had said, 'These men will throw their all in a desperate hysterical manner into any struggle.' And I realized that side by side with them he and his sons would fight and they would fight desperately too, because in their hearts there would be the hope that they would rebuild a Germany in which there would be no SS, and the swastika would be destroyed for ever. But once war comes they all become 'the enemy', for locked in battle, none can discriminate on either side.

CHAPTER VI

NAZI LABOUR FRONT

'That's too good a face to be dressed in Nazi uniform.' So said a member of the Anglo-German discussion group in the summer of 1935 as we assembled one morning to hear a talk on the Nazi labour camps.

My friend was quite right because among the three or four Brownshirts who came to meet us that morning there was one, a certain Herr Müller, whose face immediately arrested the attention of all our group and we were glad when we found that he was to be the speaker. Nor indeed were we disappointed because we found his talk interesting and, more than most speakers, he made us understand how readily youth could be led by that type of man and his appeal, for the man himself was intensely sincere. Much that he said was sound and showed an experiment which could obviously be used for good ends or exploited for very bad ends. But a little about him first. He was a middle-aged working man, lean and hardened by toil and, we felt, by suffering. He was a skilled artisan, and having spent four years in the trenches in France and Flanders, had then faced years of unemployment. It was obvious that during that time he had kept his self-respect and done a great deal of reading, but, as he said to me at lunch afterwards, 'My own unemployment I could learn to bear, for the war in France had killed something in me, and I did not feel I could recover any great interest in life afterwards. But for my sons it was different. The eldest one never had any work from the time he left school, and he has become so useless that I doubt if even the Führer can make any good out of him. The other two, thank God, were only coming out of school when Hitler came into power, and they will be saved by the Party. If an English working man had spent four years in France and then saw that his three sons might all rot away, would he not be grateful if someone started a movement that would give them work and the right attitude to work which I explained to you this morning?'

Returning to the speech Herr Müller made to our group, which that morning included a few French and American teachers. They were staying in Berlin so we invited them to join us for this particular discussion. The speech was supposed to be on labour camps but a great deal of it was given to a definition of work and the part it was meant to play in the life of the community. Herr Müller was no orator, but his sincerity and his passionate concern about the well-being of the young in Germany impressed some of the most sceptical of the British and French present that morning.

After denouncing Marxist socialism as making class war inevitable, he said there were many ways of describing National Socialism, but he liked best to think of it as 'loyalty to the common fate of the community'. He went on to say that this loyalty expressed itself in work. 'We are not out to level down all classes in the community,' he said, 'but we are out to value an individual by his ability to serve the community. No longer must we allow our children to think of work as a commodity to be bought or sold. They must be taught to share in all that the community has to give us.

'I should make it plain,' he continued, 'that none of us claims that these labour camps and this view of work gives us any solution for the terrible problem of unemployment except on the most temporary basis. But we do claim that the attitude to work I have tried to express, together with the experiment of the work camp and labour camp, is a means of creating a background for further endeavour. We – that is Germany and the rest of Europe – must find a way out of this hideous problem, if we are to survive, but we could not set our minds to work on this bigger problem unless, at least in some temporary form, we had met the dire need of seven million men rotting in the streets of this country.

'We maintain that the healthy and generally happy state of the men in our camps is a tribute to the success of an emergency measure we are carrying through before we have had time to deal with the fundamental causes of unemployment. The practical experiment of these camps together with the creating of a new attitude of mind to work seems to some of us to give the material and spiritual conditions which are the right background for the task of trying to solve the bigger economic problems.

'Many false claims are made for this experiment of ours both at home and abroad. I would ask you to see in it no more than an experiment. You may not think it is a suitable method to use in your own countries, even temporarily; that is for you to decide. But I would ask you not to sneer at an honest attempt to meet a terrible situation, and I might add that, apart from anything else, I am profoundly grateful to the Führer for this idea, which has saved my own sons from the destruction of unemployment.

'Long-term unemployment was striking down the manhood of this nation like a plague. These sick men, many of them young, are regaining health of body and mind. That is Germany's temporary plan.

'In the meantime, we here, you in England and France and America, have got to face the much more difficult question of the reasons for and the way to deal with mass unemployment. And I believe that it is only if we do see the interdependence of the working classes especially that we can find any answer. If together we could work to understand and cure unemployment and to tackle vested interests, whether individual or national, I think many of our political differences would disappear. But during your stay in Germany you will meet businessmen and economists, and you will discuss these things with them. My task is only to commend to you our labour camps and the special function they fulfil in a time of economic crisis. I might also say chaos, and to ask you also to realize that we are well aware of their limited objective.

'Before I finish I would like to say that I believe we are learning something so valuable in our camps that in the future they may become a normal part of the life and training of our young people. I mean, that we may make a law, and indeed I hope we shall, that a year in a labour camp would be beneficial training for young men before going into some career or to some further training such as the university. This we may do for four reasons.

'First, health, for there can be no doubt of the good physical condition of those who live and work on the land for a year. That you will be able to see for yourselves.

'Secondly, we want Germans who normally go into the professions to learn something of manual work, so that they may have more understanding for their comrades whose lives are spent in the fields, the factory or the workshop. We want to destroy the false attitude among intellectuals who look down upon manual workers, and we wish them to realize that they will be worth all the more if they possess a certain capacity for physical work.

'Thirdly, the most fundamental idea of our whole labour movement is that it should promote understanding between all classes and thus strengthen the spirit of national unity. In our camps class distinctions are overcome by the facts of experience. Hitherto in Germany, and still in many other countries, men have all kinds of theories about struggles between the classes. We are a movement of action and we try to abolish class feelings by the use of the spade and the forming of a fellowship in work. We believe that it is only by action of this kind that social disintegration can be overcome.

'Fourthly, it has great educational value, for round the camp fire in the evenings there is an opportunity for lectures and discussions on many subjects.'

The speaker sat down and fell to a general discussion.

'Will Herr Müller tell us,' asked a Frenchman, 'whether it is not true that these labour camps are really military camps in disguise and whether all these men could not therefore easily be turned into soldiers so that in fact Germany is building a vast subsidiary army under another name?'

'The answer is, in a sense, yes', said Herr Müller. 'But there are two things I would like to add. First the handling of vast numbers of men in groups can only be done on more or less military lines. Therefore, the labour camp has many of the characteristics of an army. It works in formation, the men have physical exercises, they march together and they get hardened to camp life.

'In the second place they are under discipline which, though not so strict, is similar to army discipline. I think, therefore, it is true to say that a member of the Labour Corps could physically and mentally be transformed into a soldier much more readily than other civilians and certainly than a mob of unemployed.

'But may I add this', said Herr Müller. 'In many countries, not excluding England, because I have heard Englishmen discussing it, the question has often been raised as to how far all that is best in army life, which many who love peace, nevertheless feel exists in a well-trained army, could be taken over and used in civilian life in peacetime. It is often said that the adventure and discipline of war could be used in the arts of peace, and I am convinced that our experiment is the best example you could get of such an attempt. Many of us feel the labour camp is beating swords into ploughshares. But, of course, I agree with you that if you have a large force of men who are undergoing this training, they could be used any time as soldiers. But I do not consider you have a right to call this a threat to peace. It would be on the other hand a threat to peace to have seven million unemployed. I assure you the men in the labour camps want no war. Most of them, victims of the last war, were unemployed. But surely you cannot accuse any country that has found ways and means of turning out healthy, strong and disciplined young men, of threatening war. Everything in a nation can be exploited for war purposes, but that is no argument against keeping your manhood from rotting.'

We argued this point for some time and it was obvious that as a temporary measure for dealing with thousands of unemployed it was good, and that there was much to be said for such an experiment in peacetime. But, as we pointed out, in a world of high political tension, and in view of the aggressiveness of much Nazi teaching, the Führer could scarcely expect the rest of the world, especially Germany's neighbours, to be happy at the building of what Herr Müller himself recognized could so easily become a powerful war organization.

'We are not convinced of the peaceful intentions of the Führer, and therefore we view all these things with mistrust,' said a British economist.

'Then we cannot argue further,' said Herr Müller, 'because the members of the Labour Front are convinced the Führer wants peace.'

There then followed all the usual arguments about Hitler having been a front line soldier, and I felt as I had done before that while there may be some in the high councils of the Nazis who both want war and believe it will come, you could not mistrust the sincerity of men like Herr Müller who are utterly convinced that Hitler wishes to avoid war. They most certainly are not deliberately devoting their energies to a war programme.

In order to strengthen our argument we turned to another point and asked: 'What sort of education do you give youth assembled in their labour camps and what do you discuss?'

Herr Müller turned to one of the other SA men present. Here was a very different and distasteful type, not a working man, probably a small shopkeeper, obviously second-rate, who poured forth all the cheap and shoddy propaganda on race teaching, etc. We could get nowhere with him because to every question we asked there came a kind of gramophone record reply. But it was obvious that the camps gave opportunity for concentrated propaganda of Nazi doctrine.

We visited a camp that afternoon and sat talking late that evening among ourselves. Here was an experiment that was a question of internal politics. We felt that it was really not our business to criticize and, what is more we were convinced that the vast majority of the members of this corps were sincere, not only in their desire for peace but, in their belief that this was a peaceful organization. And yet it was clear that it could very easily become a powerful war organization, and further, it was a skilful war of getting men together and subjecting them to intensive education along Nazi lines. We were puzzled and unhappy, and yet realized that the enthusiastic response from youth which Herr Müller evoked could scarcely be wondered at, and indeed was a sign of good rather than bad in the youth who responded.

CHAPTER VII

GERMAN WOMEN OPPOSE
NAZI EDUCATION – I

Late that summer I was staying in a remote country house in Bavaria with one of the most enlightened of German women. She had been one of the leaders after the last war of the movement for the emancipation of German women. She is a scholar and has a dignity which the intense suffering of the past three years has but strengthened. A liberal in the best and deepest sense, tolerant and generous, and with the highest standards of moral and intellectual integrity. The repression, the shoddiness, the degradation of learning in Nazi Germany, and the humiliation of the Nazi treatment of women had entered deeply into her soul.

Frau Otto had travelled widely and had been an ardent believer in the possibility of the League of Nations, though she spoke with some bitterness of the missed opportunities, both on the English and German side, of making it the means of establishing peace, instead, as she maintained, of making it so largely the instrument of what she considered French policy or at least anti-German policy.

She spoke with scorn of the type of women leading the Nazi Party. 'All the really intelligent women leaders in the nation have been cold-shouldered and you have the stupid, the sentimental, the unlettered, or the unhappy, undoing the work of my generation which tried to get openings for women in politics and public administration.'

When I asked her what German women thought of this, that and the other, she replied, 'That is the tragedy. Women no longer think in Germany.' Later I asked, 'How much can you do to help Jewish university and professional women?' And again rather bitterly she replied, 'As much as I have courage for.' As I learnt later of all she had done and all she had risked and suffered in the doing, I wondered afresh at the easy talk of people in our country about the lack of pluck among Germans in standing out against the Jewish oppression.

I have often wondered since how I should have behaved in her position, knowing all the odds not only for her but for her husband, who was in the civil service, and her children whose future was at stake. Should I have had the courage to continue, as she did, to shop at Jewish shops because I knew they had lost custom? Should I have sent parcels into a concentration camp to Jewish scholars? Should I have spent the night in a Jewish flat trying to help a Jewish friend who was ill and whose husband had been dragged away to a concentration camp? Should I have continued to do these things after my house had been searched and I had suffered insulting behaviour at the hands of young SS men?

'What a refreshment it is,' she said, 'to talk to a university woman from a country that is free and where the women's movement can go on. It is essential to us to keep these contacts, for we realize that when this nightmare is over we shall need the strength of the international women's movements to help us rebuild.

'I know,' she added, 'that some of my university friends in England will not come to Germany now because they so hate the Nazis. Tell them I understand their feelings, but tell them to come. I, and people who feel like I do, cannot get out of Germany – we are not allowed to – and we are in great need of the inspiration of your friendship and we want it to be based on the true facts of the situation. We want to tell you ourselves how we hate these things.'

As we talked on, I said, 'Do I seem a traitor to you and your friends in prison that I insist in keeping in touch with these Nazi women and asking them the questions which, as you say, you cannot ask?'

'Indeed no,' she said. 'It is true that some of my friends feel the only way is to ignore Nazi women altogether and to try to make them feel that they are outlaws from the society of professional women all over the world. But,' she added, 'they are so stupid and thick-skinned that I think your way of meeting them and letting them talk probably gives you a better opportunity to tell them what you and other people like you feel about their retrogressive movement.'

She went on: 'I doubt if anything will really affect them, because you realize with them, as with so many men in prominent Nazi positions, that they are thoroughly second-rate people, and on their merits would never have achieved any positions of authority. Only their blind loyalty to the Party has given them power and that they will hold on to.'

She then added: 'By the way, I have invited to tea here today about eight or ten distinguished and scholarly women. All of them used to be either in the educational or political worlds, and several of them are now married and have children. I thought they would like to meet you and that you would like to hear them discuss the complexity of the situation we are up against in deciding what to say to our children.'

After lunch that day I went for a long walk to think over some of the things that Frau Otto had told me and to ponder on the incredible fact that, in a country so renowned for scholarship, women of intellectual ability and integrity were no longer needed.

The tea party, at which I was the guest that same afternoon, and the bitter outpourings of parents and teachers alike still seem as though they must have been a bad dream.

CHAPTER VIII

GERMAN WOMEN OPPOSE
NAZI EDUCATION – II

On my way back from my walk I called in at a hotel overlooking the river where two of my friends, one a woman doctor, the other a mother of a small family, were staying and took them back with me, as Frau Otto had said I might invite them to join in our tea party and discussion with German mothers and teachers.

I told my friends of my talk with Frau Otto that morning, because this was their first visit to Nazi Germany and I wanted to prepare them for the discussion which neither they nor I would ever forget when we were made to realize the complexity of the situation that lay behind the daily decisions these German women were having to make.

Our hostess welcomed us in the garden and surprised my friends by saying, 'One or two of the others have arrived, but they all come at different times and by different ways so that we do not appear to be having any sort of meeting. One has come already for lunch. Another who is the wife of our doctor came with him on his visit to my old mother this morning and stayed behind, and two more will come in through the back garden.'

Then, turning to one of my friends with a smile, she said, 'Thus it is in Germany today when a few parents wish to meet to discuss their children. If you do not know Nazi Germany you will find our ways very strange.

'Well,' said my friend, 'I see now that only to stay at a hotel and to see the healthy and happy-looking Hitler Jugend and the young men in the Labour Corps is to get a very false picture of what this movement really stands for. That is why we are so grateful to have an opportunity this afternoon of meeting you and your friends and to hear what difficulties German parents who are not Nazis are having to face.'

We then entered the drawing room and were introduced to about six or seven middle-aged women. It at once became apparent that they were extremely intelligent and keenly interested to know what we were all thinking in England, as they had been to this country and knew many university and professional women who belonged to various international organizations.

Most of them were Protestant, though one or two were Catholics, but all were united in their hatred of the Nazis, even though they held different points of view as to how the whole situation had arisen and how it was to be met. Their friendship was based on a common suffering and a determination to try to find ways of preventing their children's minds being crippled by Nazi philosophy.

They did not often meet as a group; it was dangerous, and one of their members was already in prison. But they gained strength from meeting in twos and threes, very rarely all together, to try and discuss their more recent problems. They had apparently tried to find some excuse for meeting that would not arouse the suspicions of the Nazi Party officials. One had suggested, 'Let's have a meeting to sew for the Seamen's Mission.' 'No, that won't do,' said another laughing, 'because Catholics would not be likely to be present at a sewing party for a Protestant Mission.' When I was staying out there, they had not yet made up their minds. Many such groups cover their meetings by having tea parties or sewing parties to raise money for the Nazi Winter Help funds because it was thought they would fall under no suspicion. But even so, difficulties were always arising. Suddenly an enthusiastic Nazi woman would hear about the sewing party and want to join, and anyhow all such parties had to be registered and might be visited by officials. It seemed better not to meet all together, except when someone from abroad came, and then it was 'just a tea party' of friends to hear about education in England.

That afternoon they were obviously delighted to meet women from another country. Those who did not visit Germany then can scarcely realize how isolated the intelligent university women in Germany felt. They had no opportunity to visit England, and eagerly sought any chance of discussing their problems with those not affected by them. It often made me feel very humble to find we were being appealed to for judgement on a situation they were handling with such courage and enterprise.

At first our discussion turned on general lines and then, as so often before, came the very direct question, 'But how does it all look to you? Perhaps we do not see so clearly inside the whole situation. What would you do if you were in our position? It might help us to hear what you think is right, it is so confusing to us.'

'But,' we said, 'we just cannot picture ourselves without freedom in our country.'

It was with a note of bitterness one of them replied: 'No, that I can well imagine. I know England and realize how you cannot imagine it ever anything but free, but, believe us, we had never seen anything in our history that would indicate that we should lose our freedom to this extent.'

Another German woman with a family of four joined in.

'You know, if two years ago you had told me that we should be sitting in this room realizing that a simple tea party like this meant running risks of arrest, and that to tell you we hate the government of this country and all its works might mean imprisonment, and that the subject we are going to discuss is the freedom to educate our children as we wish, I should have thought you were mad.'

'Surely, Frau Braun,' said another mother, 'it is not only a question of freedom to educate, it is a question of whether we can have our children brought up not only as Christians, but as civilized human beings.'

'Who could have thought, indeed,' said a Catholic mother, 'that in Germany today, Catholic and Protestant mothers would meet together to discuss the religious persecution of their children?'

'Religious persecution,' said my hostess, 'seemed to us a thing that could not happen again. But our great mistake lay in our failure to see right at the beginning when the Party decided to persecute the Jews, that once persecution became part of its gospel, no one could say where it would stop. We were not quick enough to organize against the movement while it was still possible. I will tell you one reason why it all sounded fantastic. Because all its teaching seemed so dreary and shoddy and we relied on the solid educational system of our country to prevent this sort of thing from thriving. And while we were so slow, and I will add so tired after the last war and all the bad years that have followed, the Nazis gained such control over our lives that we woke up to find ourselves in chains.'

'But,' we asked, 'how many people in Germany are really behind the Party?'

They looked at one another. Then one said. 'I should think in all about 40 per cent, but,' she added, 'it is very difficult to know.'

'Yes,' said a friend, 'but the real point is not just 40 per cent or even 20 per cent, but what kind of a 40 per cent? All the energy, enthusiasm and strength of youth has at the moment been caught up in it. We have got to accept and try to understand how it was that people, even the young, broke away from Christian moral standards so easily. We are paying the price of some great failure here, and we have a very long road to travel before we regain freedom. God grant there is no war for if that comes, then everything is lost, because the country must stand united if there is war, and then we shall not be able to struggle within the country or even within the church.'

At this point the hostess said, 'We must not make this meeting too long, so perhaps we should discuss in particular the problems we have to face about the education of our children. Frau Wagner, I know you encourage your children to take a very strong line about false teaching. Will you open the discussion?' Frau Wagner had four children of whom the two eldest Walter and Friedrich, were aged fifteen and ten. She herself had been a teacher before her marriage and had read history at the university.

'I think,' she said, 'that the only thing to do is to follow the teaching very carefully and at once point out to the children all that is not true. Therefore, my children go over their history lessons with me and any other lessons where there is much propaganda, and I tell them what is just Nazi nonsense and what is real history. Of course it has made trouble for the boys at school. The elder boy is fairly cautious, but the younger one is both daring and intelligent. The history master happens to be extremely stupid so Friedrich always asks him difficult questions and does not hesitate to contradict him. Of course, they are both members of the Nazi Youth, but the eldest one has been told by the headmaster that he is considered a very bad influence by his form master, and if he does not improve he will probably be turned out of the Hitler Youth, and then he has no opportunity later to go to the university which is his great ambition.

'I argue with myself that this is not fair, but I think we have got to stand outside this movement altogether, and, if you once begin to compromise, then things become impossible. My husband is not quite sure I am right, but we can only follow our conscience, and I do not argue that others should do the same. I have told Walter now that he must make up his own mind how far he goes. I told him it may mean a very difficult future for him, and I do not want him to act as I think right, if he is not convinced. I have also told him that naturally we remain just as much friends whatever he does and that we only want him to make his own final judgement and that I will give him as far as I can any information and knowledge to help him. I have not told him that, if he is not allowed to go to the university here, I hope to send him to England or America, as that is not certain, and I think he should make up his own mind, knowing that it will be a hard road if he takes it.

'Friedrich I do not worry about so much, he is still only ten and he has it in him to go on fighting. Also he is so good at his work and at his games that I think they cannot do much harm to him, even if he gets punished a lot, and we can only hope by the time he gets to a senior form this madness will be out of Germany.'

'Yes, but, Frau Wagner, surely there is a risk you may run into danger by this policy.'

'Of course,' she said, 'that we cannot help, and I think it is a good thing that my husband is away from home on military duties, so that he does not get blamed, and if trouble comes, even if I go to prison, I think it will strengthen the boys, though I shall not be happy if I have to leave the little girls as the youngest is only six years old.' (Very soon after this conversation Frau Wagner went to prison and though all her friends made representations to get her out she was not released for some time.)

A number of parents present felt that Frau Wagner was right, and that they only wished they had as much courage. 'But,' added one of them, 'it is also true that some children can stand this sort of thing better than others. My son, for instance, is rather shy and reserved and though I think he is really brave, I do not believe he could fight constantly with his masters and not have his health affected.'

'That makes it possible for me to put my point of view,' said my hostess, 'because I take a very different one from Frau Wagner, and would like to tell you why. I think one of the worst effects of the whole Nazi Youth movement is that our children no longer get any peace or quiet, and I dread to think the kind of people they will grow into if they are subject to this incessant thundering of propaganda all the time. Not only at school, but at all their other Hitler Jugend activities they never have time to reflect quietly as individuals. And if in addition when they do come home they meet at once with conflict and are urged to strife, I feel the effect on them will be disastrous. My husband and I have thought about it a great deal, and we have decided the greatest necessity for our children is that there should somehow be some space and time in their lives for them to grow. Therefore, we never discuss politics or the Nazis or their teaching, unless the children ask. They know we belong to the Confessional Church and at our family prayers we pray naturally for Pastor Niemöller and all those who strive to keep faithful. We also hope that we make the whole atmosphere of the house and the things we talk about and read, something so different from the noise and vulgarity of the Nazis, that we think they will learn from it.

'Above all we want them to feel they can breathe freely and not feel themselves torn mentally and spiritually all the time. We hope that by this means they will be better prepared to fight later, for I agree with Frau Wagner the younger generation must fight it out, but I long for my children to have some peace in which to grow before they begin the fight. We are doing a great deal to encourage their interest in and knowledge of music and art. This is a twofold idea. First it takes them to saner and lovelier worlds than that they see around them and so builds up their spiritual resources, and secondly my husband says that if he can really teach them the history of art and how to judge, that also will help them to learn sound judgement which they can apply to other things.'

'But,' said Frau Wagner, to my hostess, 'if the children are in turmoil, how can it help to offer them peace, for peace will only come by working right through the struggle they cannot escape.'

And again they turned to us and said, 'What would you do?' and again we did not know and we could not believe such questions would ever come to us. But they all agreed that if only we could invite some of their boys to England, it would be a great help, for though they got a chance of going about in these larger Nazi parties, they did not get any chance of learning that way. Whereas, if they could spend a few weeks in the peace of an English country house, it would be a magnificent preparation for the coming struggle.

At this the headmistress broke in on the discussion, and went back to the question of strain on the children, saying she felt it really depended almost entirely on the temperament of the child. 'Of course, the children must not have any pressure put on them to struggle against the Nazi teachers because it would only mean they would break in the end.' On the other hand she felt other children would find it a great release to talk over the things they learnt at school with their parents, and the creation of a world in which Nazism didn't exist, even if very peaceful, might cause a strain in another way.

'In many ways I think we have got to follow the child,' she said, 'and watching many of the girls I find their reactions are very different indeed. It is so much easier with girls because the Nazis don't care so much about them and their future is not at stake as the Nazis have no future for them except that they should stop thinking and have large families. On the other hand,' she said, 'up to now there have been many teachers in the schools who were not Nazi and that was a help to the girls who were thinking, but I cannot say how it will be when so many of the teachers and heads of the girls' schools are going to be young Nazi gangsters.'

As the discussion drew to a close and some of the members were leaving, one of the mothers who had scarcely spoken approached me and said, 'I wonder if I could talk to you alone. Frau Otto,' referring to our hostess, 'has asked me to stay for supper and she says we may go into her little private room and talk while she remains here and talks with your two friends.'

A few minutes later we went into the small study, which had French windows. It was a warm autumn evening and the view across the Bavarian mountains was one of the most lovely in this beautiful part of the country. Realizing that Frau Brunner looked very tired and had probably found the small room in which we had been discussing all throughout the afternoon very hot, I said, 'Let's open the window and sit where we can see this lovely view of the mountains.'

'Oh, please do not,' said Frau Brunner, 'you forget I dare not talk near an open window.'

'How stupid of me,' I said, closing the French window again.

'I am sorry.'

'I am glad you do not remember,' she said. 'It is a help to meet people who do not live all the time in fear.' I realized as I looked at Frau Brunner that there was suffering of a much deeper kind on her face than on any of the others and that she had already met tragedy.

'Do you remember,' she began, 'you once met my husband? He had supper one night with Professor Kramer when he was visiting Berlin for a few days, and you were staying with the professor. He told me how much you liked some of his music. That is why I ask your help now.'

'Oh yes, of course,' I said. 'I did not know you were his wife, in fact I did not get your name quite clearly when you came into the room. But do tell me what has gone wrong, for I can see you are unhappy.'

For a moment she bit her lips and remained silent as she stared out of the window, through which the hills could be seen in the distance. Recovering herself with a great effort she said, 'You know, of course, my husband is a Jew.'

'No, I had not the slightest idea. Am I wrong in thinking he was the son of a Lutheran pastor?'

'Yes, that is quite right,' she replied. 'His grandfather became a Christian and his eldest son was a Lutheran pastor. My husband is again the eldest son but, though they have been Christian now for three generations, my husband has had his permit taken away by the Nazi Ministry of Culture so that he cannot sell any of his music or poetry in Germany except to Jews, and of course the Jews do not count him one of them since much of his writing and his music has Christian subjects. My husband has almost the greatest knowledge of religious music of anyone in Germany, and he has made a special study of Christian poetry. He is passionately fond of his country and feels himself entirely a German. I come from an old German family and have no Jewish blood in me anywhere, but he will have to get out of Germany and I beg you to help us if you can. It is so urgent for his health, and of course we have five children and cannot live very long if we do not earn.

'It is of our children I would tell you,' she went on, 'because a most terrible thing has happened. The two eldest boys, one is fifteen and the other twelve, both joined the Hitler movement and became enthusiastic young Nazis. I felt from the beginning that it was partly fear about their father having Jewish blood in him that had made them such fanatical Nazis but we thought it wiser to say nothing and just let them be free. Rudolf, the elder, got on well in the Party and soon became one of the leaders in the school and was very happy. Then one day he came home in a terrible state. I did not know that any boy could be so angry, especially my own son, and I can only say he behaved as if he were mad.

'His brother explained that it had been found out that their father had Jewish blood, and poor Rudolf was insulted by one of the young masters in front of the school. He was no longer allowed to be a leader and probably he would soon not be allowed to be in the Hitler Jugend at all. I could not help him by talking, he was just so mad with anger that I thought it was better to leave him alone. But I knew my husband would soon come in through the back garden and I thought I had better warn him first what had happened, because he was very fond of the boy, as he was the only one in the family who was also a musician and he and his father went to all the concerts and musical festivals together. They do not look alike at all, because the boy is very tall like my brother, and very fair, and, as you know, my husband is small and dark and not very strong. I walked into the garden, and when he came home and I told him, he just turned pale and said, "Is Rudolf alone?" I said, "I will call Margot out into the garden as I think she is in the room."

'A few minutes afterwards I heard my husband say as he entered the sitting room: "Rudolf, I would speak with you." In another minute I heard a cry of dismay and anguish from my husband, which now haunts me whenever I am still. For Rudolf had struck him in the face with such violence that he fell to the ground and struck his head against the end of the sideboard.'

For a moment Frau Brunner could not go on with the story, and then, seeing the look of horror on my face, she hastily exclaimed, 'Oh, believe me, Rudolf was mad, he is not like that. He could not have done it if he had not been mad. I rushed into the room and saw by his face he was mad. He ran past me and out of the front door, while my husband lay on the floor unconscious, with blood flowing from his head. It was impossible to prevent Margot and her young brother, Edward, from seeing what had happened, and I think Edward, who is only five years old, will never get over the shock of it all. Margot, I think, is all right because she is older and was so concerned about helping me look after her father that she had not time to think, but poor little Edward we found half an hour later sitting on the staircase hugging a toy and weeping bitterly.

'Anyhow, I got my husband to bed, the doctor came and he said the wound itself was not serious. But for many days after, my husband was in a despair I did not believe existed. When he slept I was always afraid for the time he would wake again, because it was so terrible for him to remember what had happened. He is better now and some Christian friends have done very much for him, but he has asked to see you and he feels he must get out of the country and try to start a new life. He said at first that he would never be able to play again, but I have told him it will be better if we can only get away. I was so very happy yesterday, because all his life he had said he wanted to write some music of the Passion, but that he would never have the courage to do it. But yesterday he said, "I think I could try to write some Passion music."

'If you could help us to get to England there is still a chance for him and the children.'

'What happened to Rudolf?' I said.

'Rudolf did not come back that night and I was terribly anxious because I dare not let the police know and yet I feared he would do harm to himself, but early the next day my brother rang up to say he had arrived at their house, which is about half an hour's bus ride from here, and that he would stay there for a time. You see, my brother, like me, is an Aryan and I must tell you he was very unhappy when I married my husband, but he has always been very friendly and now he is really most kind. He says it is much better for Rudolf to live with them for the time while we decide. Rudolf has told his uncle that he wants to leave school, change his name and get right away from here and then try to join the Party again. He says still in bitter anger that he wants to help persecute the Jews because they have ruined his life. My brother is wise and I only hope some day Rudolf will come back to us.

'For the other children I am afraid it was a severe shock, though, as I told you, Margot is all right, I think, especially as she has a wonderful teacher at school who was once a pupil of my husband's and she does much to help her. I feel much worried about poor Edward. He is very quiet and does not say much, but he has been ill once or twice lately and said he was not well enough for school owing to some pain or other. I feel it is just that he is so afraid of school now as his brother Rudolf never speaks to him or to his other brother. It would be better for us all if only we could get right away from this atmosphere.

CHAPTER IX

GERMAN FOREIGN OFFICE PROPER

Most of the men who moved quietly along the corridors were elderly. They moved rather deliberately, carrying important-looking dispatch cases from one room to another. Sometimes two would pass along together in thoughtful conversation. The whole atmosphere indicated that this was an important state department, and in the approach of porters and senior officials alike there was a dignity which in Germany always takes the form of a certain solemnity.

The rooms were spacious and well carpeted, with good solid furniture and although in many of them there was the inevitable picture of Hitler, I had a strong feeling that the gentlemen whose ponderous oil paintings hung on the side walls were looking across with heavy indignation at the upstart whose portrait held the place of honour. This strange, ill-shaped ruffian, with a name unknown in German history, who could he be?

In each of the rooms I entered to keep an appointment, a dignified figure rose from a large desk and came forward, and with traditional courtesy bowed and shook hands. That was the German Foreign Office at No. 76 Wilhelmstrasse, and as I entered it I was met by an elderly porter with the formal manner and rather shrewd looks of his profession. Although he greeted me with 'Heil Hitler' he looked neither surprised nor upset when I replied '*Guten Tag*' and in fact, having led me down the corridor, as he handed me over to a second porter he said 'Good morning' in English, with rather a wry smile which I somehow felt was meant to say 'I entirely agree with you!'

Across the road from No. 76 is No. 63 – von Ribbentrop's Foreign Affairs Office. Here you find something which looks and feels like a combination of a large police station and a building in a world fair or commercial exhibition, or perhaps a vast travel agency: whitewashed walls and, I think, black paint and vivid green linoleum on the floor, while bright yellow curtains fluttered from every window. Most of the furniture was light and modern, and made largely of steel. Here was neither courtesy nor quiet. As I approached the step leading to the front door, two sullen-looking SS guards stood to attention and growled 'Heil Hitler' at me as I climbed the steps. I entered the door and found more SS men. In fact they seemed to be on guard every few yards in the building, and their ugly obtrusiveness was clearly marked against the clean white walls. The porter was a disagreeable-looking man, and when I replied '*Guten Tag*' to his 'Heil Hitler', he repeated his greeting, but as I did the same with mine he gave up the competition, though obviously with a bad grace. But what a different atmosphere! Here at No. 63 all was bustle and noise. No one was old, and certainly no one was courteous or dignified. Here young uniformed Nazis of all types, mostly very intelligent-looking, rushed about with an air of importance and extreme urgency. As I went down the corridors I found that on many of the doors were names of countries. Rooms were marked Norway, Holland, Bulgaria, Iraq, Syria, Palestine and South Africa, later a large number of rooms for Britain and France, Poland, and so on. A group of young SS men were attached to each of these offices and many of them spoke fluently the language of the country with which they were concerned. I should think probably more mischief was planned in that vulgar, noisy building than in almost any spot in Europe. Here von Ribbentrop, the commercial traveller, could use all his experience of salesmanship. Here he could plan to try out all over the world any of the less reputable means he knows of cheating and unfair competition. Hence eager and dangerous missionaries went forth to the ends of the earth to stir up trouble. Thither came eager but ignorant youth from other lands, to be flattered and impressed.

Here also came some of the disgruntled and ill-adjusted middle-aged men from many lands. Men who have never succeeded in life, to be trained as the agents of this unscrupulous office, for by so doing they felt they had at last become important, and could now wield the power which had always eluded them. This was the training ground of most of Europe's future quislings.

Back to the German Foreign Office proper, a place from which at times admittedly an infamous policy has come. But within its walls there have always been some men with high standards of moral integrity and sound judgement; certainly also men of culture and learning, and men who thought of other countries not only as markets for shoddy propaganda and cheap intrigue with undesirable national elements, but as places from which they had gained inspiration and which they genuinely respected.

It was, I suppose, just because the members of the Foreign Office proved unsympathetic to the worst excesses of Nazi foreign propaganda that von Ribbentrop was allowed to set up his Party foreign affairs office which, of course, made endless complications for the Foreign Office proper. It is also, I gather, true that Hitler is completely ill at ease with the more cultured and conventional diplomats, and looks upon them as quite unsuitable agents for putting over his policy with vigour and determination. The grovelling insincerity of von Ribbentrop with his horde of keen and fanatical young men, together with the high-tension atmosphere of No. 63, gave Hitler the kind of setting and support he felt he needed. Another and equally serious side of the story is that our people were correspondingly ill at ease with the von Ribbentrop crowd, and I sometimes felt that neither the German Foreign Office nor our own was too well informed of all that went on in the office at No. 63.

I spent two mornings that week at the Foreign Office consulting various officials about a conference for educationalists, economists and philosophers, who were to meet in Berlin shortly afterwards, in order to see if they could get at the more fundamental causes of this revolution. Some of the Nazis, including von Ribbentrop, having realized that they could not exploit this show, became decidedly less keen about it, as I shall mention later.

One thing was quite obvious, that in the Foreign Office as in other civil service departments, you found this split between the Party and the state. I spent part of one morning and part of the next afternoon in No. 76 and I can only say that some of the officials must have been quite certain there was no secret microphone in their rooms or they would not have dared to talk as frankly as they did. Unless, of course, in a world so full of deceit some of them thought they would throw dust in my eyes by abusing the Nazis, in the hope that I would open up more freely, and possibly even repeat what others in the same building had said. However, except perhaps in the case of one man I met, and whom I did not trust in the least for all his charm, I rather think the others were sincere, or as sincere as anyone can be who lives in a state of deliberate compromise.

Some of the men I met on that and other occasions were obviously determined not to betray in any way what their attitude to the Nazis was. Yet somehow, most of the Nazi jargon they used sounded incongruous. If, instead of sitting by the desk of the speaker, I had been seated at the other side of the long room we were in, I should have felt I was listening to a play, and one in which the chief actor was not very much inside his part. The attitude of some of these men was formal and entirely correct in relation to the German government. After all they were government officials, and they were Germans, and any personal opinions they had must not be revealed to a stranger and a foreigner. They, no less than others, were anxious, very anxious, about the future of Europe. They did not put forward the more fantastic Nazi claims, but carefully and much more skilfully they indicated that the causes of unrest in Europe twenty years after the last war were not entirely Germany's fault. They were well versed in any writings or speeches of men in our own country who had pointed out with some vigour that the disarmament of Germany was morally indefensible unless the rest of the world disarmed.

With people like those it was well-nigh impossible to know what they were really thinking, though all the time I was acutely aware that the whole Nazi idiom was foreign to them, even though they used it formally, and indeed gave the Nazi designs a less crude and much more subtle interpretation.

Later that morning another member of this office I was visiting shrugged his shoulders and in a passing remark at once revealed his attitude. 'You know, fevers must run their course, and the only thing for some of us to do is to wait … you understand me?' He went on, to show how cleverly the Nazis were using certain national fears and sentiments: 'Take for example the fear of encirclement. People in your country are quite wrong in thinking that this is not a real fear in the mind of many Germans. Hitler knows better, and he uses this fear. You see, it is not that the Germans have a reasonable theory about encirclement that is based on facts, although this is partially true, because all our neighbours are so heavily armed. The much more dangerous thing is that facts like these can be highly coloured, and they are presented to a people who do not think of a "theory" of encirclement, but are deeply conscious that one of the most bitter experiences of their lives was the four years of the last war when in fact they were encircled by enemies.'

'I am interested in what you say,' I replied, 'because I agree we are often far too impatient, and do not look below the surface to discover the reasons for certain attitudes of mind. I well remember just after the last war in talking to German students, that, as you say, they felt that of all the experiences of the war, almost the most bitter was the feeling of isolation and encirclement which they said had a spiritual and intellectual, as well as a purely physical expression. The fact that, as I pointed out to these students, we felt it was entirely Germany's fault that practically the whole civilized world had been against her, was really irrelevant to the actual experience they were describing.'

'Well, we won't discuss the "war guilt clause",' said Herr von Friedland. 'But the relevance of their past experience to the present day is really a psychological relevance. Surely it is true that a fear very often begets the very thing it fears. There is no doubt at all that there is deep down in the minds of masses of my fellow countrymen an intense fear of encirclement, and an intense fear of Russia. Hitler knows how to use both these fears, and by feeding them he hopes to strengthen the people's belief in him and his Party. By the way,' he said, 'did you go into the Unter den Linden exhibition called "Die Front"?'

'Yes,' I said, 'and I realize that much of that, especially the picture postcards, which were bought by the thousand, tends to increase this fear. And it is visited by crowds from all over Germany.'

'And mind you,' he added, 'I would not be honest if I did not say that I also think there is an element of truth in their fears. So long as there are burning problems left in Europe from the last war, and so long as there is acute economic depression, there is always a possibility of war. And whereas I am convinced that the people of this country don't want war, I am equally sure that if they are encouraged to believe war is likely, they will give full backing to all preparations against a second defeat and blockade. Most certainly Nazi propaganda does prepare their minds by showing the vulnerability of the Reich.'

'But don't they see,' I asked, 'that if Hitler goes on doing things like walking into the Rhineland and Austria, he will certainly start a war sooner or later?'

Herr von Friedland got up and wandered to the window, and standing there with his back to the light he continued, 'You know, your country is almost impossible for any of us to understand. Although officially you protested against these things, the impression many of us got and certainly the impression given here by many Nazis in places of authority is that many responsible people in England, while regretting the way Germany acted, nevertheless felt that it was entirely reasonable that we should have the right to move our troops anywhere on our own territory. Personally I think that attitude is fair and just, but it has been represented in Germany in a most unfortunate way.

'I do not agree with the Nazis' attitude to the Treaty of Versailles,' he continued, 'though naturally I take a very different view of it from your countrymen. But you know,' he added, 'the Englishman's strong sense of fair play makes it very important that your country should not be a party to any treaty which in future years a new generation will refuse to take seriously even if it does not repudiate it all together. It was this standard of fair play in your country that made so many of your people say that the entry into the Rhineland was reasonable. Even about Austria there were not lacking voices in England that pointed out that you too were partly responsible for the disaster of Austria because you and France would not allow the economic Anschluss at a time when it was reasonable and would have saved so much suffering in that country. I think it is important that any treaty that aims at peace should be the kind of treaty that can still be taken seriously twenty years after it is signed. Some of the present generation in England as well as in Germany seem to live uncomfortably with certain of the decisions of 1919.'

Walking back to his desk Herr von Friedland did not sit down but stood beside it playing with his pen. 'Of course,' he continued, 'the most important thing is the clever way in which Hitler understands the mind of the people. You saw his latest headline?'

'No. Which one do you mean?' I asked.

'Hitler liquidates Versailles,' he replied. 'Whatever you or I may think of that treaty, whatever history may later say of it, for us, as Germans, it does stand for defeat and distress, and in a curious way Hitler has made thousands of Germans feel that he has closed a most unhappy chapter.'

At this moment the door opened and a junior secretary entered stiffly and announced that Herr von Friedland was expected for the conference in the Minister's room. 'Thank you, I'll come at once,' Herr von Friedland replied. Then turning to me as the door closed on the secretary he said, 'I must go. I hope your conference with the Nazis is a success. Ask them all the questions you can, especially the sort that it is difficult for Germans to ask them, but forgive me for warning you, in your own expression, to remember all the time that you are dealing with outsiders.'

It was during the next afternoon that I had perhaps the most interesting talk at the Foreign Office. A few minutes before two thirty I was taken up to keep an appointment with Herr von Hildesheim. I had not met him for many years, though I had known him as long ago as 1913. Having exchanged greetings and inquiries about our two families and mutual friends Herr von Hildesheim plunged straight in by saying, 'So you have come over with your friends to try and understand the Third Reich. I can only tell you that when you do understand it, you will join with the rest of us in praying God there may be a Fourth Reich and that as soon as possible.'

'Well, that's plain anyhow, it's rather a relief to know exactly what you think about it all,' I replied.

He laughed and said, 'No, I'm afraid I cannot say exactly what I think because that would not be possible in language fit for a lady, or indeed, for this Foreign Office. However, tell me more about your party.' We discussed the plans for lectures for some minutes, then I said, 'Look here, tell me plainly, do you think there is any point in our coming across here and trying to understand the Nazis, or do you think we're heading straight for war anyhow, and that no kind of informal work can therefore do any good?'

'My answer to that, I fear, depends partly on the state of my own mind at any given time,' said Herr von Hildesheim. 'I am bound to say sometimes that I think it is quite useless, that we shall certainly have war and nothing can prevent it. At other times, I feel the more contact there is between the Nazis and you the better, provided you are not the kind of people to be fooled. The type of Englishman who comes over here, drinks in Nazi propaganda and then goes back to England and talks as though he knows what is happening, is a grave menace and certainly is being used by the Nazis for their own ends. The man who will not come near Germany I understand better but it is obvious that if he does no harm he does no good because he has no touch with any of them. Yet all the same I think your party is right to come, because I know you will not be afraid to ask the Nazis many of the questions that it is almost impossible for a German to ask them even if he wishes to, and, of course, it gives the Nazis a chance of learning what people in other countries think of them, for I fear they know nothing and care little.

'Tell me,' he continued, 'what do you think of our Ambassador to the Court of St James?'

'Von Ribbentrop?' I said laughing. 'It's impossible to be polite about him.'

'Oh, please don't try,' he replied.

'We have a joke in England that will give you a fair idea. We now say that England can no longer be expected to believe Germany is short of "raw material" if she exports so much to other countries.'

Herr von Hildesheim laughed. 'Yes, that just about describes him. He is certainly "raw material", right enough.'

'I have only met him once myself,' I said. 'He struck me as having the mentality and the looks of a complete swindler. Even his receptions in London are a joke for he loses no opportunity of showing his bad taste in every way. I should think few people in England like him and fewer trust him. One of his worst mistakes is that he seems to spend half his time away from England, and we begin to wonder if perhaps he does not realize that being Ambassador to Great Britain is a big enough job, and that it might be worth his while trying to understand England instead of spending his time on propaganda and visits to Germany.'

'Oh, don't tell me,' groaned Herr von Hildsheim. 'When he was appointed to Great Britain we felt that if he were given enough rope he would hang himself, but that he would at least close down his "circus" at No. 63 before he went to London. Instead of that he is obviously much more interested in it than anything else, including his job in England. The truth is that he is as uncomfortable at the Court of St James's as he is among us at this office, and having found favour with Hitler, he sets up this upstart organization across the road, of which he has supreme control, and completely ignores us, although we are the Foreign Office. You realize that he sends his young agents all over the world to make muddles and difficulties and we have to answer for them and to pay for their ignorance and mischief though we have no control at all over him or them. It is pretty monstrous that many of our men are being used for his propaganda and all sorts of other things that are entirely alien to Foreign Office tradition. In this way he makes the position of loyal consuls and ambassadors in other countries impossible, because he plants his young men there as his spies and the unfortunate consuls have to take the blame for the activities of people who have been forced on them as members of their staffs.

'The really dangerous thing is that I am convinced that their ignorance and aggressiveness will end in war. The real international scene has changed from this Foreign Office to von Ribbentrop and his gangsters. We are now a kind of international museum, but action and decision are in the control of the men across the road.'

'What you say of the Foreign Office and von Ribbentrop's office,' I interrupted, 'is really only one of the examples of the kind of split there is between state and Party in many spheres of national life, isn't it?'

'You are right,' he replied, 'but in Foreign Affairs it is a specially dangerous thing to have this division, though I may say, it is pretty bad everywhere, for instance in our Law Courts.'

'Do you think it is partly that you are all snobs in relation to the Nazis?' I asked.

Herr von Hildesheim laughed. 'Well, go on,' he said, 'what do you mean?'

'I mean that I wonder sometimes whether you could not have cooperated more and perhaps, thereby, kept more control, if you and indeed our own diplomats had not made these men feel so jolly uncomfortable socially that they walked off and felt they must work alone and not with you. Surely, even though they are vulgar and dishonest it might be worth knowing them if only to plan opposition to their tactics. For instance, I once had lunch with a British diplomat and Rosenberg, and I am bound to say the lofty superiority of our diplomat made it impossible for Rosenberg to feel other than a fool, and I felt it was not because he was a bad man that he was so snubbed but much more the Old School tie business.'

'There have been moments,' he said, 'when I have had a conscience about this, but I don't think anything else could have been done, because I think, even if we had got a better relationship superficially, that we should soon have found that fundamentally our views were irreconcilable. But to excuse ourselves is not to avoid facing the danger, because Hitler himself is out of touch with all really responsible members of this Ministry. He prefers an "upstart" like von Ribbentrop probably because he too is made to feel uncomfortable by cultured or even educated men.

'If you are not tired,' he went on, 'I'd like to show you how seriously I feel this is affecting the whole international situation.'

'Oh, do please go on, I am most interested,' I replied.

'The Nazis have created a system, a language and a code, I was going to say of honour, it would be better to say of dishonour, of their own, and you cannot cooperate if you recognize a different standard. You either go all in or you remain all out. Here is a very interesting example of what I mean, the kind of current diplomatic language that the Nazis don't understand. I learnt from some of those who are often with Hitler that one of the standing jokes of his immediate group is the translation of the phrase you often use, namely, "The British government takes a serious view of the situation". That apparently is always met with ribald laughter and sneers and seems to them to mean precisely nothing. I gather at on one occasion someone present who knew better tried to suggest that in fact it did mean that the relations between the two countries had deteriorated and that in itself was a very serious thing. This remark was met with further shrugs of the shoulder and laughs, and one particularly crude Nazi remarked, "Deteriorated relations mean nothing. We are only interested in action and they are doing nothing, so that is all we care."

'Herr von Hildesheim, may I ask you a question?' I said. 'If you were the prime minister of England today and wanted to preserve peace on honourable terms in Europe, what would you do?'

Without any hesitation he replied, 'Arm like hell, and break through all traditions in order to deal with the people who count. Let me explain. I think it is quite useless to deal with Nazis unless they know you are really strong and determined to fight if need be. At the same time I do not think any of the slow roundabout diplomatic methods are getting anywhere. Perhaps I should be nearer the mark if I say that diplomats are getting nowhere, neither yours nor ours. For you must not mistake me, after what I have said about not being able to cooperate with the Nazis. I still think you may be able to do nothing to prevent war, but if I were your prime minister, knowing what I do know, I would realize that the German Foreign Office is not the only place to deal with under present circumstances and that British diplomats are not getting through anywhere. Neither the British nor the German Foreign Officials have got proper contact with Hitler and his gang. Whoever else tried might fail, but I would go on experimenting till I got someone who could break through the barrier. It might need to be someone with the technique and training of a psychologist rather than of a civil servant. I think you must know men in your country who would know how to warn the Nazis and who would really make themselves understood. I must add that I might not be a very hopeful prime minister but at least I should feel I had realized that a completely new situation had arisen, and that I had to meet it in a new way and that I must stop trying to deal with a situation that has long since passed away.'

'May I ask one more question which is closely related to that?' I said.

'Yes, please do,' he replied, 'it is a long time since we had a talk and it may be a long time before we meet again.'

'Do you think Hitler wants war, and in particular, do you think he wants war with England?'

'I am glad you have asked that, because I would like to know what you think of my own impressions on that question.

Remember that I am talking quite unofficially, and, as I value my life, confidentially.

'Does Hitler want war?' he repeated. 'I am quite convinced that Hitler not only does not want war but fears it more than anything else. At the same time, I am quite convinced that the way he expresses his fear, through acts of aggression, will make war inevitable in the end. Let me give you a background to my remarks. If Europe gets drenched in blood again and if it is due to Hitler's actions, then you will rightly say it doesn't matter very much whether in fact his dream started as a Napoleonic dream or whether it was purely a dream of Germany. I do not know how he may develop his visions. It is difficult to prophesy about the phases of so unstable a man and one unlike most human beings, but I am convinced that his power over Germans is partly due to the fact he was passionately sincere in his desire to see Germany raised from desolation and not because he or they wanted domination. Now to achieve this, and not because he wanted other territory to begin with, he used such fantastic and dangerous methods that he immediately began to threaten neighbouring states and in fact, to excite hostility and anxiety in the minds of all nations, including your own. That means that through his actions a fear of war became inevitable. He seems incapable of recognizing that he had created this situation, but as soon as he recognized it as a fact he became frantic about the dangers of another war and blockade, and since then he has thrown his whole energy and all his vast machinery into preparations for war. He once said that he was absolutely determined to see that Germany was ready for a ten years' war, so that there could be no question of her being starved out again. He has become feverishly anxious about the resources he needs in order to ensure that Germany is safe if a long war comes.'

'But,' I said, 'surely, to be as secure as all that, means that Hitler really needs to dominate Europe before he begins a war!'

'You have put it in a nutshell,' he said. 'All this Austrian and Sudetenland business is bound up with this, and it is quite certain that Germany can never have enough resources within her present boundaries to be proof against a blockade of any great length.'

'It is also clear enough, isn't it,' I said, 'that these unlimited acts of aggression by which he collects his resources are the very things that must bring war nearer, also that von Ribbentrop prepares very skilfully by means of his agents all over the world.'

'Yes the result is the same as the Napoleonic dream, but I do not believe the origin is at all the same, though that may not be of much importance,' he said, 'except that many people feel that Hitler will never be successful when he goes against his own vision, by which I mean when he seeks to dominate other races than the German race. It may be a long time before his downfall, and we may have a long war first, but many think that the first sign of his inevitable defeat was when he began to include non-German peoples in his plans.

'That brings me to your second question which is akin to the first one.'

'You mean about England?' I said. 'I would like to know what you think about that.'

'Well,' he replied, 'you once said you thought Hitler's power was partly due to the fact that in some ways he does reflect much that is in the German mind, both good and bad. I never thought about that before but I agree it is largely true, though it is perhaps super-fluous to point out that he seems to base his actions on the bad side rather than the good. But about this question of relations with England, I am quite certain that there is very strongly marked in Hitler's make-up an attitude of mind about England that you must have noticed in general in this country. It is a deep admiration and perhaps envy of the English. There is no doubt that many of my countrymen have a strong inferiority complex about your country. I believe Hitler really wants to be friends with England more than anything, but he has not the slightest idea how to do it. He and many Germans show this in bitter outbursts if they feel thwarted in their hopes, and of course, they fail to realize who is to blame.

'I once was present at a reception in the Chancellery just after

Mussolini's visit,' he added, 'at the time the papers and propaganda were full of the Rome-Berlin Axis. I was standing near the chancellor when a young German diplomat, who was just off to a post in British territory, came to say goodbye to Hitler. To the astonishment both of the young man and of myself, Hitler seized his hands in both of his and with hysterical emphasis he said, 'There is only one Axis I have any real care for, and that is Berlin-London. We must not have war with England again.'

'Well, I'm afraid,' I said, 'that his theory he so often gives to youth that nothing is impossible breaks down here, because it is in fact impossible for him to have peace with England much longer if he goes on behaving as he is at present.'

'Naturally,' said Herr von Hildesheim, 'but then Hitler does not know England or the English language and you know the type of men who are responsible for reading the English papers to him and how hopeless they are. Then you must add to that, that he depends on von Ribbentrop's advice because he really thinks he knows England. There is no doubt that von Ribbentrop himself does not begin to understand England and his failure there is making him a bitter enemy of your country out of revenge.'

'Yes, you probably know,' I remarked, 'of the speech he made at a farewell dinner to Germans in England when he said that he hoped he would never have failure written so large over anything he did in the future as it must be written over his Ambassadorship in England, and then added slowly, "Gentlemen, the failure is England's!"

'I am bound to say,' I added, 'that as I travel among Germans of all classes I am struck with two things, namely, the feeling that our two countries ought never to have fought and must not do so again on the one hand, and on the other, a genuine desire for friendship and an intense fear of war.'

'Yes, both these are profoundly true, but for all that, if war comes the nation will unite to begin with and I think fight desperately because we shall all be determined to avoid a second defeat at all costs.'

'I am afraid I must go,' I said rising. 'It all sounds rather dangerous.'

'It is,' he replied, 'and of course, we have only discussed today the political side of our question. There are, as you realize, other factors. I do hope your conference will deal with the economic side of the whole international situation because I sometimes think that if we could have an economic Locarno rather than a political one, we might get a good deal further. Finally, of course, I know you recognize and should therefore investigate further, the deeper phenomenon underlying the unrest in Germany and indeed in Europe today. These things are not the province of the Foreign Office but they are of very great significance for the world.'

I was going out to tea after this talk, but I found it too late, so I telephoned and cancelled the appointment, and leaving the Wilhelmstrasse I walked along to the Charlottenburg Gardens and thought about the discussions and the men I had met that long afternoon in the Foreign Office. I have only mentioned a few of the interviews, though in all I talked to about ten of the members, some holding important, and others only junior posts. I felt they were mostly honest and wanting peace, but their attitude seemed almost entirely negative and rather helpless. Compared with the vigorous sense of mission in von Ribbentrop's office, it did seem as though my friend was right when he said the Foreign Office was a kind of museum piece, and that all the real life and policy was made across the road. I wondered if we could do anything about dealing with this, for as I walked along the quiet corridors of that building that afternoon and down the broad staircase where all moved slowly and ponderously I felt tired and depressed, as though I had caught some of their helplessness and hopelessness.

CHAPTER X

VON RIBBENTROP'S NAZI
FOREIGN OFFICE

Now back to the whitewashed walls, the yellow curtains and all the young men hurrying hither and thither in von Ribbentrop's 'exhibition' building. 'Heil Hitler,' growled the disagreeable-looking porter, and then took me along to one of the doors marked 'England'. As we entered the porter again growled 'Heil Hitler' and 'Heil Hitler' came from a tall, intelligent, young SS man who got up from his desk and came across to greet me. He was very polite and eager to help in every way and tried to impress on me that von Ribbentrop and his assistants were all most interested in the Anglo-German discussions I was arranging, and that there was an invitation for me to have lunch at the Kaiserhof with a member of von Ribbentrop's staff. 'In the meantime,' he continued, 'I will introduce you to a Herr Schultz who is responsible for planning the lectures for your group on the international side of our movement, which means the relations with youth movements in foreign countries.'

We walked along the corridor again with all its noise and bustle. The atmosphere was alive and I felt all these young men were dead keen on their job and finding it very thrilling. It was obviously a place where quick decisions were taken and they made you feel that they were in competition with the world. I mean, that in sending his missionaries all over the world, von Ribbentrop chooses people who understand how to sell Nazi propaganda. These youths are probably never told that their aim must be to cheat, or that any methods can be used to further their ends. No, much more subtly they are made to feel that they are highly privileged missionaries who have a faith to which they must bear witness, and that all means to that end are legitimate.

Having reached an office marked 'Palestine' I was introduced to Herr Schultz who was sitting at his desk with another SS man and a young man, obviously a foreigner.

Herr Schultz, having greeted me said, 'Would you just forgive me for one moment while I finish this discussion and then we will find another room to talk in.

'Do take a seat,' he said, showing me a steel chair covered with green leather.

He then went back to his discussion but did not sit down again. He stood behind his chair and talked to the foreigner who turned out to be a young Arab. To my amazement Herr Schultz spoke Arabic fluently and though I could understand nothing of the conversation, it was obvious that the Arab was both flattered and extremely interested. From the other SS man present who spoke English I learned that this Arab was arranging for a party of young Arabs to attend the annual Party Rally at Nuremberg.

'I am so sorry to have kept you waiting,' said Herr Schultz as he joined me. 'Shall we go to another room?'

As we passed down the corridor he said quite frankly, 'That is an Arab student, and he is coming with a number of young Arabs to the Congress – some of them are coming all the way from Palestine. You see, the Führer is anxious to be friends with all nations.'

Whatever the designs of the Führer, many of his young followers were sincere in believing he wants friendship between his youth and the youth of the world. I felt I could scarcely reply, so said, 'How do you know the language?'

'That is just luck,' he replied. 'My father was a business man who was out East for many years and I learnt it as a child and now it is really useful.'

I found on inquiring that in each national department von Ribbentrop had skilfully collected young men who had lived in the various countries or who spoke the language, whatever it was, including Japanese.

It was really no wonder that these young men, most of them recently down from the university, were thrilled with their jobs. They felt a real importance in what they were doing and they got the chance of traveling all over the world. They were among the most dangerous agents of the Party because on the whole they were intelligent and pleasant young men who certainly did not give the impression of brutality or even aggressiveness. When I hear people say that Hitler's technique was to stir up political agitators in countries like Austria or the Sudetenland and that he then got the nationals in that country to ask the Germans to come in, I always feel that leaves out the very important first step. The first people sent into these countries were these younger men, and indeed, even schoolboys, and between them they prepared the way by enthusing certain elements among the youth in the countries they visited. Into that prepared situation the agitator went and found ready-made a number of keen disciples. I will discuss later how I saw this working at Nuremberg, especially among the Dutch and Scandinavian groups. For the moment, back to my discussions in this office, and in particular, to the lunch party and later to the evening discussions I had with two of von Ribbentrop's special men. Herr Schultz and I spent half an hour deciding about the lecturers he thought should talk to our party. I was appalled when he suggested a thoroughly second-rate man, who had been given an important post in Berlin University, to talk on education. I could not resist saying: 'But surely Herr Baemler is not very good, is he?'

'He is a very great man,' said Herr Schultz, 'and he has written one of the most interesting books on Nazi education.'

'Oh yes, I know about that book,' I said. 'But I have been told that the authorities in many universities are trying to find out who are the students who insist on writing rude remarks and questions in the margins of Baemler's books when they borrow them from the library. I was told that already five new copies had been placed in the Berlin library, each time to replace a copy in which mocking remarks had been written in the margin by some courageous student.'

Herr Schultz seemed rather annoyed at this but tried to laugh it off by saying, 'Well, students in all countries are fond of ragging.'

As we were talking, the telephone rang and Herr Schultz having answered it came back to me with a message. 'Herr von Ribbentrop's assistant, Herr Hewel, says that he is very sorry but the Führer wants him, so he must go at once to the Chancellery instead of lunching with you. He says he may have to stay there all day, and possibly to dinner tonight, so he wonders whether, if you are at the Kaiserhof, he may come round after dinner, even if he is rather late. Is that all right for you?'

'Yes, certainly, tell Herr Hewel I shall be out to dinner but back in the hotel from ten o'clock onwards.'

As I left the building I met a man I had known for many years coming up the steps. He was rather older and quite a different type and class from most of Ribbentrop's men. I had often wondered how he got involved in this group because he was gracious in manner and obviously a good man for looking after the more distinguished foreign guests, for he had travelled widely. I rather suspect that he had been without work and without money since the inflation period and, his health having given way, he could not get back into the army where he had served before. To my surprise he was in civilian clothes instead of the SS uniform he was wearing a few months before. He looked ill and tired, and when we had finished our greetings he said, 'Are you by any chance free, because if so, we might lunch together at the Adlon.'

'Yes, I'd like to do that, because my lunch engagement has just been cancelled,' I replied as we walked along together.

It was a hot day and when we had settled down for lunch Herr von Oder said, 'What will you have? You will forgive me if I eat a very light lunch as I am on a diet.'

'I shall certainly join you because during this hot weather I know the Adlon produces a very good dish of cold asparagus and an iced orange drink. I had this yesterday.'

After the waiter had gone I turned to my friend. 'Why are you in civilian clothes? Have you left the SS, or are you on leave?'

He was silent for a moment and I was very conscious of the strain in his face and voice as he replied, 'I am so ashamed at what I have seen the SS men do that I cannot bring myself to put on the uniform again,' he said. 'And the fact that I have been ill gives me a chance of leave while I decide what I am going to do.'

'If you will forgive me for saying so,' I replied, 'I have always wondered how you came to be in the SS. But tell me what has happened to make you want to leave.'

'I was sent on a special mission to Vienna and other Austrian towns,' he said, 'and although I entirely agree that Austria should be joined to Germany, what I saw of the treatment of the Jews there made me feel I could not go on. It literally made me ill or else it was the worry as to what I should do. I am not fit for the army and it may be difficult for me to get another job if I leave the SS.'

As he said this two more SS men, one of whom recognized this man, came to the next table. The conversation changed at once, but all through the lunch I realized that the man was ill and nervous. He had obviously played false to himself at the beginning of the revolution as I rather suspected, and now found himself trapped in the betrayal of his own judgement.

At 10.45 that night I was sitting in the lounge of the Kaiserhof drinking coffee with an English friend when I saw the tall heavy figure of Herr Hewel approaching. He was a crude, bullying type of man with little culture, though I should think intelligence of a kind and good organizing ability. He came across and joined us, ordering some beer. Ignoring the subject we were supposed to discuss he plunged straight in.

'Your newspapers have no imagination at all about the reunion with Austria.'

We protested that perhaps he meant that our papers did not agree with Germany's brutal methods.

'It is not a case of agreeing,' he said with some sign of anger but obviously with great sincerity. 'They just will not see what is happening because they do not like it.'

'I tell you,' he continued, 'I went into Austria with the Führer and it was the most wonderful experience of my life. There were thousands upon thousands of them all on their knees in the streets with tears streaming from their eyes.'

'I wonder,' I said, 'whether there were as many inside their houses also on their knees but in fear rather than gratitude.'

'Ugh,' he said. 'That is not true. Why must you always look on the bad side of our pictures? I just could not believe it when I came back from Vienna and read your English papers – no imagination or understanding, just your incessant attitude of a governess scolding.'

Then he suddenly burst out: 'You should have seen the Führer tonight – I have just had dinner with him in the Chancellery and afterwards he kept going over to the map of Austria and holding it in his hands and saying, "Tell me again, Hewel, is it true that Austria has come back to Germany – that Austria is mine?"'

'Yes, but look here,' we both exclaimed, 'what did Hitler promise? His memory is very short.'

'You do not understand the Führer,' he said emphatically.

'No, that's true enough,' we exclaimed, and I saw an angry look cross his face as he realized we were smiling.

'You do not seem to realize that in any national or international situation there can be what Hitler calls vital organic developments. If a complete change comes as in Austria, from within, then of course, the Führer must meet that change. He cannot be bound by a situation which has completely altered.'

Then, sipping his beer and lighting a cigarette he continued, 'That is why the democracies are never able to lead. They are so slow and live on theory instead of following life. Ah well, anyhow, no negotiations with the democracies would have given Austria back to us.'

My friend Joan then asked, 'I suppose you agree with those who say that a National Socialist is a man of action first and excuses afterwards.'

He laughed and said coarsely, 'And why not?'

Then trying to turn the conversation he said, 'By the way,

talking of action I have learnt from von Ribbentrop about your party coming over here. He says the programme is too theoretical and that you will not understand National Socialism unless you see it in action.'

To this Joan replied, 'We feel we have seen quite enough action for a time and that we'd like a little more explanation.'

'Yes, Herr Hewel, we are well aware that Herr Hitler is a man of action,' I added.

'He jolly well has to be,' retorted Herr Hewel. 'For twenty years there was the chance to deal with Germany and problems in Europe on a reasonable basis but nothing had been done. Now the Führer is right, the only thing to do is to take action. The world is very angry for a time and then gradually everyone begins to see that it is all very reasonable and things settle down. That is why I am sure the Führer must go into the Sudetenland this autumn.'

'What do you mean?' we both exclaimed, in response to this blatant announcement.

'Well,' he said, 'just that the world is already angry about Austria and it might be better to get this Sudetenland affair over in the same year and then perhaps after six months or so we could seriously settle down to being friends and making peace in Europe. There can be no peace until these wrongs are put right, and as you will not help put them right, the Führer must, and it would be better to get all these things over and then have some chance of peace.'

He was, I think, aware of our surprise at the frank brutality of this announcement, and so trying to recover himself he went on: 'Of course, it is also true that even if the Führer did not decide to annex the Sudetenland himself, the situation there is becoming so tense that the Sudetenland will come to us if we do not soon go there.'

'But,' said my friend, 'is it not true that your Party sends Nazis into places like the Sudetenland, to stir up agitations and try to cause trouble?'

'Far from it,' said Herr Hewel. 'It is our Party that every morning clears away the swastikas on the walls and pavements and also for three mornings running it has had to clear away triumphal arches put up in the night by enthusiastic Sudetenland National Socialists. We have the Führer's orders to prevent agitation, but we can do nothing against the passionate desire of those who are exiled to come home to the Reich.'

We could stand this no longer, so I said, 'Look here, Herr Hewel, you really do take us for fools.' To this he gave a coarse laugh and said, 'Well, it is not very easy for you to prove you are right, and I happen to have been in the Sudetenland for some time.'

A long and acrimonious discussion followed but we felt it an obvious waste of time talking to him so finally decided to discuss the conference.

He agreed. 'It is now well after midnight, so perhaps we had better discuss the plans for your party. I have had a letter from von Ribbentrop to say that he had seen you in London. I gather he suggested that we make some changes on one day of your programme.'

'For heaven's sake, don't tell me that in spite of all I said to him, von Ribbentrop still suggests we don't discuss theology,' I said, 'but that we go and see your new autobahn roads instead.'

'Well, yes,' said Herr Hewel, 'that is what he suggests – you see, as I said, our movement is a movement of action rather than of theory, and he thinks that if you want to understand National Socialism you should see things we have made.'

'Look here, Herr Hewel, I told Herr von Ribbentrop in London that I am not bringing over people like the members of my party to look at roads. So I warn you that we shall not go on excursions of that kind even if you do arrange them. I may add that the main thing you Nazis seem to be creating is a situation in Europe that will end in destruction and war. We are much more interested in finding out the theories underlying such dangerous action than in studying your roads, which might be valuable to you in war, but do not interest me or my friends just now.'

Herr Hewel looked annoyed but trying to keep his temper he said placatingly, just as von Ribbentrop had done, 'Why do you bring theologians and philosophers over here? They would have been more suitable to the old Germany, and discussions on theology will not be very important or interesting.'

'The answer is simple,' I said. 'It is because you people are raising a theological question of the greatest significance. When you demand that men's final allegiance is to the state, then you raise a fundamental question. Do you know, for instance, what Baemler of Berlin has written on education? Let me read you an extract I copied out this week.

'"The teaching of religion of the denominations is under the protection of the state. But the Reich is neither Catholic nor Protestant, but German ... The attitude of the individual to the denominations will not be regulated by the state. The state keeps the concordats, by which it has pledged itself, and leaves it to the individual to regulate his attitude to Religion and *Weltanschauung* for himself ... The state has no objection if the individual finds that his *Weltanschauung* has become his Religion, nor on the other hand, if he adheres to the traditional denominations, and attempts to find a balance between the two. *But the state will not tolerate one thing: namely that the principle of the teaching should lie in the church dogmas rather than in the philosophy of life of the community.*"'

'Yes,' said Herr Hewel, rather irritated, 'but that sort of thing is the business of each state and not the concern of other countries. Religion is a private matter.'

'No, you are wrong, for there are certain moral codes and standards of justice that are in fact the prized possession of civilization in Europe, and these must ultimately be the expression of the philosophy of the state that makes those laws. It may not be our business to interfere with your religious teaching, but it is extremely vital for the rest of the world to know what it is you are going to train a whole generation of Germans to believe, because their actions may affect us all.'

At this point Hewel completely lost patience. 'Ach,' he said, 'you are so difficult with your parties. I don't know why you refuse to join the Link or the Anglo-German Fellowship. In the Link we have seven thousand people who take our advice and leave us to arrange their programme.'

Then with a sneer he added, 'Some of them almost eat out of our hands and at least they are willing to go and see what we want to show them.'

Well worked up by now, he went on: 'You with your twenty or thirty people are much more trouble than the whole seven thousand of them! Why must you be so difficult? It is not worth our while.'

I too felt thoroughly roused and replied, 'I repeat, because we are not fools and because our object is different. We have not the slightest interest in Nazi propaganda as such, but we are interested in Anglo-German relations, which we should like to see improved, and I must say your attitude is not very encouraging. It may be our quest is hopeless, and we can cancel our visit if it is.'

By this time Hewel had calmed down a bit and ended by agreeing to the programme we had planned. As he was preparing to go Joan said to him: 'Where did you learn to talk English so well?' For even if his vocabulary was limited and his slang incessant, he was obviously completely at ease talking English.

'Oh, I was a traveller for a British firm in the Far East. Now I am liaison officer between von Ribbentrop and the Führer of the German Reich. You don't wonder I think National Socialism is a good idea and worth defending at all costs,' he added cynically but honestly.

Although it was 1 a.m. before Herr Hewel left the Kaiserhof and there was only one very sleepy-looking old porter left, we called him to us and asked if we could possibly have a cup of China tea. He said he would get it.

We talked for some time about the von Ribbentrop crowd – the really intelligent young university men who tried all the time to suppress their intellectual and moral judgement and to sacrifice their integrity in order to gain power. These were the men who dealt with the student groups in Germany and abroad and were able to present the case for National Socialism with some sophistication and also to travel to other countries and universities and who sacrificed all for the sake of this opportunity and responsibility. Then there were the enthusiastic but stupid and decidedly 'Nordic types' who were used for doing propaganda with the more gullible type of visitor. They were most useful in acting as guide to all the things foreigners were meant to see. They were word-perfect on all the stock Nazi answers to every sort of question. Then there was the delicate gentleman of the group who was valuable on social occasions but who was becoming ill through his betrayal of his own finer instincts. And finally there was the von Ribbentrop and Hewel type who had never held power, men who had very little integrity to suppress and who loved the power that was so new to them. They cheated, bullied and would even murder, I suspect, to gain their ends. All the tricks of the dishonest commercial traveller were in use among this crowd. No longer had they just merchandise to sell, now they were controlling a vast army of agents throughout the world, in South America and India, Japan and Holland. East and west their agents travelled round the globe and wherever they went it was to create other agents, sometimes nationals of those countries, who would prepare the way for Hitler's doctrine and make fanatical disciples.

As I tried to get to sleep that night – I kept seeing a large yellow curtain fluttering against a white wall. Somehow it seemed the right symbol in von Ribbentrop's house of betrayal. Here men were trained to be traitors to themselves, to all that was best in their own country and to go afield and seek out such men in other countries who would plot with them to bring this vile doctrine to their native lands.

Only with difficulty could I recall the other picture: quiet carpeted corridors, sedate porters, intelligent, cultured but rather old and tired civil servants and one of them saying: 'We are a kind of museum, the real direction of international affairs is over yonder.'

We have become a museum because we failed after twenty years to find any way of peace with your country for Europe.' They were powerless and I suspect their counterparts in our diplomatic service were equally powerless.

They did not even see the significance of what was happening – of young eager missionaries albeit with a devil's creed, speeding to the far corners of the globe to seek out the young who have no religion and the older men who are traitors. And they went out for a house with white walls and with yellow curtains – a house controlled by crafty and dangerous men.

CHAPTER XI

DILEMMA OF A CIVIL SERVANT
AND YOUNG GERMAN AIRMAN

I spent a week in the country with old friends who own a large estate in East Pomerania. My friend Herr von Siegersdorf is keenly interested in agricultural development and policy on which he has written a number of books. Although he is not a member of the Ministry of Agriculture he is often called into consultation with the authorities and last week he was attending a conference in Berlin on a number of problems in connection with food production.

As I stepped out of the train at a little wayside station I expected to see Herr von Siegersdorf who had promised to meet me. Instead of this a tall, fair and very handsome young officer of the Luftwaffe stepped forward, saluted, then kissed my hand saying: 'You may not remember me – it must be several years since we last met when I was over in England studying. I did not then know you knew my uncle so well.'

'Oh yes,' I said, 'of course I remember you, Ernst, but you seemed little more than a schoolboy then. You have changed a great deal.'

'I must explain,' he continued, 'why I have come to meet you. My uncle and his cousin have been in Berlin for an agricultural conference and they hoped they could travel with you on this train and you would have driven home together. But a wire came an hour ago saying they had missed the train and asking me to meet you.' As he said this he closed the door of the car in which he was to drive me home. The estate was a good quarter of an hour's drive from the station and Ernst von Schoningen said: 'I would like to take you a rather longer way round as it is a lovely drive and it will give us some opportunity to talk, because I think of things rather differently from my uncle and I would like to tell you that perhaps he is a little extreme in his views about the National Socialists.'

'Yes, do tell me. But surely you are not a Nazi?'

'No,' he replied, 'not exactly. There is much that they do and say that I hate, so much is vulgar and false, but then the leaders are not educated men. But I cannot forget two things. First of all I and most of my friends did not know what we could do because there was no opportunity in the army or in the air force, and now Hitler has made it possible for us to have a future and I cannot forget that. Secondly Hitler has given some of us an idea that there must be more fair play for all classes and that whatever class people belong to they are Germans and that in the days of Germany's disasters all Germans must hold together.'

'Yes, my dear Ernst, that is all very well, but what about concentration camps for those who do not agree, and what about the church and the press and the universities, all of which have lost their freedom?'

'I know, and at times I have felt very troubled about these things, but is it not true that you always get excesses in times of revolution. I am sure that when things are more settled in Germany and there is no fear of a counter-revolution there will be more freedom again. In wartime we all give up freedom and I think Hitler is right and that the state of Germany in 1933 was much worse than war and that we all must give up much to get things right.'

'Does your uncle agree with you about this?'

'No, I am afraid he is quite sure that only evil will come out of this revolution. One of the big differences between us is that my uncle is still attracted by conservative ideas. I think some kind of socialism was due to come after the last war and after all the confusion that followed we must have big social changes.

'Of course my uncle realizes this and we all know that if we do not have Hitler and his socialism, we should certainly have communism and that really would be worse. If Hitler has done nothing else he has prevented communism here and I think we can be patient for a time and hope that some things in the revolution will improve. I do not like it myself that Nazis are so vulgar but it might have been worse and it is only fair to be grateful for what he has done. I want socialism but not communism – my uncle wants neither.'

As Ernst said this we got out of the car and, leaving the luggage, we wandered down the garden path to a small lake in the grounds, where a number of children were playing watched over by their grandmother. Frau von Seigersdorf, who was tall and dignified with grey hair and lovely eyes, came forward to greet me saying: 'Would you like to stay down here for a little time, the sun is so lovely, and in spite of the snow it is quite warm.'

'Yes, I'd love to,' I said as she led me to a wooden seat under a tree where we could still watch the children at play. 'The nurse has gone out today so I'm looking after the children for an hour or two.'

'How is your daughter, is she here with the children?' I asked. 'No, she has gone to be near her husband who is stationed in Hanover. Nowadays the army officers never seem to get any leave at all.' I soon discovered that not all of the children were her grandchildren. The other two were from the village, one, I believe, the child of the postman and the other their chauffeur's small boy. It always interests me that so much more in Germany than in England the children of various classes play together. I have often found simple peasant children spending a whole day in the nursery of the squire's house. I'm never quite sure what the word *Junker* as commonly and rather carelessly used is meant to imply, as it is nearly always used as a term of disparagement. Perhaps this family were *Junkers* but there was not a trace of the sabre-rattling officer about them even though they were a Prussian family. Although people like them lived on large estates, there was always a certain simplicity about their way of life and they seemed to have a very happy relationship with their labourers.

The wives and daughters of this type of landowner, however beautiful when young, made little attempt to preserve their looks, and when middle-aged were often homely. They dressed well but not fashionably. In fact it interested me once or twice at social functions to realize that one could generally recognize the aristocracy by the simplicity of their dress and hair style, whereas the wives of self-made men, especially industrialists, were extravagantly dressed though often with very little elegance.

To hear a conversation between a successful industrialist and a landowner about the 'working class' was to realize how different were their attitudes. The landowner of the best type certainly felt there was no class war, but then this was partly due to the very deeply laid assumption that classes were of the very structure of society – almost that squires were squires by divine right. However limited their ideas, the welfare of those under their control was part of their very religion. I always felt, therefore, that their opposition to socialism was by no manner of means that of a wealthy capitalist, who seeks to exploit men for his own profit. The standards of these landed gentry were simple and their sense of responsibility great. And whereas for many of them there was, especially among the older generation, an instinctive dislike of any big political or social upheaval, they were really concerned about judging any new social or political scheme on its fundamental principles and were primarily interested in the cultural and religious aspects of such movements.

It was certainly true that while living simple lives they maintained a high standard of personal integrity. After the collapse of the mark many of these families were almost destitute and the manner in which they bore their adversities was an inspiration. I met some of them at that time who had left lovely country houses and were living in a few rooms with only a remnant even of the family libraries and heirlooms – all the rest had been sold. Some took in paying guests, often foreigners. Many were grateful to receive presents of food and even small gifts of money.

Anyhow the fact remained that neither during the period of

Social Democratic government, nor of National Socialism did these people base their opposition or support on any purely selfish motives of gain for themselves. They had lost practically everything, and they saw no real way of recovery. With great fortitude and dignity they had accepted poverty as their lot for the rest of their lives but when they saw a good opening for their sons in the army they certainly felt their chief anxiety was allayed. Discussion with them was totally different from many in commerce and industry, who gained and lost fortunes as political situations changed, and who were far less concerned with the underlying principles of any system, and far more concerned as to whether it meant a way of financial recovery. I do not wish to malign the industrial people or to generalize too much about their principles, but there could be no doubt that for a great many of them moral principles were not the first concern, whereas for the landowner class they were matters of vital significance.

'I think I hear the car coming,' said Frau von Siegersdorf, 'let us go and meet my husband.'

As we approached the car two men got out and she explained: 'Oh, my husband has brought his old cousin – he is in the Ministry of Agriculture – at least if he has not resigned today. He so hates the Nazis that he is always on the point of resigning.'

During dinner that evening I realized how irritated these two men had been at the conference in Berlin where Nazi officials had apparently been throwing their weight about, although they knew very little of the technical side of the agricultural subjects under discussion.

Later we settled down to talk. Herr von Siegersdorf was an example of much that was best in the traditional landed aristocracy of Germany. Tall and handsome, he was over six feet high and looked more like a judge than anything else. At one time he had taken an active part in politics but had been sickened by many things that had happened and of late years had concentrated almost entirely on agricultural matters. He was well known and liked by the farmers for miles around who knew they could count on his interest and advice in many of their difficulties. He was a very devout Christian of the extreme evangelical type, and in the summer on Sunday evenings he would sometimes hold a service for the tenants and surrounding peasantry. There was a tiny chapel but this was seldom used, and the Sunday evening services were generally held in the large entrance hall of the house. He had lost both his sons in the war and at the time of the inflation many of his most valuable heirlooms had had to be sold, but he had managed to retain the estate and his quiet courage and dignity in distress had not only helped many of his relations and friends, but had given new heart to many of the tenants and peasants. Herr von Siegersdorf had spent a great deal of time in England where he had many friends and I look back with pleasure to days before the last war when he and his two sons used to delight me and their other guests in London by singing German and then English and Russian songs, for they spoke both languages beautifully.

'Do forgive me for being very frank,' I said, 'but after all the things you and your cousin have said at dinner about the Nazis I simply cannot understand why you both serve them by being in the Ministry or constantly consulting with them. Surely by putting yourself and your knowledge at their disposal you are keeping them in power.'

'Believe me,' he said, 'your question has caused some of us more mental agony than I can describe. Let me tell you how we argue about it and how we have come to certain decisions. I believe we do right, though at times it is almost impossible to go on. My brother, as you know, is in the Ministry, and I may say is very valuable to the Ministry because he has so many years of experience. Fritz, won't you explain the kind of position you find yourself in?'

Taking his cigar from his mouth Herr von Holzkirchen said: 'There is not much to tell, it is quite simple. I now have a young Nazi aged about twenty-six at the head of my office. He knows almost nothing about agriculture and he hasn't even got any feeling for the country as he is a Berliner, born and bred. In addition he is an insufferably rude young man and exercises his authority in the most ridiculous way. For instance, last week he laid it down that in order to carry out practically what the Führer said about all classes being equal as Germans, we should all arrive at 7.30 a.m. at the office. Thus I was put on the same level as the lift-boy. But the point is that he would not care at all if I resigned – in fact I think he would be glad if I did. These young Nazis are so appallingly ignorant that I really believe he thinks he could replace me with some young upstart like himself, probably one of his relations.

'The question now is, what will happen to agriculture in this country, if this sort of thing goes on too long?'

'You see,' added Herr von Siegersdorf, 'that is the crucial point. It seems to us that Germany is suffering from a sort of plague, but it is still Germany and nothing is more important than that our agricultural policy should be carried out by men with adequate knowledge and experience. It seems to us our task is clear. We must be patient and put our knowledge at the disposal of those who are in control, however unpleasant they are. We believe that Germany must survive this political crisis but that after all the economic difficulties we have had to face, it is essential that anyone who knows anything about food production or land reclamation should serve his country and not just retire because it is so difficult.'

At this point Frau von Siegersdorf joined in and said, 'But the strain of living and working with people like that is terrible. This last twelve months has taken years off the lives of my husband and his cousin. In all their family history wherein for hundreds of years the von Siegersdorfs have served the state, they never had to do it in such difficult circumstances.'

'Of course,' I said, 'I do see your point and I think it is entirely right, but you will also see how few people in my country and indeed other countries realize circumstances of this kind. It just seems to us that the whole of Germany, apart from a small underground movement, has put itself behind Hitler and that is a very difficult thing for us to accept and understand.'

'Well,' he said, 'you can tell your friends in England that the position of the civil servant is the most difficult of all. So many of us felt we must continue to serve Germany, and yet it is perfectly true that by our holding together the structure of the state, as it were, we also keep Hitler in power.

'The international situation is not too good and even if we think that Hitler is partly to blame for it, we as Germans care very much, if there is another war, which God forbid, that we have enough food.'

As the evening came to an end Ernst von Schoningen came up to me to say goodnight and added rather quietly: 'I do not want you to misunderstand me. I am not really a Nazi and I agree with most of what my uncles have said tonight. It is just that it is very difficult for young men like me who have been given a chance in life not to feel that we owe a debt to Hitler. Also,' he added, 'I think it is true that he does some very good things. The country was in such a terrible state that the ordinary machinery of government was too slow and too conservative to deal with it. Hitler made the country feel it must find a way out of its difficulties.'

'Yes, but, Ernst,' I said, 'if he drives Europe into another war it will be even more terrible for Germany and all of us after that.'

Very sincerely he replied: 'Ach, pray God that does not happen,' and then he added eagerly, 'I would hate to fight England. Something inside me makes me feel I would always like to fight against the French because my home is in the part of Germany that the French occupied with their black troops. But I would hate to fight England, for I think our two countries could so easily be friends.'

It was Sunday and the last night of my visit to my friends. It was early in January and their Christmas tree still stood at the end of a long room, though it was nearly time for it to be dismantled. Young Ernst who had seemed increasingly restless during my visit got up during the evening and, walking across as though examining the tree, came back to our group saying to his aunt, 'Aunt Maria, could we not light the Christmas tree once more – there are still candles and it would be nice to sing 'Stille Nacht, Heilige

Nacht' round the tree while our English guest is here. Next year it may not be a 'Stille Nacht' any more, if the war which she fears does come.'

'Certainly, Ernst,' said his aunt and went over to light the tree. It was a scene I shall never forget. There was not a trace of self-consciousness about the young airman and his family as we all stood round the tree and sang one old German Christmas carol after another – the tall landowner and his charming wife, the shorter stockier cousin and the handsome restless airman. As we finished the third carol Ernst said, 'Let's end by singing "Adeste Fideles" as that belongs to all nations. The lights fluttered out and the others returned to their seats while the airman stood beside the tree still talking. It was obvious that the discussions we had had in that house during the past few days had disturbed him deeply. 'How complicated it all is,' he said. 'I love my country deeply and surely you can see I must be a loyal German and fight for Germany whatever government we have. You have made me realize that perhaps too often we try to forget the terrible things the Nazis do. We hope all the time that things will get better but also there is always the other side that there is now little unemployment. I do not feel that anyone in any other country or in this cared enough to do anything about that. Then Germany had to rise again. As a young German I longed for that to happen and I give thanks every day that the army is once again respected and that I have a job. But you have made me unhappy because, if it is all to end in war, then whoever wins, it means a lifetime of misery. Also I love England – don't you think there is any way to get our countries to understand?'

'No one can understand Hitler,' said his uncle from the other end of the room. Ernst took no notice, but looking at me said, 'What do you think?'

'Well, Ernst, I see no hope unless these gangsters are thrown out, and I think sooner or later perhaps it will have to be the army that throws them out. I can see no other way.'

'Then you think it means another civil war or a European war?'

'Yes,' I said, 'I begin to think so and I am quite certain that if we do have a European war now, you will also have a civil war.'

'No,' he said, 'if Germany fights, we all fight together.'

'To begin with,' I repeated, 'but in time there cannot be peace between the SS and the army.'

He stood silent for a moment and then running his band over his hair, a habit I remember he had when quite young, he said thoughtfully, 'I wish I could visit England again, but we work so hard now that there is no chance.' Then weary with the struggle that was going on inside him, he clicked his heels, kissed my hand and without a word to his uncle or aunt went out and up to bed. He was nineteen years old and still showed signs of the turbulent but generous nature I had often watched in his early childhood.

As I joined the others Herr von Siegersdorf said, 'It is very hard for these young men. They are keen on the army and love Germany, but they are in a terrible dilemma.'

The next day when I sat in the train as it wound its way slowly past pine forests and snow-covered fields, I thought of this family and felt how complex life was. I was convinced that if we were dealing with people like these and, indeed, their peasant farmers, there would be peace. After that I went first to Latvia and later I left for the Balkans – Bulgaria and Hungary. In every country I met students and country people. Among the young I found a curious interested alertness about Germany – a kind of deep stirring within them that the German youth as well as the Russian youth had somehow got a purpose. There was something that made life worthwhile, and these young people were many of them impatient with their parents' criticisms which at times drove them into defending much in Russia and Germany, which they knew in their hearts they did not really accept. They all want change and they all want a chance to play some part in that change, but so few have any religious faith, which means they have few standards by which to judge between falsehood and truth in revolutionary movements.

I was in eight countries that year, never in hotels and generally among students and their parents. Among the younger folk there was eager questioning or bitter hostility. Among the older in every country and almost more in Germany than anywhere else, an intense fear of war. This was summed up by one German woman who said, 'How is it possible that when all Europe cries out for peace, we are still hurled towards war and destruction? How can it come when so many among the people in every land dread it – and want to stop it?'

CHAPTER XII

THE COURAGE OF CHILDREN WHO OPPOSED NAZIS

Earlier I mentioned how a Nazi headmaster said that men were better at persistent propaganda than women. The more I travelled the more convinced I became that what he said was amply borne out by what I saw and heard. It was apparently true that there was much more individual breaking away from the Hitler girls' movement than from the boys' organization. Of course, this was partly due to the fact that it was much more serious for a boy's future than for a girl's to be outside the Party. But here are four pictures drawn from very different homes and different parts of Germany, which all indicate the kind of difficulty and show the courage of a quite young generation.

In the senior form of a very large girls' school in Silesia an ardent Nazi teacher had been giving a lesson on the Treaty of Versailles which she described as the most vindictive and brutal treaty of modern times. At the end of the class a fifteen-year old girl said, 'Excuse me, Fräulein Schmidt, what sort of a treaty do you think the Germans would have made if they had won the war?'

Fraulein Schmidt was furious and the girl was sent out of the room. That evening, at the home of this girl, five other schoolgirls met and, their mother told me, spent two hours in hilarious and ribald mirth, but would not tell her what they were doing. Later they borrowed a large sheet of drawing paper, red sealing wax and ribbon, and wrote out a long document.

It was only later that the mother learned that her daughter, together with the other five, was punished for drawing up the sort of treaty Germany might have made against England and France and had left a note with it to add that they had found the Treaty of Brest-Litovsk a great help! They had put this document on the teacher's desk.

The mother was rather worried, though she admired her daughter's pluck, and said to her, 'But you must remember even if you are not Nazis you are good young Germans.'

'Ach,' said the daughter, 'we are bored young Germans. That teacher goes on and on with her propaganda till we nearly go mad. Now we hope she will change a little. Anyhow, it was great fun to make her so angry.'

◇ ◇ ◇

It was the simple house of a Lutheran pastor in east Pomerania. His little daughter of eleven looked younger than her years and very frail, and I was interested in her courage when, just before evening prayers, at which we used to sing a hymn, she said: 'Daddy, can I open the window, because you said in church today we should let other people know that we are as proud to sing our Christian hymns as the Nazis are to sing their songs.'

So the window was opened and the little girl and her small brother of six sang lustily 'Ein feste Burg ist unser Gott'. The small boy insisted on standing by the open window and made a pretty sight as, with a defiance he did not understand but felt was the appropriate mood, he sang Lutheran hymns into the dark night.

After prayers Esther, as she was called, said, 'Shall we tell you about our secret society?' Then, with all the enthusiasm of a small schoolgirl for a secret society with secret pledges and secret signs, she told me she had started an 'Evangelisches Bund' and had got thirty-seven members in three different schools. They were all pledged to resign from the Hitler Girls during the ensuing six months – many had done so already – and they also had a scheme for Bible reading and prayer.

While Esther was talking to me her small brother was on the

floor playing with his bricks. He was building a street scene and in addition to trams and motors he had people on his pavements. Suddenly to the astonishment of everyone Fritz spat into the middle of his street scene.

'Whatever are you doing?' said his mother.

'It's a Jew,' said Fritz.

'What do you mean, Fritz?'

Again the emphatic reply, 'That man in my street is a Jew and the teacher at school said we should spit when we passed Jews in the street.'

In consternation his mother and sister reproved him, though it was obviously true that Fritz, as yet anyhow, had no anti-Semitic feelings, but was delighted to find authority for an action that caused much consternation.

Later that evening I sat talking to the father and mother. The father had already been to the school to protest, and I think he felt satisfied that the headmaster, though a Nazi, did not approve of anything as crude as the instruction given by his junior master.

'But,' said the father, 'I little thought we should have to watch even the babies lest they get contaminated by this poison. It is a tricky business bringing up children in this country today.'

◇ ◇ ◇

'Where can Hilda be?' said her grandfather as lunch was nearly over and she had not arrived. 'She knew that you were coming to lunch specially because she had a half-holiday and that you were going to take her out,' he said, addressing Hilda's father and mother.

Hilda was the only daughter of a retired officer who was a large landowner in Westphalia, and whose four sons were all in the army. During the school term Hilda lived with her grand-parents in order that she could attend school in the town. Today, however, was Whit Monday and her parents had come over to lunch because Hilda had said the school was all being taken to the Lutheran Church in the morning and that, after the service was over, she would have a holiday for the rest of the day. She promised to be home well before lunch.

Turning to me her father said, 'You will find our daughter has grown a great deal. Unfortunately, she has joined the Hitler Maids which distresses us, but she now has rather socialistic ideas and thinks she should go in with other girls. Lately she was very upset because a very famous Protestant pastor, Dr Niemöller, was sent to prison. Hilda knew him and I think it gave her her first shock and the idea that perhaps she would not agree very long with the Nazis, but we shall see. My wife and I think it is better she should make her own decisions.'

As he finished speaking the door burst open and in came Hilda. Without a word of greeting to anyone, she stood, one hand still holding the door handle, while with the other she pulled her cap off a mop of lovely golden brown hair. With flushed cheeks she announced, 'I have forced my way into the presence of Herr Koch at his own lunch table, and I told him that I and many like me will leave the Party and that we hate him, and if he goes on like that we shall hate Hitler too in the end, and I told him he could send me to prison if he liked.'

Her mother turned pale but the old grandfather said slowly, 'But, Hilda, what do you mean? Herr Koch is the head of all the Nazis in this province and has guards at his front gate. No one can get in.'

'Well, I did,' said Hilda. 'I treated the guards as though I were a princess and they had to do what I wanted, and somehow it worked. I then got past the maid and finally the wife. She was the most difficult, but she had to go and tell her hideous husband that I would not wait till his lunch was over, I must see him at once. So he said I could go to the dining room. You can do things if you are angry enough. *Nicht wahr*, Papa?' said Hilda.

Her father who had remained silent until now was not lacking in courage; he stared first with complete amazement and then with delight at his very beautiful daughter of fifteen and a half.

She suddenly appeared to him in an entirely new light. Hitherto she had always been the baby girl in a house that was predominantly male and military. Then his surprise gave way to a good laugh as he turned to me and said, 'I think in England you would probably say, "Well played, Hilda".'

'Anyhow,' he continued, 'come in and shut the door and tell us exactly what you are talking about. Remember we don't know.' Hilda sat on the back of the sofa and told her story. 'First of all,' she said, 'when I got to school I found my friend Ingrid terribly upset because her father, who is not only the most loved pastor in this town but a most courageous ex-officer, the stories of whose bravery in the last war are known in the whole school where he gives religious instruction, had been sent to prison. By order of Herr Koch the Gestapo called at seven o'clock this morning at his house to arrest him. They said they would only allow him time to put on some clothing. The pastor replied, "I will call my family, because we always have family prayers before we start doing anything in the day, and even before going to prison it would be a good idea to keep this Christian custom." Ingrid says even the Gestapo men seemed embarrassed and all the family and the maids sang as well as they could. It must have looked strange with only her mother properly dressed and the Gestapo men standing in the doorway.

'That was bad enough,' said Hilda, 'but when the school got to church we found that the preacher was one of these "German Christians", and he did nothing but talk against the Jews and also against Christian pastors who did not agree that Adolf Hitler is like a second Christ. It was terrible, Grandpapa, what he said, and if that is what the Party does I will not belong to it, and I decided I would go and tell Herr Koch. I have told him that I will write to Hitler myself, and that my eldest brother who is an officer will give my letter to Hitler because he knows him and is in Berlin, and I would tell Hitler that I and lots and lots more girls were keen members of the Nazi Youth groups, but that we cannot belong to it if he sends such a terrible man to Westphalia.'

Breathless after this long outburst Hilda stopped for a moment, but not long enough for anyone to say anything before she turned to her father and said, 'You, Papa, can't you do something about the pastor? He was such a good officer and loves Germany and he has been sent to prison because he is a Christian and because he said it was wicked to treat the Jews as the Nazis do.'

Then suddenly laughing she added, 'None of the girls thought I could get past the guards. Can I go round and see Ingrid and tell her?'

Her old grandmother, who had remained completely silent till then, said, 'Well, I think it wouldn't be a bad idea if you tidied your hair and had some lunch and, as you have talked till all our coffee is cold, we will have some fresh made.'

After Hilda had left the room the old lady, who was obviously proud of her granddaughter, but at the same time very perturbed, turned to her son and said, 'I found it difficult enough when you and your brothers got into trouble by fighting the village boys who were communists, but what you are going to do with a daughter who starts fighting with a lot of Nazi gangsters I just don't know.'

'I am thankful,' said the father turning to me, 'that I have retired and do not come into contact with the Nazis. It is a good sign when the younger generation like my daughter rebel. I may be optimistic, but I think a lot of the bad things that are happening are due to the fact that the men at the top are ignorant and vulgar. I really don't know what to make of it all, because undoubtedly Hitler has done some good things. This city was a nightmare of unemployment, and anyhow we should have had some sort of revolution. Perhaps even Nazis are better than communists, who also put their clergy in prisons. Naturally, my sons are glad that there is once more a chance of a career in the army, and they know they owe that to Hitler. I hope somehow when the army is strong enough and when people have got tired of the propaganda, that the excesses that come in every revolution may also die down here.'

A quiet voice came from the depths of the armchair into which the old grandfather had sunk. 'You deceive yourself, Karl,' he said.

'While you sleep the Nazis are going to get such a control of this country that we can never get free again, unless we have a war or some terrible internal upheaval.'

Then turning to me he said, 'I am an old man now and I have perhaps more time to think than my son, and certainly more time than my grandsons who are so busy with their training in the army. I am convinced that the apathy in this country, which is largely due to exhaustion from the last war and all that came after, is going to mean that we have let something so evil get hold here, that Germany will now face fifty years of dictators and wars to get free from it. We are trying to compromise with evil so that we may have an easier time now, but it is not possible and we shall pay bitterly for our apathy and our compromise.

'Of course, as my son says, it is true that in Russia there is no freedom. But that is only so because in spite of some good things Russians are not used to freedom. But in this country we are turning our back on the freedom we have had, which is a terrible thing to do.'

'I am afraid,' said the son, 'our English guest will find it hard to judge what is happening here as we all say different things. The fact is we are very confused in this new situation.'

'And our confusion,' said the old man almost in anger, as he put out the stump of his cigar, 'will be our damnation.'

At that point Hilda came back for her lunch just as we all rose to leave the table. The old man, glancing at his granddaughter with pride, said, 'I'll stay and see that the child gets into no more trouble till she has had lunch, and then we will join you in the garden.'

◇ ◇ ◇

Lest I should appear to over-emphasize the power of the girls to resist, here is a most moving story of a boy of sixteen who lived in Frankfurt and was the son of a retired civil servant, a well-known engineer and prominent Protestant layman. Johann was a quiet and rather diffident boy with a great deal more interest in scholarship than in sport. He was extremely clever and had inherited his father's love of reading. His parents were strongly anti-Nazi, but decided they would not forbid their children to join the local Hitler Jugend groups if they wished. 'In fact,' said his father, 'I am quite sure in the end Johann will disagree as much as I do when he sees what it all means, but he had far better discover that for himself. In the meantime it will do him no harm to go on their marches and to their camps, for he does not take enough outdoor exercise and works too hard. As you see, he does not look strong.

'At first Johann used to talk about the Hitler Jugend and what they were doing and seemed very happy. He had taken great interest in being asked to help lead a study group on German colonial demands, as all the boys in this and many other schools were being specially trained in this. But by degrees Johann became more silent. He had obviously discovered that the Nazi master who was in charge of his study group was more concerned with propaganda than with truth. He had in fact been to a public library and had looked up many things about the British Empire and found how much of the stuff they were being taught was both unjust and untrue.

'Then in November 1938 came the terrible attack on the Jews. Late one winter evening Johann was on his way home from school with some of his friends and had seen some helpless old Jews being beaten up in the street by some young SS men. Most of his schoolmates had joined in and jeered. Johann arrived home looking deadly pale and, saying he did not want any supper, shut himself up in his room.

'It was very hard to watch him after that,' went on his father. 'We would never discuss anything with him but we knew there was a terrible conflict in his mind about it all. Up to now he had always hoped to stay an extra year at school, but now he gave us hints, though without saying why, that he would like to leave soon. It was quite obvious that he was very unhappy, but we decided that, unless he discussed it with us or the pastor, we would say nothing. He looked ill and for the first time in his life he began to stutter.

'Now I must tell you what happened a few weeks ago. It was a bitterly cold winter's afternoon just a week before Christmas. The school bell rang and three hundred boys flocked into the school assembly hall for the closing ceremony for that term. In front on the platform there was a large lighted Christmas tree, and the custom was that the master addressed all the boys and that then they had Christmas carols before separating for the holidays.

'That day there was now the familiar sight of a Nazi Gauleiter, crude and unlettered, sitting on the platform with the headmaster. The master just said a word or two and then the Gauleiter got up and, after a eulogy of the Führer, let out a great diatribe against the Jews, and as usual urged the boys not to care for learning but for physical strength and toughness. It was a vulgar speech with many coarse jokes and, though most of the boys seemed to enjoy it, the headmaster looked ill at ease. The Gauleiter then suggested they should sing some of the Nazi songs, and chose one of the most crude anti-Jewish songs of the Party, ending with the famous "Horst Wessel". One of the masters sitting on the platform noticed the tense white face of Johann as he stood in the second row of boys, silent throughout all this proceeding, with his eyes fixed on the Christmas tree which seemed to belong to another world.

'The headmaster rose to give the word of dismissal and, as he did so, there was a sound of scuffle as Johann pushed past the boys in front of him and shot up the platform steps to the piano which the young Nazi master in uniform had just left. Johann, who is a good pianist, sat down and began to play the favourite German carol "Stille Nacht, Heilige Nacht".

'It all happened in a second and threw everyone into a strange bewilderment. Some boys looked round, others began to hum the tune under their breath. The bullying Gauleiter stared at the slender pale-faced boy who now sat silent at the piano. The fear he had momentarily lost had returned and he seemed unable to move.

'The headmaster dismissed the boys and then, as he passed off the platform with the Gauleiter and the other masters, he patted Johann on the head and said, as though wishing to appease the Gauleiter without being unkind to the boy, "Poor boy, he's got it so much in his blood that he cannot get rid of it, but he will in time." By way of explanation he told the Gauleiter that Johann's uncle was a famous theologian and that they were a very religious family. Johann then made a dive for the back door and, running through the snow and bitter wind with no coat and without the books he wanted for the holidays, reached home and locked himself in his bedroom. We were distressed but greatly relieved when an hour later one of the older masters known to us as an anti-Nazi arrived, bringing his coat and books. He told us the story of his courage. After that our son was able to take us into his confidence, and when he returned from a week's stay in Bavaria with this master who was his friend, he had gained strength and resolution and sent in his resignation from the Hitler Jugend.

'"Of course," said his master, "his struggle has been bitter because he knows the cost. Unfortunately now, a boy, however clever he is, and Johann is brilliant, is not allowed to go to the university unless he shows himself a good Party member. It is a terrible blow to him to give up the university, but I try to comfort him by telling him that after he has done his year in the Labour Corps and his military service, this madness may have passed from Germany and he may yet get to the university. Certainly he is happier now and stronger, even with this disappointment."'

CHAPTER XIII

IN THE EARLY DAYS –
A STUDY IN CONTRASTS

As the Nazi Movement became increasingly brutal, it was diffi-cult at times to recall that in the early days there was much which impressed the casual traveller, for there were signs of renewed vitality and even a happy sense of freedom among the youth.

To those who knew where to look, there was always a hinter-land of suffering and distress, but it was not always easy for the foreign traveller to discover what was happening.

I remember well going over early in 1936 and on the very first day I was there I was deeply impressed by the vivid contrasts between the apparently good and harmless aspects of the Nazi Movement and the sinister brutality always lurking just out of sight.

It is obvious that those who visited the country – especially those who stayed in hotels and only saw a great renewal of vitality everywhere and never got behind the scenes – often got an entirely false view. It is equally true that those in our country who showed their repugnance to the evil side by refusing to visit Germany at all, may have failed to realize the full significance of what was happening and in so doing they may easily have underrated its vitality and the dangers inherent in the very fact of its healthier and happier superficialities. But, in that one day, I moved quickly from light to darkness, from a gay and joyous side of the Move-ment to bitter sorrow and degradation behind the scenes.

When I left the hotel that morning, I found that there was a great youth rally in Berlin and I watched the march past of thou-sands of boys who looked in perfect health and were singing lustily.

It was a most pleasing sight and when I remembered how many of their older brothers had just lounged at street corners with no particular aim in life and no prospect for the future, I could not help feeling that the calling forth of this energy and enthusiasm was very attractive and might, if rightly directed, prove very valuable. Certainly that morning I felt I was witnessing nothing more than a Scout rally on a grand scale — grand enough to embrace the entire youth of the country. I remembered, too, that a few years back I had seen in Vienna and indeed in Germany constant processions of children, each carrying a different political banner, even though most of the children knew exactly nothing of what they were representing. It seemed a good idea to discountenance a large number of youth movements organized by contending political parties, and when Hitler said 'We will only have one children's movement in Germany' he sounded reasonable.

But if there is to be one youth movement only, it was vital that its aim and purpose should be sound. That it should be harnessed to a gang of criminals was a terrifying thought.

However, with all my questionings and doubts I could not help being impressed with that morning's ceremonies, merely as a spectacle of youth and energy and the undoubted happiness and contentment on most of the faces. It was as well perhaps that I should so soon see the other side of the picture.

Leaving Unter den Linden I had a hurried lunch as I found it was later than I thought, and then took a bus to the Kurfürstendamm and began walking down some streets where there are many boarding houses and blocks of flats where Jews are allowed to live. Along these streets I met some other young people — Germans too but Jews. They were not in procession but walked singly or stood at the pavement's edge, utterly dejected. The streets were mainly desolate and many shops were boarded up. I was on my way to visit an old lady whose married children and small grandchildren were out of Germany and were friends of mine. They were deeply anxious about their old mother who had not wanted to leave her home to come abroad with them.

Now another of her sons had had to leave Germany for Palestine and I had promised I would go along and see her and try to persuade her to come over to join her daughter as soon as possible, in fact with me if she could be ready in time. To my dying day I shall never forget that old lady. She was very small and gentle-looking with lovely silver hair and blue eyes. I sat down on the sofa next to her and told her who I was. She put out a frail little hand on mine and looked at me slowly and with a dignity and courage that would not let her break down. Or was it just that she had suffered beyond the point of tears? She said: 'My dear, I am not frightened of death – I am now eighty years old and I await death, it is the next step for me, but I am so afraid of this waiting time with so many of my family away – but please don't tell them. You see, I dare not go in the streets, one never knows what will happen in this part of the city, and sometimes I am afraid to stay in alone. My neighbours are kind but the time is long – yes, I'm very much afraid of the time till I die.'

Then her face changed, as though, having drawn away the veil for a moment, she would again draw it over the tragedy of her lonely waiting time, and with a happier smile and eager interest she asked me about her son and daughter and their children. We spoke of each in turn and she was hungry for news and agreed that when the summer came perhaps she would travel to them. Then she began making up little parcels of chocolates for her grandchildren.

'Worth nothing,' she said, 'but just that they know they are from grandmother.'

We talked of other things for she was a well-read woman and suffered bitterly from the denial of cultural amenities to Jews. Even when I left she was serene and dignified and showed no sign of the distress that had been summed up in her first tragic words, 'I am very afraid of the waiting time.'

I felt stifled as I left that house and walked back to the west end and the hotel at which I was staying. I had some sandwiches and coffee in my room while I talked to an English friend who was with me and together we set forth on one more errand made necessary by this Nazi philosophy. When I left England a week earlier I had been asked if I would take five Cook's travelling tickets to Berlin. They were given to me by a German pastor in London who wanted to get his family to England. It seemed that the only way to do this was to give them tickets from Germany to England. These were made out as return tickets so that it should not be thought they were trying to escape from Germany but just going over to friends for a summer holiday.

I had been worried about these tickets and wanted to deliver them, but knew I must carry out my instructions carefully. 'Go after 9 p.m. at night,' said the pastor, 'and give three knocks at the door – that is the sign to my wife you are a friend – and then her companion will open the door.'

It was not easy to find the right maisonette, especially as the pastor had asked me not to ask the way of any stranger nor to let anyone realize I was visiting his wife, as my being a foreigner might arouse suspicion. We had therefore to leave the hotel and take a taxi to a different address and then in the dark work our way back to the right house.

The German pastor's wife was very typical. She had a direct honest look; her hair was drawn straight back and she had no frills in dress, manner or in speech. I gave her her husband's letter and the five tickets and explained to her that he thought it wiser that the tickets should be made out from Leipzig where she could go and spend a few days first with some relations as they often did, and travel to England from there. This rather appalled poor Frau Pastor for she had four small children and had felt the journey to England would be hard enough if she left from Berlin.

'Oh dear, I wonder why he did this. Doesn't he realize how difficult it is and that I shall want to take as much luggage and to attract as little attention as I can.'

We sat for an hour talking out the practical details till my head grew dizzy with all the complications involved in getting a loyal German woman with her children who should have been a credit to any country away as an exile, leaving her home, her elderly parents and all her friends. As we finished discussing the details she turned to us and said: 'It all seems as if it could not be real that we should go as fugitives from the country of our birth and which we love and go into an unknown future with everything uncertain, and now to have to go a long roundabout journey to get there. And why? Because my husband would preach in his church the Christian Gospel. He is not political, but he felt he must go on saying, specially to his younger people, that they must not worship an idol, and when in this neighbourhood the father of a Jewish family was taken to prison we looked after his family. A brutal Nazi Gestapo man struck my husband for that, and it was only because another young boy who is in the Nazi Party but is very ashamed though he won't say so, warned my husband to leave quickly that he got away, for the day after he crossed the frontier into Holland the Gestapo came to arrest him.

'It must seem terrible to you,' she said, 'I myself cannot believe it is real. I had thought of religious persecution as something of the past and even in Russia, well, I thought the church had been political and that they were afraid a counter-revolution might come from it. But here in Berlin my husband is not going to lead a counter-revolution and yet he cannot preach the Gospel. It is utterly impossible. I cannot understand why they think we are worth persecuting.'

She drew a breath. 'Perhaps I do not see deep enough, for my husband says that it is inevitable that they should persecute us because although the church does not seem very powerful, its teaching does strike at the very root of the Nazi teaching, and that in time men must choose. But I must not keep you and it would not be wise for you to leave here in the middle of the night. Thank you very much for bringing the tickets.'

Then just as we were leaving she called us back and added, 'Do not tell my husband that I am greatly worried about this Leipzig business, for he does not realize all the money difficulties and he is only so anxious to have us in England without rousing suspicion.

He does not fully realize what it means to escape secretly with four children under nine years of age. You see, the youngest is only a year old. But thank you and I will see you in England, I hope, some day.'

As we walked home that night the three scenes came back; the gay, happy, healthy youth group marching down Unter den Linden with unmistakable signs of life and inspiration; the tragic little old lady; the plucky pastor's wife trying to escape secretly with four children – all these are the results of Nazism and we realized then that as it was developing it would be the gay happiness that would pass, since a movement that suffered these other things to happen carried within it the seed of death and destruction to all that is good.

But even then we could hardly have imagined to what lengths of brutality and ruthlessness the Nazis would go in Germany and throughout Europe. So that these early stories scarcely seem worth repeating except as indicating the sure signs of a movement that was going to lead to the grim terror of Poland and occupied Europe.

CHAPTER XIV

TRIBUTE TO AMBASSADOR

A tall, handsome and most gracious man, followed by a small dog, crossed the room to greet me, with the words 'Forgive me for keeping you waiting for a few minutes. An ambassador is the slave of many people.' It was Baron von Hoersch, Ambassador to the Court of St James's, speaking. Surely few ambassadors have suffered more cruelly at the hands of a perfidious government and, whatever the cause of his death, Baron von Hoersch suffered keenly during his last months as he tried to maintain standards of decency and honour while acting on behalf of a government that knew neither.

'I am so glad you are taking over to Germany a group of educationalists to talk with the new Nazi educationalists, for you will be in a privileged position to ask many questions that our own educationalists do not get a chance to ask.'

Then, summoning all the art of the diplomat's gentle insinuation, he indicated his hope that we should not be misled by the Nazis into believing that any real scholars and educationalists in Germany could tolerate the dreary and shoddy stuff being given out by upstart young Nazis who really know nothing either of education or scholarship. He added discreetly, 'Sometimes your countrymen are so tolerant as to give a wrong impression.' Reassured that we had no intention of refraining from free and frank criticism, he said, 'I have had a letter from Berlin about your party. They make one or two suggestions I will tell you about.'

Without comment he stated that they would like to make a few changes in the suggested programme because it was considered too theoretical. National Socialism was primarily a movement of action rather than theory. Therefore on the day when we had put down the discussion on the more fundamental principles of education they proposed we should go out to see some of their land schools instead. 'How absurd they are, Your Excellency,' I said. 'Is it not strange that the country from which one has always felt there came a challenge to *Grundsätzlichkeit* in the approach to any subject should now try to avoid all the more *grundsätzlich* questions about education and philosophy? Would you be good enough to tell them in Berlin that we expect Germans to be *grundsätzlich* and that we are travelling from England in order to discuss the fundamental principles of National Socialist education, not its passing manifestations.'

'I thank you. I could wish for no better answer to send them.'

We then fell to a franker discussion, and he said how he hoped that the traditional standards of scholarship and criticism in Germany could withstand this cheap and often ludicrous teaching about race, blood and earth, and suchlike. I rose to leave and once again he and the small dog accompanied me to the door. When saying goodbye he added, 'Afraid to be *grundsätzlich*. How right you are. That exactly describes the change in education. I beg you to continue to take English educationalists over to Germany who will have the courage to ask my countrymen there for the fundamental principles of all their new theories.'

PART II

CHAPTER I

THE TRAGEDY OF THE UNEMPLOYED STUDENT

The Nazi doctrine as expounded by young men with no learning and little judgement is alarming because it is such a jumble
of good and bad ideas. Even when the ideas are good, they are
worked out in bad ways, and it is obvious that in repeating all
sorts of Nazi clichés, many of the young men do not recognize
the significance of what they say, or the sinister consequences of
all this superficial claptrap. Far more revolting than these ignorant
young enthusiasts were the middle-aged men who had been second-rate teachers and lecturers but who, owing to their devotion
to the Party, were given positions of responsibility and at times
professorships. They now turned their shoddy minds to finding
some kind of philosophical interpretation of the Nazi revolution.

A group of us listened to lectures by several men of this kind,
and we felt that they had sold themselves to the Party, and that
in so doing they had degraded not only themselves, but also the
famous chairs of learning which some of them now occupy.

A week or two after hearing and deploring these second-rate
scholars, I stayed with friends in the Rhineland. The parents,
cultured and Christian, were anti-Nazi, but all their children,
including a brilliant son, had joined the Party, and their home
was a meeting place for the children and their young Nazi friends.
'Sometimes,' said the father, 'I am inclined to forbid them to enter
the house, for I feel it is being defiled by much of their silly talk,
and it is not easy for the older generation to be treated like a pack
of fools by some of these ardent and ignorant young men. Most

of all do I regret that people, like my eldest son and some of his friends who have good brains, should be so easily misled by much that is utterly false and even ridiculous. But of course they have had a hard time in former years because two of my boys were unemployed for a long time and they felt their training at the university was useless, and now at last they know they are wanted and have a chance of leadership and authority.'

His wife, who had been silent until now, joined in and said, 'I know my husband is right that this Nazi business is vile, but formerly it was terrible to see the children so unhappy and useless. I hope that, if many like our boys go into the Party, perhaps they can do something to improve it. It is wonderful what my sons have done for some of the boys in this town already. You would not recognize them, for they have become different altogether in body and spirit. They were just wasting on the streets, and now they have a new self-respect.'

'My wife says truly that superficially this movement seems to have done much, but I know something of the people who are in control, and behind all the youthful enthusiasm there is much that is dark and ugly. Any movement that degrades standards of learning, mocks the Christian religion and denies the right of free speech must end in disaster. But I think my wife is right that we should let my sons and their friends meet in our house, but that, as she says, we should try in every way to let them see we stand for certain positive values which are irreconcilable with Nazi teaching. Of course, by doing this we run certain risks, as some of these young fanatics may decide to report what I say to the Gestapo.' Then dropping his voice he added thoughtfully, 'My own son – the really clever one – sometimes I wonder if even he might not do that.'

'Hans, how can you say such things?' cried his wife.

'My dear, I will tell you why. It is not that Walter does not love us, but he has been more hurt and disillusioned by his long unemployment than most, and in order to accept the Nazi teaching he must all the time suppress his intellect and be dishonest in a sense. Sometimes I think that what we and this home stand for are an almost unbearable challenge to him, and that one day he may become so hurt by it that he will take the way of the fanatic and harm those who challenge him, most deeply.'

His wife turned to me and said, 'Don't take my husband too seriously. Today he is much depressed for he had such great hopes of his sons. Of course, all his fears are groundless.'

Were they, I wondered, for there are stories of just such parents being betrayed by their children.

Among the friends who came in constantly to visit this house was a young doctor of philosophy whom I had met on one or two occasions before both in England and Germany. He was one of the students who during his university days would not have been able to continue his studies if it had not been for the relief that had been given to him by the International Students Service.* This organization after the last war went into the universities to help students in need in all the countries that had been at war, and among the students helped was my friend, Wilhelm.

He had visited England, which he admired greatly, and was anxious that the two countries should be friends. A year or two back he had been profoundly moved because he had been staying in an English home on an Armistice Day, and when he had gone into the drawing room that morning he noticed two small bunches of poppies lying at the foot of a photograph of an English officer who was the eldest son of the house and had fallen in France in 1916. Wilhelm did not know about Poppy Day, so his hostess, Mrs Curtis, explained and added, 'We always buy a bunch of poppies and put them with Harold's photo, but this year I bought two bunches – the second one is there today in memory of your father because I understand he too was killed in France.'

---

* During the years 1920–5 about £ 475,000 was collected by students in forty different countries. This was used to give relief to students in need throughout central and south-eastern Europe as well as Russia. At the present time I.S.S. is helping students who are prisoners of war and refugees and is making plans for relief work among students in Europe at the end of this war.

'After that,' said Wilhelm, 'I realized that to all the other qualities I admired in the English could be added the fact that they are
not all cold and reserved. Already I had met an English gentleman,
but now I knew also the courtesy of an English lady in her home.'

Wilhelm knew I was staying with his friends and came in for
coffee one afternoon. He realized that I was surprised and distressed to see him in full Nazi attire, so having got me alone he
said, 'Could you spend a few hours in Cologne tomorrow? It is not
far from here and I am told you have recently been with English
friends in Berlin meeting some of our Nazi leaders. I care so much,
more than anything, that my English friends should understand
this movement and should not believe all the lies about it in the
foreign papers. Could we talk about it together?'

'All right, Wilhelm, let us meet in the big hotel near Cologne
station and have coffee there tomorrow morning at ten o'clock.'

'That is excellent,' he said, and then almost to himself he added:
'It is easier to talk in a big hotel because in a restaurant you are
much nearer other people.'

I sat in the corner of the large lounge and watched Wilhelm
enter the next morning. My corner was rather dark and it took
him a moment or two to find me. He was a handsome young man
of just under six feet in height, slender in build, with dark hair and
eyes and a sensitive and extremely intelligent face. His uniform
was beautifully cut and became him well, for in those days the SS
uniform had not yet become the symbol of all that is bestial and
insolent. Wilhelm came from a simple middle-class home, but his
bearing was aristocratic and his intellect penetrating. It seemed
impossible that he should pay even lip service to the kind of nonsense that a man like Baemler was writing.

We ordered our coffee and he inquired eagerly: 'Who were the
British group of educationalists you took to Berlin and who were
the lecturers on the Nazi side?'

I showed him the programme and when he had glanced at it he
said, 'Tell me, did your people see something of the inspiration of
the philosophy of our new movement in Germany?'

To which I replied: 'Wilhelm, how can you ask me that? It is a rotten philosophy and those of us who know and love Germany felt humiliated that a country so famed for scholarship, should have such second-rate people teaching in your universities.'

Almost angrily he replied, 'Oh, you have grown so old in your country that you do not know new wine when it is there.'

'Old wine or new wine, it is rotten, Wilhelm, and not only am I distressed for your country that so many are being misled, but I cannot think what you are doing to your mind, if you allow yourself to accept such stuff as that.'

There was silence for a time, and I realized that Wilhelm was almost too deeply moved to speak. When he did, his face was pale, as he turned to me, and said very quietly, 'For God's sake, don't raise any further conflict for me.'

He then started talking of his student days. 'Do you remember the days of International Student Service and the terrible struggle it was for some of us to remain at the university? We stuck it out because we really believed two things. The first was that we were needed by our country – the desolation left by the last war meant that Germany was in great need of trained men of all sorts and that we should really be wanted in the reconstruction of everything here. The second thing was we all belonged to the international youth movements because we thought the League of Nations meant that there was going to be more chance of understanding; it was enough that our fathers had killed one another, and we were determined it should not happen to us. You know something of how hard it was to struggle on at the university, and many of us could only do it because it seemed here was a future worth preparing for. Do you remember, for instance, my friend Karl, the medical student in Leipzig? But I will tell you about him later.'

'But,' I interrupted, 'Karl was brilliant. Surely there was room for him as a doctor?'

'There wasn't room for any of us,' he said. 'My generation that worked so hard and with such terrible suffering just was not wanted. Karl is dead.

'At the end of my time at the university,' he continued, 'I was unemployed for a year, so I went back to do some research work in the hope that perhaps times would improve. But for five years I remained unemployed and was broken in body and spirit and I learned how stupid were all my dreams in those hard days at the university. I was not wanted by Germany and certainly if I was not wanted here I was not wanted anywhere in the world. Even more futile were all our international youth movements, for the League of Nations was not interested in peace, it was only interested in maintaining the *status quo*, and it never had the courage to put anything right in Europe. Heavens, how the younger crowd were duped into false hopes for the future! At any rate, life became for me completely hopeless.

'Just then I was introduced to Hitler. You won't understand and I cannot explain either because I don't know what happened, but life for me took on a tremendous new significance. After all, Germany would rise again; after all, I was wanted. I have since committed myself, body, soul and spirit, to this movement for the resurrection of Germany. I can only tell you that I cannot go back, I cannot question, I am pledged. I beg you not to try to set up conflict in my mind. I dare not let that happen for I am as much committed to Hitler as the fundamentalist is to his Bible. Believe me, I cannot face uncertainty and conflict again. No, for me it is Hitler and the resurrection of Germany on one side or suicide on the other. I have chosen Hitler, leave me in peace with my choice. By the way, talking of suicide that was the way Karl took.'

'But' I said, 'the professors at Leipzig told me Karl was one of the finest students they had ever known. What do you mean? There must have been a place for him.'

'God, how awful it was!' he replied. 'You remember he had no home. His father died of wounds after the war and his mother had died when he was very young. Perhaps you didn't know that for the last two years of his student days in Leipzig he took a job as a night watchman and sat by a fire in one of those huts by the roadside? He used to study all night with a lantern and then get a few hours' sleep before going to the university and again before he went on night duty. It meant he did not have to pay for lodgings, and, if he was ever free in the holidays, he used to come along to me. In spite of all, his work was excellent but his health could not stand it, and when he was qualified and I think, might have been given one of the few jobs going, he was turned down because they feared T.B. He left me a note and went out that night and shot himself – it was always the same story – "I am no longer of any use to anyone."'

Wilhelm turned on me again almost angrily and said, 'How can you in your country just criticize and say we are anti-Christian? It may be some silly things are said by some leaders in the Party, but, tell me, is it not religious to believe that there is a purpose for everyone in this life? For myself, I am again religious, for I now believe that I was created for something and that there is design and meaning in life, whereas for five years I could see none, not only for myself but for my generation, and for my country. We were left out. Now even if war comes and we die, we die for a purpose – the rebirth of Germany.

'You keep on talking of lack of freedom, but if you look at the young generation in Germany today, you will see they have a wonderful new freedom born of a devotion to a great task which demands their all. We cannot help it that some of the middle-aged churchmen are disgruntled. They have failed to save Germany, so we must do it. I agree,' he added, 'that sometimes the approach to the churches has been clumsy, but they have been so blind that it is their own fault. I see it this way. Here is a movement, chiefly of the young, but open to all, which demands the total mobilization of the spiritual as well as the material resources of the country. We dare not, in fact cannot, accept our tremendous task unless we can bring into our service all the available resources of strength. Therefore I think the churches simply must come in.'

'But, Wilhelm,' I said, 'surely you see that you cannot talk about the spiritual resources of the church as though they were bits of meat you put into a sausage machine to help make it up? The church has her beliefs and creeds and her life cannot possibly be separated from her faith.'

'A great many things are happening now which no one thought could happen,' he replied, 'but I don't think we get anywhere by arguing, because I and thousands upon thousands of others are living by an experience which people outside just don't understand. But, as we achieve the resurrection of Germany, I hope you and my English friends will understand our actions and our life, even when you do not agree with our theories. I beg you to tell your students that for many of us there never has been a more passionate assertion of our faith in God as Creator than this revolt against despair, not only against physical death but against spiritual and intellectual death. Tell them we may not talk their language about God and religion and the church; tell them we cannot argue, but we live by an experience, and that experience is the determination to show there is purpose and meaning in life and that we all know now we have a part to play.'

As Wilhelm left me I crossed to the cathedral and sat there for some time thinking, and there came to me the memory of something that a very wise old German statesman had said to me a week or two earlier and which I had not understood at the time.

'The really tragic thing about this movement,' he said, 'is that I believe it must end in war. There will of course be political incidents that lead on to war, but actually below all that, I believe that there is a kind of momentum or, if you like, hysteria in this movement and in the devotion of many of its individual members that will drive them to some kind of ultimate sacrifice. Something has got hold of them that will hurl them to death as the final surrender to their devotion. Perhaps you think I am talking nonsense but I am convinced that what I say is true, though I find it difficult to put it into words that will make it sound sensible. The reasons the politician and the historian, unless they are very profound, will give for the next war will be the superficial reasons. Below all these there is a philosophy leading to destruction.'

That afternoon as the light streamed through the glorious

windows of Cologne Cathedral I sat and thought of Wilhelm and felt that he too had committed himself to destruction and I began to see what the German statesman meant.

CHAPTER II

A PROFESSOR MEETS THE SS AT MIDNIGHT

You do not often meet in Germany a man who is a profound scholar and at the same time a man of the world in the best sense of the term, with keen and astute judgement in current affairs both political and social. I sometimes think that Hitler would never have made the progress he has if German teachers in schools and universities as well as in the church had not so often been purely academic and remote from life and in particular from the life of the young.

However, I want to talk about one of the most remarkable Germans I have ever met. He was a professor of philosophy but his interests and his knowledge were unusually wide. Apart from having serious discussions with him at various times, I have spent some hours with him at such different places as the London Zoo, the Parthenon Museum in Berlin, and the Art Gallery in Dresden, and I always found him not only a delightful companion but a mine of information about the particular things we were seeing or hearing.

First, of a scene in his home, then later, in his own words his interpretation of some of the more fundamental reasons why even intelligent and by no means only unscrupulous young people were caught up in this Nazi movement. I am bound to say I think his comments are among the most penetrating I have heard. It was so easy in Germany as well as in England to shrug one's shoulders in horror at the vulgar and brutal aspects of the movement, without realizing that the real tragedy of the revolution in the centre of

Europe lay in the fact that there were more profound reasons for it than a superficial reading of such aspects would lead one to suspect. Perhaps I should say that the real tragedy lies in the betrayal of a whole generation of youth looking for leadership and eager to serve.

But, returning to Professor Braun who, I should add, has a delightfully keen sense of humour which serves him well in handling situations that throw others into panic or anger.

On one or two occasions Professor Braun had fallen foul of the Gestapo who suggested that at times he harboured Jewish and other scholars, which I believe was true. I know within one month he and his wife had had about twelve visits from Gestapo men, but it so happened the men in the particular district in which his house was situated in a small town in Silesia were younger and less brutal than the average. Anyhow, these young SS men could not understand, and in the end could not resist, the good will and good humour with which he always met them and even welcomed them.

If they arrived in the middle of the afternoon, he would invariably say, 'Well, you chaps must choose this time to come because you know it is when we drink coffee. Just decide which room you want to examine while I tell my wife that this afternoon it is coffee and cakes for four.' Or if they arrived at 6 p.m., 'Oh, I see the idea, a glass of beer on your way home.'

At first the Gestapo men were suspicious and rude to him, refusing all refreshments. But after a number of visits their resistance broke down, largely, I think, because in fact Professor Braun was profoundly interested in them personally. However hostile he might be to the beliefs of the movement and its gangster leaders, he felt somehow partly to blame that intelligent young men should have been ensnared by it. Certainly only the students who knew the professor intimately realized how many young men owed everything to his friendship when the truth about the Nazi Party they had joined came home to them. This is the story of one of these.

In their earlier visits it was obvious the SS men did not feel they ought to take that glass of beer with the professor, whose premises they were inspecting, and of course it's always difficult with two Nazis together because no two Nazis dare trust one another. However, one of them said in an aside to the other, 'Maybe we'll get him talking,' and thus they settled down to the glass of beer.

'Herr Professor, why do you oppose our Party?' said one of the young men.

'Well, you know it has to be that I oppose you because I believe in God,' said the Professor.

'But so does the Führer,' came the quick reply.

'Does he really?' said the Professor. 'Well, it's funny how differently it takes different people!'

Late one night two of them called again, but the professor was as imperturbable as ever. 'Look here, this is a bit absurd both for me to be wakened up at midnight, and for you to be working such long hours. I propose if you call after 11 p.m. you should sleep here. When you have been round the rooms tonight you will find there is no bed free, but we will stoke up the oven in my study and you can sleep there if you like. Meanwhile, my wife and I would like to go to sleep now, so if you want something to eat, you know the kitchen and you must help yourselves. Please leave something for breakfast,' he added, 'especially if you wish to join us then.'

The men were rather confused and explained that they only wished to go round the rooms to see the professor had no strange guests and that they would be gone in a few minutes.

So they were, but a quarter of an hour later, just before 1 a.m., there was another knock, less rude and insistent than usual. Professor Braun wondered momentarily if it could be a fugitive from the Nazis seeking refuge. But as he opened the door he found it was one of the SS men who had come back. The light from the entrance hall flooded his face as he stood in the darkness on the landing of the maisonette. He was pale and obviously distressed as he said, 'Herr Professor, after all, may I come for the night, because I must talk to you and I have no other opportunity.'

As 2 and 3 a.m. struck it must have been a strange sight to see the professor in his dressing gown sitting back in his chair smoking a cigar as he sipped his beer, and the young SS man, who had thrown his cap, belt and revolver on the table, sitting with his service coat unbuttoned and resting his elbows on his knees. He ran his hands through his thick dark hair. He was not the perfect Nordic type; in fact, he came from eastern Silesia and might have had Slav blood in his veins. For nearly three hours Hermann, for that was his name, poured forth a story of bitter disillusionment.

'I was unemployed,' he said. 'No, I didn't go to the university because my father too was unemployed, but I read a great deal and did any odd jobs I could find, and always thought if I studied I might be more likely to get a job, but nothing came. Then I heard about this Nazi Party. Many of my friends joined and I heard the Führer speak and I was inspired because I believed that he really had something for me to do, and he made us all feel there was something to live for. I still think Germany and the Führer are worth living for, but I did not know that it would be my job to go into the homes of good Germans like you who also want Germany to rise again. You are no enemy of Germany, and I cannot see that it helps anyone never to leave you in peace.

'But, Herr Professor, there is something worse, I am frightened they will make me go on guard in a concentration camp. They are terrible places and I could not do it. I know the Jews are the enemies of Germany because the Führer says so, but it is horrible in those camps and there are not only Jews but pastors, social democrats and Catholics. One of my friends went on guard there and in three days he committed suicide. It is dreadful down at the headquarters of the SS. So many of the men like to tell revolting stories of torture and all the things they do to Jews and others. If they like doing such things they must be mad. I cannot, I will not, believe that the Führer knows about it. Herr Professor, what can I do, where can I go? I joined this Party because it seemed like a new life opening for me, and now I cannot sleep because I see death everywhere – I am caught in something horrible and I cannot escape.'

Just after 6 a.m. the professor's wife wakened to find her husband had never come up to bed at all, so going downstairs she opened the study door quietly lest she should disturb them if they were both asleep. But she found the professor sitting at his desk writing, for he had not felt he could sleep after that long talk, while his guest who was huddled up in an armchair slept feverishly, and might wake and need his company for he was obviously unnerved.

The professor followed his wife into the kitchen and they discussed what they could do to help Hermann out of the Party, or perhaps first on to a different kind of work. It was difficult, there were others in this position, and yet he was only nineteen and ought to be helped, because too often the professor had seen how some of them had got over this kind of initial revulsion and later became brutalized and pathological members of the Party. 'Anyhow,' said his wife, 'I will get breakfast, for we must get him away early for his own sake.'

The professor's children were delighted when they were told that breakfast was to be nearly an hour earlier and that they might get up at once. Soon the two eldest came tumbling downstairs and were rather taken aback when they found their guest was an SS man. Although they had never actually seen any trouble in their home, Edward, who was eight years old, knew enough from his school friends to realize there was often trouble when they came. However, he greeted him in a friendly way, but Liesel, aged four, a timid little girl, was not so sure and decided to sit on her mother's lap for family prayers, which they always had before breakfast.

Liesel never took her eyes off Hermann, for she had all the child's sure instinct for recognizing suffering, and somehow she felt he was very unhappy and during the singing of the hymn she even suspected he was trying not to cry.

As soon as prayers were over, she climbed from her mother's lap and, going across to Hermann, she put her hands on his knees and looking up into his face said, "*Warum bist du so traurig?*" ('Why are you so sad?')

I have mentioned this story of Professor Braun because I

wanted to show the kind of man he is before I talk about his teaching and above all his interpretation of post-war developments in Germany.

I wrote him a line before I went to Germany again to say I wanted to speak to him, and asked him to leave a note at my hotel to tell me when we could meet, not just for a chat but with enough time for him to tell me at leisure why he thought so many students had been caught up in the Nazi Movement. I felt that more than most he saw the relation of what had been happening in the universities for a number of years previously to the fanatical devotion of many of the students to the Party.

CHAPTER III

THE PROFESSOR DISCUSSES NAZI PHILOSOPHY AND STUDENTS – I

I was staying in Berlin in the autumn of 1937 and had dined out one night, and as I came into the hotel about 10 p.m. the head porter told me that a small boy of about fifteen years old had come in with a letter for me, but he would not leave it. He said he lived nearby and that he would come back at 11 p.m., as he wanted an answer.

An hour later the messenger came back with a pencilled note with no signature and, addressing me by a nickname I recognized as the password, let me know that the writer was Professor Braun. The passage read, 'Railway stations are very good places to meet. Everyone moves and changes around at the tables and one attracts very little notice, even if one stays a long time. Will you meet me at Friedrichstrasse at 10 a.m. tomorrow, and we can talk all the morning? I have a luncheon engagement at 12.30 till about 2 p.m., that is why I am in Berlin, also to see the friend with whom I am staying and whose son brings this letter. If you would like a second talk and will meet me at, say 2.15 p.m., at the Anhalter Bahnhof, we could spend several more hours together before I go south again. Please send a reply by the boy with this letter.'

The next morning just before 10 o'clock I got to the Friedrich-strasse Bahnhof. It was a hot day late in August and only a few days before the annual Nuremberg Congress of the Nazi Party, so that already all the stations and trains were packed with troops, SA and SS men on the move. We glanced into the restaurant, which was crowded out and at first it seemed hopeless, but men began moving off and we soon discovered to our delight a table for two in a remote corner.

'These troops are a good screen,' said Professor Braun. ' In fact, we are protected by the German army!'

After inquiring about a number of English and American friends the professor said, 'I am glad you want more than a super-ficial explanation of this revolution. It is most important it should be thoroughly understood, because its greatest danger lies deeply hidden. But if you really want to understand and to explain to some of my English friends in your universities what is happen-ing today in Germany, you must have much patience, because I want to take you right back to the period after the last war and tell you of the kind of intellectual, moral and spiritual milestones on the way.

'In fact,' he said laughing, 'I have prepared two whole lectures for you – one for Friedrichstrasse this morning and one for the Anhalter Bahnhof when we meet this afternoon.'

'How marvellous,' I said. 'But wait a minute, let me get out paper and pencil to make some notes.'

'Those also I have made for you because we only have this one day together, and I want you to understand as much as I can tell you. So I have written down some notes and we can discuss them and you can make your own notes at the side. But let us order some coffee first.'

As we waited for this he continued, 'Of course, you realize I shall only deal with one aspect of the problem. I do not deny the economic chaos which made revolution and dictatorship easy; I do not deny the political blunders our leaders have made; and forgive me, I do not deny that England and France and America by their foreign policy must accept some blame that such a revo-lution came in this country. But even if all these things are true, I am convinced there are some reasons even deeper why Hitlerism succeeded. This country had had many parties and programmes before. Why has this one set everything alight? I will try to tell you what I believe to be the reasons.

At that point he took out his notes. 'Of course they are very brief for many libraries could be written about these things. But I have chosen this subject because, although one of the causes of revolution in Germany may operate outside, indeed revolutions elsewhere are certain to be of a different character, nevertheless I think some of the things that I am going to indicate, besides being true of our own younger generation in Germany, may in other forms and in varying degrees become true of younger people in many parts of the world.'

Thousands of troops and SA men must have come in and out of that restaurant as we stayed on and talked for nearly three hours. I think the best thing I can do is to recall the notes of these two talks. I cannot attempt to report the full discussion, but the notes in the professor's own words may be more interesting. I agree with him that they raise many a question in one's mind about the general tendency to spiritual bankruptcy and I sometimes think we in our country are living on past capital, and that there are many disquieting signs both in England and America and, I suspect, even more in France.

I

'In order to understand the historical and philosophical background which explains the attitude of the young generation in Germany, it is necessary to consider its attitude at the time of the advent to power of National Socialism. First, then, let me give you a brief review of the past.

'The development of German Youth after the last war and before the National Socialist regime can be described roughly in three stages.

'The first stage was that immediately following the war. The expressionistic Youth Movement was at its height and was shaping the life of the young people. We can still remember the outward and inward characteristics of that time – the elaborate romanticism, the overflowing vitality and the quest for novelty.

'The old order of life had been destroyed in the war and a new order had to be found. The old political world had broken down and people tried to compensate for this in a mystic "new birth". It was a desire for life in a young generation which had lost the old standards of life.

'Today we realize the grave error which lay at the bottom of this philosophical and historical expressionism. It was not the beginning of a new era, but the end of the old one. It was the death struggle of the age of humanism, and, although it proclaimed itself as the enemy of the spiritual heritage of the nineteenth century, its battles were fought with the old weapons. Many thought that the new era had arrived. Today we know that expressionism was not even a bridge to it but simply a vanguard which exploded some of the tottering strongholds of a passing age. Small wonder then that this young generation of expressionists disappeared quickly and completely.

'The second stage was the turning away from expressionism, from the intoxication of feeling and the mystical worship of things new, to realism, to the present, or as it was termed at the time, to the new "matter-of-factness". This movement ran parallel with the stabilization of finance and was, in fact, a sort of spiritual stabilization. The flight from subjectivism and individualism was now complete. Instead of the ideal of the creative individual we find the ideal of the community. The ideals and ideologies of the past were really dead now; they had lost all power of persuasion. Interest in sport and technical achievements were the means by which life and the world were to be mastered. A new kind of realism had at last arrived and was coupled with a new respect for reality.

'Yet even this stage was not the final development. The "stabilization" in finance as well as in philosophy turned out to be a deception. And therefore there followed one of the most difficult and painful chapters in the development and fate of the young generation in my country – it might be called the process of complete disillusionment.

'This is the third stage. Looking first at outward conditions, one realizes that the position of youth was becoming increasingly insecure and hazardous. Financial insecurity was a cruel reality. Unemployment, especially depressing among youth, was made even more so by the almost complete lack of hope for the future. This was particularly the case among university students, a section of youth whose carefreeness had once been proverbial. In 1931 seven thousand left the universities and thirty thousand entered. In the same year there were about forty thousand unemployed university people, and it was estimated that in ten years' time only about 50 per cent of all university people would find employment. A terrible outlook for a university-trained proletariat.

'The result of this was that the young generation could no longer look into the future with anything like happiness or confidence. They knew well what it was to fear for their very means of existence. This was a threat to the bourgeois desire for security.'

II
The Spiritual Condition

'Against this constant fear, often existing in the subconscious mind, the will to live of the young generation revolted. It was almost like a hidden testimony to the existence of the Creator, that this desire to live of the younger generation could not be strangled in spite of the hopelessness of their position. The instinctive, one might almost call it the animal will to live, would not die. In this connection a fact arose which was often not understood by the older people. The young generation broke away from the old standards and values, at first slowly and carefully and then completely. The term "new primitivity" was coined. The sociologist Rosenstock used it in order to prove that the young generation had voluntarily severed itself from the spiritual world and the older generation.

'Compared with the many-sided and versatile world of pre-war generations this "new primitivity" seemed an impoverishment, which in fact it was in a certain sense. The reason for this was that these young people had absolutely no ties with the pre-war generation; this was equally true of the "nationally minded" youth. This then was the very condition that made possible the creation of something new in the political sphere. And so it happened that this primitivity and spiritual impoverishment was born of a profoundly distressing fact and at the same time held great promise for the future. The distressing fact was that the older generation too had lost so much of the old values that they could hardly be counsellors to the younger generation. The great promise for the future was the realization that now that old values had been thrown overboard, the way was clear for a new discovery, in fact, for a spiritual revival, at least among the younger generation. Its significance lay in the fact that the young recognized a certain spiritual bankruptcy in the general outlook, and that it was no longer any use to try to gloss over this impoverishment with an out-of-date theology or philosophical formula. This primitivity showed that the will to live had not been strangled, but that it was capable of shaping new systems from the broken old ones. Without a clear grasp of this point, it is impossible to understand the rise of the new political movement in Germany and its tremendous influence on the youth of that time, also that such fundamental things as discipline, order and community life once again came to play so important a part.

'Another characteristic is important. The new primitivity was nothing formal and empty and was totally different from the general mystical longing for something new, such as we find for instance in Rousseau's desire for a return to nature. In these years, Hans Grimm, the great novelist and poet, formulated the new spirit in this way: he called the younger generation the "youth with the great desire for service" and with this he characterized one of the finest qualities of these young people. In place of the old intellectual reasoning which ruled the idea of post-war youth, we now find a will to sacrifice, if necessary to sacrifice life itself. It may be counted among the great surprises which only real history can have in store, that out of the muddled and often emotional intellectual conditions of the period immediately after the war such an attitude could arise. It was doubtless one of the most important and most sincere preparatory movements for some political change in Germany, and perhaps the greatest tragedy of our time is the wicked exploitation of a mood and attitude that might have been used for the highest ends.'

III
The Political Change

'This desire for sacrifice and service was very soon to find a focus in a convulsion leading to a political re-birth of the nation. It must be remembered that for many the question of the simple naked existence of the nation as well as their own survival stood out more clearly than at any other time. The individual circumstances in politics and economics that constantly stressed this fact need not be enumerated here. That new ways had to be found, if the nation was to be preserved from chaos, was perfectly clear even to the older generation. The difference between the older and younger generations lay in the fact that the young had so little faith in the old political recipes, that they refused to consider them at all. In the place of these old political ideas came an experience quite new in our history, namely the experience of the people as a community. Thus an object for service and for the general desire to sacrifice was found and called forth a tremendous response for the youth of the whole country.

'This train of thought shows clearly how very different the political experiences of the younger generation were from anything that had called itself political thinking. Very few political changes can boast so logical a development as that of 1933.

'There is another factor of decisive importance – the conception of a political and racial leader and his followers. This characteristic is by no means as alien as it seems to many critics from outside, for it grew directly out of the spiritual change preceding 1933. It shows again that the younger generation did not consider this political change in the light of an intellectual change of programme, but rather as a change in their attitude as human beings.

'Much was written and said in those days in the attempt to explain this change. It was said, for instance, that Man, no longer capable of coping with historical problems, was projecting all his expectations of new and better times into the figure of a Führer. The conception of the Führer quite naturally took the place of the humanistic pictures of Man and History, and it is most significant that, in place of the old abstract conceptions, there appeared the living, heart-and-soul embracing, concrete idea of following the Führer. In this we see the greatest historical change of our time, and no one was more thoroughly ready to accept it than the young generation in Germany.'

The professor then left to keep his luncheon engagement saying, 'If you are not weary we will meet again this afternoon and I will talk of the underlying philosophy in this historical and political development.'

I will not make further comment beyond saying that the professor's description of the attitude of German students during the period 1919—33 falls entirely into line with my own observations, although it will be obvious that there was no hard and fast line between the various periods.

CHAPTER IV

THE PROFESSOR DISCUSSES NAZI PHILOSOPHY AND STUDENTS – II

The same afternoon I met Professor Braun again at the Anhalter Bahnhof, but the crowds were so great that we could not get a table at all. So we took a bus to the zoo, for it was a very hot afternoon and there we sat under a tree for many another hour. Here again, in his own words, is his interpretation of some of the underlying philosophy of this revolution.

'After having given a general description of the historical development of Nazism, it may be useful to add a few words about its underlying philosophy and its implications for the younger generation.

'One of the main features of this philosophy is the fact that it constitutes a comprehensive philosophy of life. The superficial type of criticism which consists of discussing almost exclusively the question of practical political life will always be unable to grasp this new vision, which called forth the unconditional enthusiasm of the younger generation. In fact this may be found later to be a turning point in the history of modern political thought. It is not the first, but so far it is certainly the most striking example of politics replacing religion. In the merger of these two most powerful influences, the intellectual and spiritual forces in politics are definitely taking the lead. This must be taken as a guiding principle in trying to understand why all spheres of life are being conquered by the new movement?

'It is the younger generation which participates fully in this comprehensive change in the general outlook on life. They are filled with the conviction that they are marching ahead of the older generation, which is still tied up with old-fashioned patterns of thought. This fact also explains why a full understanding of the new ideology must be traced back to the religious element of this conviction. It is no longer the question of different political methods but of a total change in outlook upon life itself. This is proved beyond doubt by the fact that this new movement is able to make the most definite demands upon its followers, that it is asking nothing less than real self-surrender, sacrifice and faith. Nothing of that would be possible in the case of a mere theory of economic or political life. Such a demand can only be made by a real religion or by a philosophy of life that equals religion in the strength and fervour of faith and conviction.

'This is essentially the case in the new movement in Germany. It also explains why the most sincere and candid followers of the movement are to be found among the younger generation. It was precisely this element that appealed to them more than any previous political philosophy. The typically bourgeois thought with its shallow rationalism has no meaning whatever for them. It is now discussed by the young as something to be ashamed of, which was forced to give way to the new attitude with its characteristic elements – dedication, sacrifice, discipline, obedience and the overwhelming experience that there is a new aim in life worth living for.

'It is most important also to notice that many of the traditional elements of religious life are losing their meaning entirely. Substitute religions that were founded in recent years have little attractive power. The new political conviction takes the place that in former generations religion held – that is all. The new substitute religions were found to be artificial and lacking reality, while the political faith was asking for all the enthusiasm within the hearts of the younger people.

'One other important consequence is that today rationalistic arguing has little meaning to the young. Conviction and obedience mean more to them than arguments. The rationalistic period of political thought has definitely passed for the time being, and the political prophet and his believers have taken the place of the arguing diplomat of the past. If one asks for a more technical explanation of this new philosophy there are two elements that ought to be considered as basic.

'First there is the conception of the race and the experience of the *Volksgemeinschaft*. Try to argue with young Nazis and you will find it is not essential to them to know what is the scientific explanation of these problems in detail, for they say what is essential, is that our experience is the basic experience of historic reality. So they feel that the revolution of the totality of life includes a revolution in the philosophical thought and methods as well. And this field of human activities is in their mind just one more illustration of the fact that a total change in the whole outlook on life is necessary. Even within the Party there have been some who have offered criticism, but the majority do not understand what is happening. The first and most comprehensive of all criticism centres round the psychological nature of this revolution. For to many the change seems to be a change of psychological approach to the problem of political reality rather than a change in political facts.

'Though the undeniable successes in practical politics are not to be ignored, one must emphasize that the new political faith means nothing less than that a whole generation deliberately puts its longings and expectations, and therefore its readiness to sacrifice, upon one man thus making this man – as they put it symbolically – the image into which they put all their hopes.

'More radical critics go on to say that this new political faith is bound to collapse if a serious crisis occurs which demands the real forces of endurance, forces which no illusion but only a genuine faith can provide. It is of course the duty of all who think in this country and abroad to continue to keep on asking these critical questions, for they are essential.

'The second critical consideration grows out of Christian thought. For it is clear this total faith in one man and one movement is contrary to the First Commandment: "Thou shalt have none other gods but Me." It has been stated constantly by German pastors that this problem is the dominant question of the present epoch of our church history. It is difficult to say how far the young caught in the Nazi movement will be influenced in any way by these critical and important considerations. The one thing that may be said is that the discussion about these problems in Germany is widespread if not public, and will become intensified as the implications of the movement become apparent. But one must hesitate to give estimates as to the probable figures of those among the younger generation in my country who really are concerned about these questions. It is extremely important they should constantly be urged to study them, and it is of inestimable value when British students and British university people get to know our younger generation and challenge them to think about these things. They can do this with more effect than many people here, but they must understand how deep this movement goes and concentrate on asking the more fundamental questions.

'In judging this situation, never forget that one of its essential factors is the new atmosphere of conviction and dedication which stresses life more than thought, enthusiasm more than argument, obedience to the Cause more than intellectual questioning. And most of all to thousands of them, I mean the thoughtful ones, there is a new purpose in life and no comparison is possible between the present and a past in which for them everything seemed hopeless.

'These are only rough notes,' said Professor Braun, 'and this movement is still capable of moving in different directions or rather perhaps of adopting stronger emphasis on some attitudes than others. But I am not optimistic, as I think the control of it will fall into the hands of the worst elements and I expect that if it doesn't make war sooner, it certainly will do so when it sees its hold on the nation diminishing. I feel the need for the thoughtful people in each nation to examine very carefully what it was in the experience and attitude of the younger generation in our country that made it possible for Hitler to gain their fanatical devotion.'

We discussed these points for some time and I am quite sure the professor was right, that there is real need for investigation into the more fundamental problems underlying the allegiance given to National Socialism by German youth.

CHAPTER V

AUSTRIAN PRIEST AND
NAZI HERESIES

It was wonderful to have escaped into the Austrian mountains again. I always feel when I cross the frontier into that country that even Nature herself reflects a greater tenderness and gaiety and a gentler attitude to life. Some say the Austrians are less reliable and less efficient than the Germans. Even in peaceful days I felt that was a relief after the too ordered efficiency of a Prussian state, but in Nazi days, German efficiency strikes terror into my mind as I realize their efficiency is now so often expressed in ruthless and cruel suppression and persecution.

But I want to forget all that and tell of a lovely evening when I sat on the wooden veranda of a simple peasant home in the heart of the Austrian mountains. I was the only guest because those people did not generally accept visitors except during the skiing season. After a month in Germany, ending up with a visit to the Nazi Party Congress at Nuremberg, I felt I must be alone for a while and I hoped in time to sort out some of the bewildering impressions of the past five weeks.

Have you ever wakened up from a nightmare and felt you must turn on the light and get up for a moment, just to make quite sure it was a bad dream and that if you slept again the horror of it would not come back?

Nuremberg, in 1935, was such a nightmare that I felt I should need many days alone on the mountainside to let that bad dream fade. Slowly, very slowly, the tramp of thousands upon thousands of uniformed men with sullen faces, the eager march of youth going unconsciously to destruction, the roar of aeroplanes and tanks, the raucous voices of the Nazi orators, and the most persistent, almost maddening beating of the drums and the 'Baderweiler March', at last began to fade.

I wandered about the hills all day and on that lovely September evening I was reminded of the words 'the silence clings about me like a gift'. Away in the distance men gathered the last crop of hay and nearer at hand along a narrow mountain path there passed some peasants with rugged, honest faces who, as they met me, murmured in friendly tones 'Grüss Gott' as they went on to the small church at the foot of the hill where the bell called them to Benediction.

I followed them down and after the service spoke to the priest, as I had been told he knew England well. He was a good scholar and had travelled widely, having spent ten years in America and two in England. Now in his old age he was writing a book while he looked after this little country parish. He seemed interested when I told him I had come to this remote and beautiful village for a rest after Nuremberg and in order to write some notes on my impressions of Germany.

But almost irritably he replied, 'You should not go to Nuremberg. It is a sort of madhouse and if so many foreigners go and are polite to the Nazis, they will only use it for further propaganda.'

I tried to explain to him that my visit to Nuremberg was only part of an attempt I was making to try to understand the fundamental reasons for the vitality and energy that this movement had let loose.

Not unkindly but very firmly, he replied, 'It ought not to take a month to find out that this movement is evil. Its origin and its value are easy to judge.'

'What exactly do you mean?' I said. 'Do you think that it is perhaps just another outbreak of the Prussian militarism in a new and more vulgar form?'

'Maybe,' he said, shrugging his shoulders, 'because in any country where there is a revolution it will dress itself in a national dress, and military uniform is almost like the national dress of the Germans, so that it is not surprising that the movement takes a semi-military character and also that it takes on all the worst excesses of militarism rather than anything good there might be in it.'

'But I was not thinking of any kind of superficial characteristics of this movement. Its origins are much deeper than its external appearance. Surely the only true explanation is that when men cease to worship the true God they will make themselves false gods.'

'It has happened before,' he said with a smile, 'that men in a wilderness have made unto themselves graven images. The whole world today is full of false gods, and it is not surprising that in Germany they have chosen particularly brutal and violent gods. That makes it easier to see what is happening but there are also other false gods being followed in America and England.'

As we talked we reached the little wooden peasant farm at which I was staying and I would have said goodbye but the kindly farmer's wife came out and said, 'Please, Hochwürden, come in and have a drink of wine.' I was delighted when the priest agreed and we settled down on the veranda overlooking the mountains now lit up by the setting sun. Sipping his wine the old priest began.

'Surely anyone with insight must have realized for many years that there has been growing in Europe a kind of spiritual bankruptcy and that this was bound to find some expression in political upheaval. For long I have felt there would be vast historical and economic changes for "things happen in the reality of the mind before they are made manifest in the reality of history". We now see the beginning of these changes and no one knows where they will lead. You rightly felt that at Nuremberg you were witnessing a religious festival centred round false gods. This same spiritual bankruptcy lay within the Russian revolution and I wonder if the political confusions of France do not indicate the same kind of loss of spiritual and moral health in the people.'

'And England,' I questioned, 'you have lived in my country, I understand.'

'In England things always develop differently and it is dangerous especially for a foreigner to judge. I would say that on the one hand the progress of secularization has not advanced so far as in many parts of Europe. On the other hand I would suggest that it has advanced a great deal further than many of your countrymen realize and that there are signs that you live on a kind of spiritual capital on which you draw very extravagantly. There has not been the same aggressive attack on a spiritual conception of life but the drift into a purely secular form of life is there and even among educationalist and social reformers there are many assumptions based on a humanist and not a spiritual conception of the world. If that trend is not challenged, then in time men in your country too will make themselves false gods.'

'Early in our talk,' I said, 'you quoted Nicolai Berdyaev, the Russian philosopher, and what you now say is in line with his contention that we have reached the end of an age – in fact the end of humanism. Do you agree with that?'

'I am deeply impressed with his writings,' he replied. 'I think he is one of the most profound thinkers of our time. I do not agree with many things he says but his analysis of the spiritual sickness in Europe is very penetrating. As a matter of fact I've got one of his books with me,' he replied, pulling a small book out of his pocket. 'I was reading it this afternoon and thought I might read some of it during my sermon tonight. Sometimes,' he added smiling, 'I forget I am no longer preaching to students in New York and I am afraid my people in this village would not have understood Nicolai Berdyaev, at least not in the language he writes. But let me read these passages to you because they illustrate so well the sort of things we are discussing. Listen to this. "At the moment it is almost as though there is a Christian foundation in the souls of many Europeans so that a great deal of Christian teaching and morality lives on in a kind of secularized form. But if men go on living away from the foundations of their spiritual life in the church then disintegration and, in a period of crisis like this, false gods will arise. We shall go through a very dark time of disturbance, suffering and paganism, but the very fact that man is now so busy building and defending false gods indicates that his faith in himself has been badly shaken."*

'Or again he writes so vividly of the kind of unendurable loneliness "that humanism has brought to man who now seeks escape from that in all sorts of forms of collectivism. That humanism has not strengthened man but weakened him is the paradoxical denouement of modern history. In the very act of affirming himself, he has lost himself. European man strode into modern history full of confidence in himself and his creative powers to which he put no limits; today he leaves it to pass into an unknown epoch discouraged, his faith in himself in shreds, that faith which he had in his own powers and the strength of his own skill – and he is threatened with the loss for ever of the core of his personality."'

'And yet great and noble things have been achieved during this period of humanism,' I replied.

'Surely,' he said, 'but at the cost to man of losing faith in himself. It is to restore his faith that the Nazis point men to the image of the German race and tell their followers that there they will find the source of life and faith in themselves.

'It is,' he said, 'to quote Berdyaev again, a hopeful sign "that man in asserting himself has become lonely".'

'Yes, it is probably true that the Nazi Youth were not really aware of the depth of their loneliness or "spiritual homesickness" but the Nazi revolution would never have called forth the fanatical allegiance if it had not made them first of all perhaps dimly aware of a spiritual evolution or rather that they were cut off from the true source of their spiritual being. They responded so enthusiastically – so tragically – because this teaching, however false it is to us, seemed to have some connection with the foundations of life and to give some answer to the desolation of pure

---

* *End of our Time*

individualisms. Within this tragedy there is hope because it means we move into a religious age again even though at first we follow false gods.'

'But' I said, 'returning to the actual situation in Germany today, what is the church's answer to Nazism?'

A slow smile spread over his old face as he replied, 'Forgive me but your question is put in rather a Protestant form. For a Catholic there is no question of the church finding an answer to Nazis. It is Nazism that is being judged, not the church. The Catholic faith is the answer because it is the truth and that remains untouched by the Nazi or any other passing heresy. To challenge is from our side, and Nazism is but one of the spiritual sicknesses of the many there have been and will be in the life of the church.'

As the sun set behind the mountains the old priest rose to go, saying, 'I am glad we have had this talk because now I understand better what you mean by trying to investigate the origins of National Socialism. It is, after all, perhaps important that people in other countries should understand how this kind of thing has arisen so that they will understand more quickly when false gods arise in their own country.'

I sat for some time on the veranda as darkness fell and watched the old priest make his way back to the presbytery.

I was puzzled on the one hand by the way some Protestant groups seemed thrown into confusion by the Nazis and sought feverishly for answers to their claims, while on the other hand some Catholics like this old priest assumed a lofty indifference to a revolution of this kind. I am sure there must be an attitude of compromise between these two points of view which, while maintaining that truth must prevail and is its own best witness, nevertheless will recognize that it is because the church has failed to appeal to or to hold the youth of Germany that such a movement became possible.

While I was away among those hills I wrote a number of notes on this question of religion and the Nazis. Later I will discuss these and of my impressions of some of the talks I had that year with individuals and groups. I became more than ever convinced that the Nazi dynamic, which for Germany and the world is much more important than anything else, is dependent on the pseudo-religious conceptions and practices of the Nazis. I doubt very much whether the leaders had any conception of the significance of the particular form of appeal they used, and I doubt equally whether youth was conscious of its need and how it was being met. Germany is famed for ersatz material and I rather wonder whether in producing National Socialism she has not in fact produced a most dangerous form of ersatz religion.

CHAPTER VI

TWO SIDES OF THE SAME STORY – HITLER JUGEND AND LUTHERAN PASTORS

While I was staying in Austria recovering from my visits to Germany and the Balkans, a long-distance call came through from Dresden. 'I heard you were in Simonshof after your visit to Nuremberg and that you propose to go on to Switzerland. Could we meet and travel together?' The speaker was an English friend who knew Germany well and who had been present at some of the Anglo-German discussion groups. This particular summer we had not met in Germany and I knew it would be interesting to compare notes with him. 'Yes, that would be excellent,' I replied, 'if you are willing to travel via Vienna, as I want to spend a few days there next week.'

Ten days later I met Mr Langham as he stepped out of a train in Vienna early one morning, and as we came out of the station we were surprised and delighted to meet a Dutchman who was known to us both and who had meant to set off for Switzerland that morning. We persuaded him to remain with us for the day so that we might all travel by the night train. After having coffee, we visited some of our favourite haunts and then decided to go out of the city for the day. The weather was sultry and we knew we should have a better chance of quiet conversation if we went away from the crowded city restaurants. A bus took us to a lovely old inn we knew well and which was run by a staunch Catholic who hated the Nazis and feared lest they might come to Austria.

The Dutchman, whom I will call Dr Holland, spoke fluent

German and ordered lunch and we then settled down to compare our experiences not only in Germany, but in other countries where the repercussions of Nazism were being increasingly felt, such as Hungary and Bulgaria.

After discussing the dangers of the whole political situation, our talk turned to the question of the youth in Germany and in particular to the vitality and enthusiasm of the Hitler Jugend as we had seen it not only in big assemblies of youth, but in the activities of village groups or small summer camps.

'Yes,' said the Dutchman, 'I certainly agree with you that the reason for this dynamic outburst in Germany is the thing we need most to understand. It is a great pity that so many people dwell only on the more superficial demonstrations of this highly significant phenomenon, for it is in fact much the most powerful and indeed the most dangerous aspect of the whole revolution in Central Europe. We must remember also that it bears a very close relation to the rest of the world. The form of this revolution is typically German, but its deeper spiritual causes reveal a need that is common to a great many people outside Germany, causes that in the end may well lead to disturbing developments elsewhere, though not along Nazi lines, for there are many false gods besides those the Nazis worship.'

'I think,' I said, 'that what has misled visitors to Germany and puzzled them is the obvious sense of freedom and purpose that has come to the young members of a movement that in fact takes away all freedom.'

'But think for a moment,' said Dr Holland, 'what sort of "freedom" these people have had. Think of the years of unhappiness and insecurity in many of their homes. Very few people who have not stayed with German families in recent years realize the appalling strain through which the ordinary household has passed since 1914.

'After all the horrors of war and blockade came the collapse of the mark, which was perhaps the most tragic blow of all.'

'But wasn't that the fault of German financiers?' I asked.

'Opinions differ,' said the Englishman, 'but the suffering was the same. You remember something of that?'

'Goodness, do I not,' I replied. 'Money seemed mad, and the most careful housewife dare not keep even a few shillings for a day or two because it might be worth nothing. I remember one mother who had bought dozens of pairs of boots and shoes with every penny that came her way because they would have permanent value, which their money had lost. Then again you will remember our mutual friend, the professor in Leipzig, who bought opera tickets for his boys for three months ahead, though they had scarcely enough to live on. Whoever was to blame, it was one of the most desperate situations I have ever seen in a nation. I shall always remember going into a china shop in Dresden I knew well. It was kept by an old widow whose son had been killed in the last war. I can see her now sitting behind her counter, old and thin and ill and, I found later, very hungry. I asked her the price of a vase and in a voice broken with sobs she replied, "I don't know." Stupidly I had gone in during the lunch hour and it was during that time the value of the mark changed each day and no one dared sell anything between noon and 2 p.m. when they would learn what the new level was to be.'

'Anyone,' said Dr Holland, 'who knew Germany then and has since seen this terrible unemployment, will realize that many young Germans came from homes where there was not only physical and material insecurity, but also little moral or spiritual health to be found. Many parents, feeling that their very existence was at stake and having no real philosophy or religion to fall back on, did not give their children a happy or positive outlook on life and I don't think many young Germans were conscious of freedom.'

'Anyhow, I doubt,' said Mr Langham, 'whether there is anything more shattering than to face unemployment at the threshold of life, and after a great struggle to get through the university to find you are not wanted. I'm afraid that some of the cruel young Nazis are really pathological as the result of their deep sense of injustice. It is hardly surprising that the unemployed intelligentsia have crowded into a movement that not only tells them there is a big future ahead for them, but immediately offers them posts of influence and sometimes of real power. They are also told that in helping to lead this revolution for the resurrection of Germany, they are part of something of tremendous historic significance.'

'Oh yes,' I said, 'I see how attractive and tempting the work. But it is terrible that some of them who know better should betray their own intellectual integrity.'

'I rather think many of them rationalize that by saying that if they are all in the movement they may influence it along sounder lines,' said Dr Holland. 'What is certain is that a situation involving thousands of students without faith or work is likely to provide a prophet – be he true or false – with a following.'

'As I see it, there is something much more profound in the movement than can be expressed in either political or economic terms. It has got hold of the younger crowd because it has met certain fundamental needs which can only be called religious.'

'That is exactly the impression I gained,' I said, 'and yet it is an aspect of the revolution, the significance of which people in England, at any rate, are extremely slow to grasp.'

'Well, of course,' Mr Langham replied, 'it is not very easy unless you have been at youth camps or Nuremberg. But do tell us your impression of Hitler's speeches on youth.'

'I should be very much interested in that,' added Dr Holland, 'because I have never actually heard Hitler speak and I remain puzzled by the immense power he wields. He looks such a horrible man and his voice is harsh and ugly.'

The anaemic-looking waiter who evidently understood English was just placing a dish of *spätzli* on the table and in an anxious tone whispered to Dr Holland, 'Excuse me, sir, it may be all right for the lady to talk about the German Führer like that, but for you it may be very dangerous when you return to Germany, for even in Austria there are many spies.'

'For heaven's sake,' said Dr Holland, 'don't take me for a

German. Thank God I am a Dutch citizen and not a citizen of the Third Reich.'

At this the waiter, after taking a quick look round leaned over the table and with a wry smile said, 'Then please talk very loud.'

We laughed and then went on with our conversation. 'Let me tell you,' I said, 'of some of the things Hitler says to youth which strike me as being particularly dangerous because the principles he states are often true, though his application of them is entirely false. To illustrate this I will tell you of some of the things he said in the early days of the movement when I was listening to him in the hope that I should hear him declare his programme. Imagine my surprise when I tell you that during a speech lasting for an hour and a half, he made no reference to either economic or political plans. He cut right below all the practical side of the revolution and hammered at what he called their faith. Mind you, a great deal of what he said was pure mumbo-jumbo, but he did say two very important things and said them again and again in different forms, and it was these things that roused the almost delirious enthusiasm of the crowd before him.

'As usual he started by drawing an exaggerated picture of the policy of various parties since the war and their failure to bring unity, peace or prosperity to Germany. It was a completely distorted account, but one could scarcely expect boys of that age to be able to check up on what he said. He went on to draw a really terrifying picture of Germany when he came to power. This was the more impressive because so many boys in his audience must have been well aware of the despondency and discouragement of their parents, and many had also experienced the dire results of mass unemployment.

'With consummate skill he got his audience to feel the despair and desolation of Germany, and then, working himself up into a frenzy, he thundered at this youthful crowd. I do not remember all his words, but the main points remain vividly in my mind.

'"You must realize that however dark things are, there is no such thing as deadlock in the affairs of men. The only deadlock today is in the minds of men. You need never be defeated by your circumstances. Man is only finally defeated by himself. That is true of you, my young comrades, and that is also true of your country."

'He went on, "For years this country has been ruled by men who were defeated in spirit. Their favourite theme was that there was 'no way out' and that the fault was everyone else's but their own. You have heard them say again and again that all the desolation and distress in Germany was due, first to defeat and secondly to forces outside this country. I deny all that. Germany was never defeated except in the minds of cowardly politicians. It is true that outside enemies have tried and will continue to try to crush Germany and to keep her from taking her place among free and great powers. I am not afraid of outside powers. You are not afraid, you know your destiny. The destiny of the Fatherland is not decided by a lot of chattering politicians in other countries. No power, no country in the world can stop Germany from rising again."

'He had worked up his audience into a frenzy of excitement now, but he went on with unabated fury. "Politicians all the world over talk of difficulties – let them do it. We are not interested in difficulties, we are only interested in success. I tell you to strike out the word 'impossible' from your vocabulary. There is a way out and you, my young comrades, will find it. I tell you the resurrection of Germany from dust and ashes to a powerful and unified country does not depend on outside forces, it does not depend on fainthearted politicians – it depends on you."

'Hitler halted for a moment, overcome by his own passion, while the youthful audience seemed almost intoxicated. He wiped his brow and his voice became quieter and more appealing as he held out his hands saying, "You, my young comrades, are Germany's future and her future is safe with you. Germany has been kicked, scorned and driven to despair and none within her have had the courage to revolt and to defend her right to live. If you are passionately, blindly loyal and obedient, then I tell you that in five years' time from now things will happen that will startle the world. I bring you a faith that cannot be defeated."

Then, ingratiatingly, he went on, "But, my young friends, you cannot achieve this miracle as individuals. You cannot achieve it unless you realize that it is the community and not the individual that matters, and unless you give yourselves up completely to the service of the Fatherland. That means that you care about Germans because they are Germans and you do not care any more what their fathers earned, nor what their religion is. Don't think the mere wearing of a brown uniform makes you a good National Socialist. You are only a good National Socialist if in your heart you are deeply unhappy while a single German is unemployed. Thanks to the cowardice of her politicians, the divisions of Germany have been one of the causes of her despair. What country wants twenty-three political parties? No, some of the old people may still like their divisions, but I tell you, the youth of this country must be one. We will never again have the ridiculous picture of children marching against one another under different political banners."

At this point Mr Langham interposed, 'For goodness' sake have some more coffee, or you will get as exhausted as the Führer.'

Laughing I replied, 'Well, you know, it is almost impossible to recall that scene without becoming aware again of the tension and hysteria in that vast gathering. It was almost terrifying, and yet, as you say, men just shrug their shoulders and say "what rot all this Nazi stuff is" and don't begin to see what it is doing to a whole generation in Germany.'

'If only the foreign powers could be brought to understand,' said Dr Holland. 'For the future of Europe it may yet prove more important and indeed more dangerous than anything else that is happening. A movement of this sort has dynamic power which will have repercussions throughout the world, because there are present at most of their great youth rallies young men from many other countries who are likely to be impressed with all this. And in addition you have these unofficial ambassadors of von

Ribbentrop's – the cream of the Nazi Youth, travelling to all parts of the globe.'

'I know well enough,' I answered, 'that some English students travelling through Germany and staying at youth hostels are profoundly impressed, and when I ask them why, they reply, "It is wonderful to meet people so intensely alive and so full of aim and purpose; they at least know what they believe and what they want."'

'What gives all this an alarming and even sinister character is that some of the things that Hitler says to them are in themselves true. It amazes me that some people in our own countries seem to imagine that Hitler stands up and describes all the beastly, sadistic orgies he can imagine and thereby attracts the wholehearted enthusiasm of youth. Were he to do so, he would be far less dangerous and certainly far less powerful, because he would then only attract the criminal or the pathological types, whereas now he gets the energy, the enthusiasm and the generous response of the best elements in the youth of the country.'

'Then again,' said Mr Langham, 'the other factor that is too often forgotten is that the youth Hitler lashed into a frenzy of excitement and determination by the vision he gave that day of what miracles might happen in Germany in a few years' time are now able to see that much of what he promised has already come. And even if his speeches this year were, as you said earlier, much less effective, the youth had the demonstration of the vast throng gathered at Nuremberg and must have felt that the promises Hitler made had indeed been fulfilled.'

'What a land of contrasts it is,' said Mr Langham, 'for while you were listening to Hitler addressing thousands of young Germans, I was seeing a very different picture – a secret meeting of Protestant pastors.'

'Could you tell us about that,' we exclaimed.

'Yes,' he replied, looking around, 'there is no one about just now' – for even the waiter had moved off. 'But I will mention no names.

'I was staying with a Lutheran pastor in south Germany, when a letter came from one of the leading pastors in that district. The letter was brought by hand because it would have been dangerous to post it. A copy of it had been sent to all the pastors in the district who belonged to the Confessional Church group and to any who lived beyond the district but who could arrange to stay with friends for a few days.

'The letter was a summons to a secret meeting in a small hotel on the outskirts of the town. A well-known leader in the Confessional Church had arrived from Berlin at this hotel to report to those who wished to hear the results of a recent meeting between a delegation of pastors and the Nazi Minister of Church Affairs Herr Kerrl. The man who owned the hotel was a keen churchman and was prepared to risk this secret meeting in one of his back parlours. So many pastors managed to get there under cover of darkness that the meeting had to be held in two shifts, one group of pastors waiting outside while the other heard the report.

'I went into the room,' said Mr Langham, 'just as the first lot had settled down. The room was small and it was packed to suffocation with pastors, young and old, some sitting, some standing. At a table at one end of the room sat the speaker and next to him one or two well-known leaders of the Confessional Church. When we were all packed in, the speaker rose and spoke for half an hour.

'Very quietly, without emotion, but with a deep sense of the significance of the occasion, he gave an account of the dealings with the Minister of Church Affairs. He told them that all their latest hopes of agreement had been completely shattered by recent conferences with Kerrl. Shattered, he said, by Kerrl's own attitude, as he did not come within a cry of understanding what they were about in their opposition to Nazi teaching and control.

'The delegation had had to remind Kerrl that the Gospel was not for sale, that it was absolute in its demands on them and that their vocation was obedience to God. The silence in that back room was tense and you felt that here were men whose families and livelihood as well as their lives might hang on this report, but who were quietly and unshakably determined to go on with the struggle.

'Some of the older men looked worried and ill, while the younger ones had a kind of elation about them as if the Gospel and their task had suddenly become real to them in a new and powerful way.

'The speaker came to the end of his report and paused for a moment and then with a dignity born of deep conviction, he added, "Brethren, you want to know what to do. There is only one thing to do – to go straight ahead, looking neither to the right hand nor to the left, remaining faithful to the Gospel and preaching the word of God. Do not let us be troubled by the world. It hated our Lord. It may hate us. He told us that it would. That is not our concern. It is for us to be faithful. Amen."

'He remained standing for a moment and then slowly one pastor after another got up and walked out of the room into the night. Some went away talking in twos and threes, some walked home alone. Others had a long bicycle ride along country roads and would only reach their homes in the early hours of the morning.

'I wondered,' said Mr Langham, 'how many pastors in our own country really understand the nature of the struggle that these men are up against.'

So long had we sat discussing that we suddenly realized it was nearly 3 p.m. and that we had the inn to ourselves. Noticing that our conversation had ceased, the waiter grew bolder and came over and talked to us for he was obviously anxious to do so once he knew we were not Germans and were anti-Nazi.

'It is impossible to prevent the young from following Hitler,' he said. 'My boy is eighteen years old and he has never had a proper job since he left school. Now he enjoys all sorts of adventures because he belongs to a gang of rough boys who call themselves Nazis. They don't know or care what it means, but they like going out at night and painting swastikas on public buildings and pavements and then watching the authorities clean them off the next day. It is just an excitement and something to do – at least that is how it started. But now I think something more serious is happening. I believe the Nazis have got hold of some of these gangs and that they are paying them and telling them what to do.'

'You really think they are in touch with the German Nazis, do you?' asked Mr Langham.

'I cannot be sure of that, but something happened the other day which worried me. Suddenly my younger son got angry with his elder brother, who is in a job and very much against the younger one's adventures. He turned on his elder brother and on me and said, "When Hitler comes to Austria, I shall be telling you and a lot more people like you what you have got to do." I don't know whether it was mere stupid bragging, but I have the feeling that the Germans are preparing the ground for invading this country one day, and that at the beginning they will use boys like my son and his friends.'

As the waiter was helping Dr Holland on with his coat, I said to him, 'Tell me, what is the attitude of Austria to the Nazis? Surely the country as a whole wants to keep its freedom?' A bitter look crossed the face of the waiter as he answered, 'Since the last war the only freedom we have had in Austria is the freedom to die slowly of starvation. Many people now hear that there is no unemployment in Germany and I'm afraid they think it would be better to let the Nazis come rather than to go on as we have gone since the last war.'

On the way back to the bus, we reflected sadly on how little had been done in the past twenty years to deal with economic and political situations in Europe created by the last war and which were obviously dangerous. Against a background of moral and spiritual bankruptcy, charged with a profound inner restlessness that might manifest itself in the form of violent social upheavals, there existed focal points of political danger. And yet political leaders in Europe seem unwilling to recognize that these focal points were particularly likely to cause disturbance in a situation where there was not enough moral and spiritual stability to enable men to grapple with these problems sanely. Certainly very few of the democratic statesman and thinkers seem to have been able to read the writing on the wall.

As the train steamed out of Vienna that night, we all agreed that no city in Europe had had a more tragic history since 1914. A beautiful city almost without a country and one in which from 1918 it had always been possible to see tragic signs of the aftermath of war – and now there fell on it the long shadow of Nazi intrigue and approaching aggression.

CHAPTER VII

SWISS BARRISTER AND NAZI MYTHOLOGY IN WESTERN CIVILIZATION

We had just left the frontier town of Buchs and having replaced our baggage on the rack we went into the corridor. Here we should get a good view of the Lake of Wallenstadt and a little later the glorious Glarus Mountains would come into sight.

'How wonderful,' said Mr Langham, 'it is to be going back into freedom where the shadows of the Gestapo do not fall.'

'As a matter of fact,' said Dr Holland, 'they did have trouble in Geneva in the spring when a flat belonging to an Englishman was ransacked and his manservant injured, but fortunately the Swiss authorities took a strong enough line to discourage any further attempt of that kind.'

By this time students from other nations were in the corridor and Dr Holland soon got into conversation with a Dutch student, while Mr Langham and I told an English student who had joined us something about the chief lecturers who were to take part in the international summer school we were all attending.

'You will find a Swiss barrister called Dr Zürcher by far the most illuminating,' I said, 'especially as he has just completed nearly a year visiting universities in most European countries.'

'Yes,' added Mr Langham, 'get to know him, you can't miss him as he is massive in form and has a massive brain and combines sound scholarship with sound judgement. I always think,' he continued, 'that it is a great tribute to his sympathetic imagination, as well as his great learning, that men in so many nations are keen to hear his observations on their own countries as well as the political and social undercurrents of other countries.'

'He speaks many languages,' I added, 'and this gives him an excellent chance of getting to know what people are thinking and saying. But the thing about Dr Zürcher that has interested me most is his theological knowledge. He himself is a Calvinist, but he has made a careful study of current trends in theology and in addition to an academic knowledge, he seems to be able to enter with understanding into the worship and traditions of Russian Orthodoxy and Roman Catholicism, as well as those of the Protestant Churches.'

'It is, I think,' said Mr Langham, 'this combination of political and theological knowledge that makes his observations particularly interesting just now when experiments are being made on a huge scale to make of politics a form of ersatz religion.'

Having reached Geneva we parted from the students and went to our hotel where we rang up Dr Zürcher and he invited us to dine with him the next evening. He and his charming wife received us in their beautiful flat and we decided we would leave the Nazis and all their works till after dinner was over. In the meantime he entertained us delightfully with stories of some of his European journeys, dwelling on the lighter side of his experiences, though interspersing this with penetrating comments which made us want to ask many questions.

Coffee was served in a sitting room with French windows opening on to a small balcony. It was a hot evening and through the open window we could look across to the Salève Mountain.

'Now do tell me what it is you would like to discuss,' said the doctor. 'I gather it is about the significance in Europe of certain aspects of the Nazi revolution. If so, that is what you in England call a "tall order".'

'Let us say,' I replied, 'that it is certain religious aspects of the general situation we would like you to talk about. If Mr Langham will allow me, I would like to tell you why we want to hear your views.'

'Yes, go ahead,' said Mr Langham.

'You know, I think, that we have both spent some time in Germany in recent years, studying the situation, especially in regard to youth. The more I have reflected on the fundamental aspects of the Nazi revolution the more concerned I felt to discover how this linked up with what was happening outside Germany. For spiritual necessities do not live within national frontiers, even if "solutions" take national forms and the nature of this breakdown in Central Europe indicates that some of its causes will be found in different forms in the civilization in which it has occurred. So much is known,' I continued, 'about the false and indeed evil solutions tried by Germany, but we want you to talk of aspects of the necessities that called for solution and which have universal significance.'

'It is surely only natural,' said Dr Zürcher, 'that most people should be more concerned with the falseness of German teaching and its dire consequences, but you are certainly wise, if you wish to understand what is happening, to try to see it in a much wider context. For instance,' he continued, 'in my country here I often hear people sneering at all the things the Germans are saying about "blood and soil", and yet a too ready denunciation of this teaching means that they completely fail to realize that, however false the answer is, it is at least an attempt on the part of the Germans to give some answer to certain fundamental human needs.'

'You mean,' said Mr Langham, 'that it is an attempt to give an answer to the question of origin and destiny?'

'Exactly,' he replied, 'but I would like to elaborate that, if you are interested.'

We both assured him that it was precisely because we were so interested that we had decided to stay in Switzerland before going back to England. Dr Zürcher rose and fetched some drinks.

'It's a hot evening,' he said, 'and it's a long story, so do help yourselves to an iced drink while I try to give you my "impressions".'

We accepted the invitation and settled down to listen. I will give Dr Zürcher's own words as far as I can recall them and at the risk of over-condensation.

'Man has two questions, or rather two groups of questions,' he said, 'insistent in his mind –whence and whither? Through all the ages and in every race, religion has been concerned with these two fundamentals and, in a sense, two different kinds of religion have come into being according to which of the two questions has been held of more importance.'

'Hold on a minute,' interrupted Mr Langham. 'What do you include under those two questions – whence and whither? I can conceive of their being answered either in scientific or in spiritual terms, but neither answer quite meets the case of this blood and soil business, does it?'

'Let me take the two questions separately, then,' replied Dr Zürcher. 'First, whence? Every one of us is confronted with the mystery of his being – the date and place of our birth, the blood in our veins, coming to us from our parents and ancestors; the race, nationality, the historical epoch to which we belong. Now all these facts are beyond the reach of our wills and of our reason. They represent the vast, non-rational hinterland of our lives. The same is true of the fact of death and of the way in which, between birth and death, our life is swayed by the great non-rational force of love, or Eros. All this raises the question, whence? And that demands an answer. It is, if you like, a man's fate – his roots in the whole vast cosmic process, in which he is himself a tiny incident. Religion has given many different answers, but it has never been able to evade the challenge. I should call this aspect of religion, the aspect which looks back to the past and searches for origins, static religion.'

'That seems a curious phrase,' I said. 'Is it really true of the great pagan religions whether of antiquity or of today? I should have thought they were too powerful to be termed static.'

'Well, I don't mind very much about the word, though I cannot think of a better,' said Dr Zürcher. 'I mean religion which is not as much interested in the future, in where history is going to, but in the past and where history has come from. But perhaps I can make myself clearer if I go on to the second question – whither? Man is not only the child of the past, he is also the parent of the future, moving towards an unknown end. And he knows it. Therefore, he is aware of a world that has not yet come into being, a world that ought to be. And religion has to answer questions about that too. I call this forward-looking aspect of religion dynamic, because it is the power that drives man forward.

'Now, in the Christian religion this means the coming of righteousness and the Kingdom of God, or, if you like, the kingdom of that which ought to be, the rational kingdom of the moral law. There man is confronted with God with all that that means of judgement and mercy, forgiveness and reconciliation. But – and this is the point I am trying to make – we need answers to both our urgent questions: whence and whither? Religion can only be effective if it assigns to a man a place in the cosmos adequate to his complex nature, and he is both mind and spirit and flesh and blood. He needs an assurance of significance both in regard to the rational, forward-looking side of his nature and in regard to his non-rational past. To use my terms, religion, to be effective, must combine the static and the dynamic aspects in one whole or it will leave man unsatisfied, fundamentally divided in himself and therefore uncertain of his destiny.'

'I see,' said Mr Langham, 'you mean that we may have been overstressing one of these two aspects at the expense of the other and this rebirth of paganism is a violent corrective?'

'Yes. I do not know whether you will agree with me, but I cannot help feeling that institutional Christianity, especially of the modern Protestant type, has been more concerned with the dynamic aspect of religion than with the static. It has spoken a lot of man as a rational person, and has had little to say about his cosmic origin. I consider that this has brought about what I should like to term "the rupture of man with the cosmic forces", and to my mind, this rupture is one of the most important contributing factors of the present crisis of our Western civilization. Here I would like to emphasize that this is in no way a crisis limited to Germany. You and I know too well how far back in history the process of secularization begins, starting with the glorification of man and man alone, and ending in the most appalling distortion and annihilation of the image of man in our present secularized and machine-made world. To my mind it is very important that we should not be so concerned with false teaching or brutal action in Germany as to fail to recognize that at least she must be credited with feeling keenly the present atomization of society and the loneliness of man, and being wise enough to realize that this was due to what I have called "the rupture of man with the cosmic forces".'

'But just a minute, Dr Zürcher, you don't surely suggest that many of the Nazi leaders were really conscious of any such rupture and that they set out to find an answer!'

'That is a question which it is difficult to answer, because,' he said, 'it is obvious that a great many Nazi leaders would not have the slightest idea what we are talking about. But there were earlier writers in Germany who were thinking in these terms, and certainly some of the Nazis knew of this point of view and were at least partially aware of this rupture which was probably true to their own experience. The Nazis generally expressed these things in vulgar and non-intellectual terms, but I do not believe that it was just chance that so much of their teaching and symbolism is directed towards answering the spiritual needs of this generation, if they had not somehow sensed the nature of these needs.

'Anyhow,' he continued, 'the important thing is that the Nazis did attempt to give a solution, and however much we may deplore this we must recognize that this problem is not merely their problem, but also the problem of Europe and Western civilization. Their solution is a new gospel for the Nazis, called "Blood and Soil", the attempt to give to the *Volksgenossen* inside the Reich cosmic significance without admitting that the cosmos does not belong to the Germans but belongs to God alone, who is its creator.'

'Well, whether many Nazis understand what they are about or not, there can be no doubt in the minds of those who study German youth just now,' I said, 'that they have found a genuine inspiration in the thought that their individual lives have taken on a new significance because they can identify themselves with the German race in which they have their origin and roots and see their destiny secured within the destiny of the Third Reich, which gave them a sense of purpose and fulfilment.'

'Before we go,' said Mr Langham, 'there is one other point we have been discussing, and about which we would like to hear your opinion, namely, how does all you say about "blood and soil" teaching link up with their teaching on *Gemeinschaft?*'

'Yes,' I added, 'I am very anxious to hear what you say on that because as I have talked to young Nazis I have been aware that some of their deepest experiences which gave them fanatical devotion are bound up with what they call the experience of *Gemeinschaft.*'

'Certainly,' said Dr Zürcher, 'I would like to talk of that but it cannot be said in a sentence, so you must forgive me if I give you what will sound like a short lecture.'

'Yes, please, go ahead,' we said.

'You see, you have raised the question of the second major cause of the crisis in Western civilization,' he replied. 'When we say that man has become atomized and lonely in our machine age, we mean not merely that he has been uprooted and severed his ties with his cosmic origin, but also that there has been disruption of organic human relationships, through the lack of true community. In the old days man had a place definitely assigned to him, whether high or low, in an organic society. This had its limitations, but also its great advantages, and on balance the advantages far outweighed the drawbacks. We talk today a lot about security, collective security in the international field, social security at home, but we talk very little about a much more important security, namely, the inner feeling, and acceptance of a place in the social fabric of the nation. Once again, the Germans were among the first to become acutely conscious of this aspect of the crisis, and the Nazis offered their own methods of solution. We may not like it, but there is no doubt that they created a new sense of community for the rank and file of the Germans. In doing so they attempted, not without success, to permeate industrial labour with a new sense of the dignity of its function in the community. In fact, they tried to do the same for all the large groups in the nation: youth, the universities, the liberal professions, the theatre, the press, etc. They also understood the hunger of the lonely and atomized masses for a principle of authority which is not abstract, but embodied in a living and concrete personality. Hence the 'Führerprinzip', which starts with the Führer himself, and goes down the line to the smallest Gauleiter or 'Unterführer' throughout the whole hierarchy. This was again a way to restore meaning to the masses, to save them from senseless loneliness, to restore to them greatness, by giving them the feeling that the humblest among them shared the greatness of the whole. But here again the Nazis committed the fatal and tragic mistake of building up this pseudo church. They built up a tribal community and a tribal loyalty. They sacrificed freedom for the sake of restoring a sense of meaning and greatness to the humble. They thought it possible to evolve a system of double morality, one valid among Germans, and another appropriate to other nations and races. They forgot that the dignity of man is derived from God and God alone, and that no amount of symbolization of the new community feeling by "marching together" and other activities could overcome the distortion of the human image. Neither did they grasp that a national community's true greatness resided in the acceptance of the will of God and in that alone.'

Mr Langham and I thanked Dr Zürcher for the extraordinarily interesting points he had made, and extracted from him the promise that he would visit England in the near future to lecture in the universities.

It was a lovely evening, and Dr Zürcher said he would walk part of the way back to our hotel with us. As we said goodbye, and renewed our thanks, he said, 'I have welcomed the chance of talking about these things with you, for I feel deeply the tragedy of Germany. Remember,' he continued, 'we Alemannic Swiss who have been nurtured in the great tradition of German culture, are probably more sensitive to the new German heresy than the English or the French, because we have a closer insight into the unique endowment of the German nation, and therefore we can measure more accurately the Nazis' betrayal of the true German mission in the world – perhaps some day we may talk of that.'

Mr Langham and I continued to discuss some of these points after we reached our hotel, and we realized that Dr Zürcher had given us a great deal to think about, for whether we agreed entirely with all he said or not, we felt that in this and in subsequent lectures he gave us something of the wider setting of the Nazi betrayal, which reinforced our conviction of the need for a careful study of the relevance of the Nazi revolution to the general European situation.

CHAPTER VIII

A TRAITOR TO HIMSELF

'If you and one or two of your English friends could come to coffee at my house tomorrow night, I will invite some of the student members of the Nazi Party and a few teachers to meet you for a discussion and we will explain to you what I mean when I say how happy the younger generation is about the revolution.'

So said young Dr Hartmann, who held a senior post in a large boys' school in Munich. He had a good university record, but would scarcely have been appointed to this particular post if it had not been for his enthusiastic membership of the Nazi Party. After dinner the next night, three of us set out for the Hartmann flat. On the way we called to mind that less than a week before we had gone to another flat in Munich, which was the home of a young German lawyer. He was passionately anti-Nazi and had been most anxious that we should meet some of his friends in the legal profession that they might tell us how bitterly they deplored the degradation into which they felt Germany had fallen and how they resented the fact that all decent standards of justice were being subordinated to Nazi aims and manipulations.

The night we met the lawyers we had had to take great precautions about our meeting. We were all to travel by different routes and to arrive at different times. It was deeply moving to see the intense relief and delight it was to those young lawyers to be able to tell us what they were thinking and as one of them said, to meet English scholars – and to realize that sanity still existed outside Germany if not within. Our host had written a long paper, which he read, and then we asked many questions.

As the party drew to a close, one of the German lawyers present said, 'Perhaps the best illustration we could give you of the kind of slavery into which we have fallen is to point out that if a Gestapo man knew of this meeting and of what we have been saying, it is certain we should all be in a concentration camp very quickly and it is possible that some of us might be shot. Dr Sachs, the lawyer who read the paper, will have to burn it in case his home is searched.'

But that was the first week I was in Germany on this visit and now I want to recall another evening with the Nazis. This time we could go openly to the Nazi house and there was no anxiety about the meeting. We were welcomed by Dr Hartmann and his young wife, also a keen Nazi, and three or four youth leaders and teachers together with three boys aged from fourteen to sixteen. One, I think, was a younger brother of Frau Hartmann, the other two were his friends.

As we were drinking coffee our host said, 'I found since I saw you yesterday that one of the most important younger Nazi leaders in our Ministry of Culture is in Munich for a few days, so he will come and open the discussion tonight. Sometimes the English papers say of the Nazis that they are not intellectual. I can assure you Dr Weber is brilliant, and I think he will make you understand that all Nazis are not unintelligent.'

Just as Dr Hartmann finished speaking the door opened and Dr Karl Weber came in. I realized at once that I knew him, and on shaking hands I recalled where we had met. 'But surely, Dr Weber, you remember we have met before. About three years ago we were together at an International Student conference in Switzerland where we discussed Christianity and internationalism late into the night.'

Dr Weber was obviously embarrassed that his Nazi friends should hear this and was quite determined that I should pursue the subject no further. He replied rather coldly. 'Oh yes, but those were the days in which we lived in a kind of fantasy about the League of Nations. Now, thank God, we in this country have become realists and know that neither Christianity nor the League of Nations could save Germany from destruction.'

At this point others came up to be introduced and I had no further chance of talking to him.

After coffee we settled down to listen to Karl Weber and at first I found it difficult to concentrate on what he was saying because I was so interested in his face. The marks of a deep conflict were all too apparent, and his thinly veiled cynicism could not hide his unhappiness. It seemed as though he had sold his soul to this movement and as I reflected I realized what the temptation had been. Dr Weber had been among the thousands of unemployed intellectuals, and now he was in a really important state post and was looked up to, not only by young Nazis, but by many of the crude and less intellectual types who greatly admired the skill with which he expressed their theories in high-sounding intellectual phrases and who found in him a past-master in the art of rationalizing Nazi actions.

Dr Weber talked to us for more than an hour and then answered questions for another hour. I must select some of the points he made which seem to me to explain what I mean by the fundamentally religious appeal to the Nazi Youth in much of the teaching given to them.

However I must repeat a warning I have given before when telling these stories. It is easy enough for people in England, especially those with some kind of education and judgement, to see how utterly false and even ludicrous much Nazi teaching is. But I am not concerned as to whether the intelligentsia in our own country are deceived by Nazi teaching, whereas I am concerned with trying to show how plausible it all sounded to young Germans with no particular religious, intellectual or moral standards by which to judge what was being said, a generation who even in early years had been faced with uncertainty about their future. Many of them were the sons and daughters of unhappy parents who had not recovered from the last war and were far too bewildered themselves to be good guides to their children

– and many also had older brothers unemployed and bitter. A very astute traveller in Europe in 1925 remarked: 'The old world is dead and the new is waiting to be born.'

That was profoundly true and none could have dreamed that so terrible a new world would be born in central Europe. I must not enlarge further on this point but I am convinced that we shall never rightly assess the full significance and indeed the full dangers of this movement, if we fail to realize who were the eager disciples of this new faith and unless we understand something of their background and of the genuine human needs they felt were satisfied by Nazi teaching. But, to get back to Dr Weber with his tense, unhappy face as he started to address us.

'I find my English friends talk a great deal about loss of freedom in Germany, and yet as they travel in this country they must become aware that the youth seems much freer and certainly much happier than for many years. Even the more prejudiced foreigners have told me of their amazement at this outburst of new life, energy and purpose. There are many reasons I could give you for this, but I will select a few, though I must first remind you that people mean very different things when they speak of freedom. I am not going to enter into the various aspects such as freedom from foreign domination, freedom from economic slavery, freedom from poverty or unemployment. You know of these and many others, but I want to suggest to you that the younger generation in Germany needed above all the freedom that comes from security, and the kind of security I mean is that which comes to those who give complete obedience to an authority they know they can trust.

'For youth in Germany the terrible time of uncertainty is over. In National Socialism they are finding the reason for their existence, the chance of living fully and with a purpose. The state control of the young in Germany today is not to be thought of as tyranny and oppression, but rather it is control or care in the same sense that in former days the church undertook the responsibility for her children. In the Middle Ages the church was concerned about the whole life of man, and man gained a sense of freedom from trusting in the authority and judgement of the church in all important departments of his life.

'When man broke from the family of the church he drifted more and more into individualism. Strength and security began to fail him and by degrees he felt himself not so much free as desolate. In Germany you have seen the greatest extreme of individualism and you have also seen the greatest collapse.

'In this situation the Führer arose, and now the German state gathers men, not back into the broken bits of various churches which are relics of the past, but instead into the great family of the German Reich. It offers the young the same authority, the same strength, and the same freedom in that comes from an unquestioning belief in a creed and a way of life. It is also true that, just as the church did not ask the individual to formulate his own faith and creed, so we do not ask the young Nazi to do this either. He must enter into the faith without question.

'He may not understand it all, he may not even like it all, but he must realize that the wisdom of the state is greater than his own.

'But I must here remind you,' continued Dr Weber, 'that when a young man becomes a good Nazi, it is not so much intellectual change as a yielding to a new and comprehensive view of life, and he will find much joy and a sense of release in following it. Foreigners find this difficult to understand because they use their own conceptions in interpreting it. Nazi philosophy cannot be explained in terms of any previous ideas, for it is bound up with the historic fate of the German people. In National Socialism the ideas of race and community represent a new experience of reality which has come almost like a revelation to many of us.

'We may still share with you and with all mankind in the political and economic crisis in the world,' continued Dr Weber, 'but in what you regard as merely political events in 1933 we found a new experience of existence. This experience belongs to the realm of the *unsagbar*. We feel we must begin here with that which is new in life. From this experience we begin to see that the distinction between private and public must disappear, and we have made the discovery of the great reality of cooperation within the family of the German race. For all now, especially for the young, we recognize the authority of sacrifice, of decision, of responsibility and of absolute obedience.

'This for us all is a great educational and I would say, inspirational event, a transition from an attitude which merely enjoys reality theoretically to one which recognizes the demand of reality. The Führer experienced in the last war that the eternal values of a common human life and fellowship were discovered by men under stress of war, which led to new respect among all classes. It was in complete opposition to this discovery that the acute class conflict arose again in our country in post-war years. The National Socialistic Revolution is the reassertion that the common fate of blood and race are more profound than any class distinctions. You will see that our philosophy has reacted against abstract theories, and that we now have the concrete conceptions of *Blut und Boden* and we believe that all culture is based on and bound up with race.

'It is plain to all who are willing to see, that this philosophy involves a call to the younger generation to heroic living, for this reality of race is something which claims them, gives them a standard and orientates their whole life. This great inspiration does not only come from intellectual conceptions, it comes because there has been called forth in this country what we term a deep feeling for life (*Lebensgefühl*) which is inevitably bound up with the fact of blood and race. The Führer expresses what all of us in some measure have experienced, that we have passed from mere existence into inexhaustible life.' Then he made a most significant comment.

'Theology in Germany has been very largely what we call an "unobedient theology", that is a theology which is mainly thinking about God, not a standing before the demands of a living God. Our philosophy puts obedience to the demands of reality as essential for every young National Socialist.'

Some of us could scarcely keep quiet any longer, especially as the youths in the group were drinking in all he said. So we interrupted, 'Do excuse us, Herr Doktor, but could we ask some questions about all this?'

'I would be glad,' he said, 'if you would allow me to develop one other important point in relation to this, and then we can have a discussion on it all.

'I spoke earlier of youth being lonely and in need of fellowship. It is true that there were all sorts of idealistic youth movements and especially international youth movements, but the Führer has shown us that it is ridiculous to think of a world fellowship. Men can only be creative within a fellowship they can recognize, one that has certain limitations. The world fellowship of youth is like the League of Nations, only a hazy figment of the imagination that crumbles as soon as political difficulties arise. But the fellowship of German youth is a real thing and every member of the Hitler Jugend knows to what he belongs and that he has himself an important part to play. He knows also that he does not play that part for himself but for the sake of the community.'

'But,' we said, 'in this family what is the place of the German Jew, and indeed what is the place of anyone who opposes the National Socialists?'

Only the flash in his dark eyes revealed the fact that Dr Weber was a traitor to himself as he replied, 'Again let me refer you to the church in the Middle Ages. The church knew it was the faith that mattered and showed in the Inquisition what she could do with those who were heretics. Germany and the destiny of Germany is what matters, and, even if we are thought ruthless or cruel, we must exclude all who would poison the life of the state.'

On this point we challenged him again and again but we could get no further. In fact the more we pressed the more extreme did Dr Weber become. Even the young boys joined in this part of the discussion and talked of the Jews as the great evil they must fight relentlessly. We realized that in an almost religious sense they had created their own devil against whom they must wage ceaseless warfare. So we returned again to the question of opposition within the Party, saying to Dr Weber, 'Surely Germany is famed for her critical mind and for her standards of scholarship. It seems to us wildly unlikely that even among National Socialists you all agree. Can a good National Socialist oppose certain things the Party teaches or does and be safe? The fact that you all give the same sort of parrot answers to our questions puzzles us, because we cannot believe that suddenly you all agree about these important points, especially such things as the race problems, when the whole world is against your decisions and teachings.'

Hard pressed but with complete urbanity Dr Weber replied, 'Let me put it this way. It is obvious that there are different points of view in the Party and often different points of emphasis, and anyone in the Party has within its councils the right to put his own point of view. We express this by saying 'Innerhalb des Glaubens,' many points of view may be held. Again let me compare it with the church. Within the councils of the church there was often serious disagreement, but early Christian missionaries did not display or discuss their doctrinal disputes with the heathen.'

At this we laughed, feeling we must be the heathen, but Dr Weber rounded on us with passion and said, 'I would go further and say if the Christian missionaries in the world today had kept their differences to themselves and given only the message on which they were united, there might be more Christians in the world. It is not very impressive when men parade their quarrels before those they would convert. We feel youth at least must be saved from the confusions and uncertainties which even the church presents.'

Then recovering his composure, he added more persuasively, 'Believe me, any contribution that any good Party member has to make is very carefully considered and often accepted, but no one in the Party may organize opposition if his opinion is not accepted.

'Not only have we now got this recognizable fellowship in which each young National Socialist knows he has a part to play, but you may be surprised to learn that, to a far greater extent than in any other youth movement I know, our National Socialist songs constantly remind us of our spiritual fellowship with those who have died in our cause. I would remind you of such favourite songs sung so often by National Socialists such as 'Ich hau einen Kameraden' or the lines of the 'Horst Wessel' where we recognize the spiritual fellowship of our fallen comrades. The Führer has thus instilled into youth not only all the inspiration of a visible fellowship on earth, but strengthens it by the constant recognition of the fellowship of the spiritual world.'

It was many hours before that discussion ended. We felt we had made no impression on Dr Weber or Dr Hartmann because their very fear of facing any conflict made them fanatical in their defence of what they knew to be largely false. In the younger, less intellectual Nazis present, we had a very good example of Dr Weber's theory that they really had passed through some personal experience and that, however false the teaching they had accepted, they were quite impervious to intellectual assault. In our hotel that night we talked it over, for we had been particularly interested in what Dr Weber had said about recognizable fellowship. I believe this is an important point because in a world where so many barriers are being broken down, the group becomes too big for the average individual to grasp.

It may have been easy for John Wesley to think of the world as his parish, but for most of us 'the world' is far too vague. We realized as we talked that even in our lifetime many of the more familiar groups to which we had belonged had now largely disappeared. Most of us in childhood were taught to think of ourselves as within a certain class and a religious denomination, and we were all 'either a little liberal or else a little conservative'. Many such barriers are becoming less marked, and possibly we have not realized that, good as may be their passing in some ways, with the knitting together of the world so closely by modern means of transport we find ourselves in a very large and intangible setting. Hitler struck a powerful note when he told his youth that though they were in a wide, rich and diverse fellowship, it was a fellowship they could comprehend, and in which they could play their part individually.

Also it was clear how some of the young had been deceived by the kind of argument that Dr Weber put forward so skilfully; we even wondered how far the youth in Great Britain, growing up without definite religious teaching and fellowship, would be proof against false teaching, given similar circumstances.

What appalled us was that Dr Weber and the young master in whose house we met should be such traitors to themselves. I was almost relieved when I heard later that Karl Weber had already broken down once and that the doctor whom he had consulted – a courageous non-Nazi – had told him he could do nothing for him physically or psychologically until he had the courage to be honest with himself. When Weber left that nursing home and recovered sufficiently to return to work, the Party, with their usual skill sent him off to Japan or somewhere far afield with a group of Nazi students to visit foreign universities and to teach them something of German culture and tradition. It was a clever move because Weber would not need to produce much of the Nazi stuff he disbelieves, and would be able to give a good many perfectly honest and rather brilliant lectures on Germany. And as he was the head of this particular mission, he would not be under further Nazi supervision. That I imagine would stave off a further breakdown for a while, but for how long?

As far as I can see, the most cruel and ruthless elements in the Party are in the first place those who have seen in a movement based on force the chance for the free play of their own more brutal tendencies, and in the second place the intellectual who is a complete traitor to himself. The latter type is, I think, vey likely to become a cruel oppressor of anyone who makes him conscious of his self-betrayal.

When I thought of Dr Weber in former years and remembered he was not ignorant like many Nazi leaders but did really know the meaning of Christianity, both practical and theoretical, I was horrified to see him using his scholarship for something he knew quite well to be false. A friend of his told me he thought the reason was that Karl Weber had always been ambitious and this opportunity of gaining power and prestige in the Party was too great a temptation.

I did not believe his self-deception could last but while it did he was a skilful and powerful tool in the hands of the Party leaders. I believe Hitler himself looked upon him as a marked man. I wonder what his end will be? Probably like Judas, he will go out into the night.

CHAPTER IX

RELIGIOUS FOUNDATIONS
OF NAZI SPEECHES

Last summer I decided to spend some weeks in the Austrian mountains in order that I might study some of the notes I had made on my visits to Germany during the past five years. I found a great many notes of speeches I had heard Hitler or other youth leaders make, and of the discussions I had had with Nazi Youth leaders. It would take too long to give the details of each of these speeches or of all these discussions and the kind of setting in which they each took place, and yet their religious trend is of real importance. I shall, however, give a brief summary of some of the conceptions which seem to underlie all the Nazi teaching to youth.

I shall quote from speeches and discussions, which I think will allow a better understanding of what I mean when I say that I become increasingly convinced that no purely political or economic explanation of the Nazi revolution is adequate. I believe that these facts will reveal some of the secrets of the great dynamic within the revolution.

I do not suggest that we can afford to underestimate the economic and political factors that prepared the way for National Socialism. I think it is true that widespread and acute economic distress and in particular unprecedented unemployment amongst the younger generation, together with considerable political insecurity offered the best possible opportunity to National Socialist teaching. Without such conditions, I imagine men might not so readily have recognized their own moral and spiritual bankruptcy, or have been willing to accept false teaching.

Further, I believe that propaganda must always fail unless it appears to give an answer to some fear or to meet some need of which man is at least dimly aware.

But, given the profound restlessness and insecurity that German youth, and indeed most Germans felt, and given their scepticism about political or economic remedies for their dire necessity which twenty-three political parties had failed to relieve, I am wholly convinced that neither youth nor anyone else would have been even remotely interested if Hitler had declared he had founded a twenty-fourth party to solve their problems. Any explanation of Hitler's rise to supreme power, not only as political head, but as the idol of a whole generation of youth, which is based solely on a complex story of political intrigue, must, I think, remain unconvincing to anyone who knew something of the political apathy and disillusionment in Germany at that time. I do not believe it is possible to understand this revolution nor indeed to combat its evil power and teaching, until it is realized that the Nazi message spoke to men in the sphere of their religious understanding, and gave them a new conception of their value and of their place both in the cosmic order and in the society around them.

Economic necessity laid bare man's desperate physical needs, but the success of totalitarianism reveals clearly his spiritual and moral needs as well. To sneer at the falseness or the intellectual and spiritual inadequacy of the answers that seemed to meet these needs may be legitimate, but in itself it gives no adequate explanation of what happened. Of course, I do not mean to imply that Hitler and his gang sat down and thought out a new religion, for I doubt very much if Nazi teachers were aware of what they were doing. I have been told on good authority that Hitler and the rest were taken very much by surprise at the overwhelming enthusiasm and energy which they let loose in Germany, and were baffled to find an explanation. So much so, that some of the leaders paid a visit to an eminent psychologist outside Germany to ask him to visit their country and to explain to them if possible where all this enthusiasm had come from!

It is equally true that, if the leaders did not know what they were doing, then certainly the younger crowd caught up in it could not possibly give any rational account of why they had been so deeply stirred, nor did they understand how they had been made to feel they could surrender everything and that in so doing they had acquired a great sense of freedom.

The following few points on some of the conceptions introduced into Nazi appeals to youth show how striking they were when looked at all together. The quotations I give are extracts from my notes of speeches by Nazi leaders, or else taken at random from discussions with young Nazis.

Infallibility

'Some of the things other leaders in Germany have said were true, some were false, but I give you now something completely true. I give you also a way of life. This truth must be preserved and we will have no mercy on any who try to interfere with it. The age of uncertainty is over for you. Your future and the future of Germany are now secure.'

Eternal

'Your fathers – even you – have seen government after government fail, and there have been many experiments in Germany. I tell you that in two thousand years National Socialism will still be here. I give you something eternal. No more experiments, no more disappointments. If a man or if a nation is to be creative, it must be against an eternal background. You can now plan your lives.' Again: 'We go with the Führer feeling we have passed from mere existence into inexhaustible life.'

Comprehensive

'Your lives have all been divided up into compartments, your social life, your educational life, your home life, your political life. Sometimes these compartments had no links with one another. National Socialism affects all of them and is greater than them all.

'Your life must no longer be in bits and pieces, it must be one whole and you must subordinate everything to this one aim.

'Our art and our music, our buildings and our teachers must give themselves to the underlying purpose of National Socialism and the resurrection of Germany.

'If your educational life is so organized to one great end, so you will find in National Socialism an internal harmony and a kind of spiritual integration.

'The foreign press likes to cackle about the lack of freedom in Germany. It does that because it is envious of the great new freedom that has come to her because the youth of Germany have now only one aim and one purpose in life.'

Personal

'Germany is far-famed as the most theoretical nation on earth, which only shows how far she had got away from real life. Germany has nearly drowned herself in theories especially since the last war, for, as things got worse and worse, so we had more and more theories. The Führer doesn't offer you any more theories – he offers you a person in whom you can always believe.'

Purpose and Practical Expression

'Germany before Hitler had no use for its youth. What of a country that let its youth rot in the streets? The Führer has made all youths realize that each of them has a great purpose in life. Also it is not big and vague like the international youth movements, which are only a fantasy in the mind. It is something you can recognize and in which you can play your part at once. And you play your part no longer only for yourself. It means sacrifice and hard work. It is no good merely talking about and sighing for a better, happier Germany. You have got to create it. And what is more, you are really important in so far as you contribute to the life of the fellowship and hold the faith.'

Fellowship

'You are no longer alone. Remember that your real life and activity is that of your society and your race. You will gain your strength in this fellowship as you help to build this unity. In Germany's dark days of distress after the war, the darkest thing of all was that the Fatherland had no unity, even though we stood alone and desolate. As Germany rises to her new life, she may stand alone, but she is not afraid because this new unity in the nation is unbreakable.

'Perhaps a few older people in our country still like to be divided. Let them be. Youth has become one because we know how terrible it was when youth opposed youth. Now we belong to a fellowship that we can recognize and in which we each have a part to play.'

Purpose for the Fellowship

'Not only will you all find your individual purpose in this movement and understand for the first time the purpose of creation, but remember also "every movement in history is directly related to God". We judge history by the fulfilment of the destiny of each people.

'We have travelled a long road and now we near the end with the Führer leading us. We need to mobilize the whole spiritual resources of the race that we may attain our destiny. You come from the German race and your destiny is bound up with the destiny of the Third Reich.'

Evil

'You must never underestimate your foes. Be ruthless in defending the faith against those who would destroy it. There are those who seek to destroy all that is best in this life and we must wage ceaseless war against them. You know your enemy. It is the Jew.'

Symbols

'We have our ceremonies and our uniforms. In our ritual, in our songs and stories of the past, we are helped to realize that life is much higher than we see and that we belong to a world much greater than the world we perceive around us. We are gathered into the fellowship of the whole German race and you have as your comrades who march beside you unseen, those who have died for our cause. Whenever you see a man in SS or SA uniform, you can say to yourself: "He has found the way. His uniform testifies to the faith he holds and to the fellowship to which he belongs." That fellowship is not only just you, but all those who have died or will die for the good of Germany.'

PART III

CHAPTER I

NUREMBERG

The stories of this book have dealt mainly with the bitter struggle in the minds and spirits of individual Germans who wished to avoid and break away from Nazi enslavement. I want to end by saying something of the vast and impressive background of organized pageantry against which this struggle was waged, and finally to give a personal impression of the central figure in this tragic drama, even though I am aware that Hitler defies all definitions and will remain one of the great enigmas of his age.

This war has revealed on a European scale the devilish efficiency of the Gestapo, and the whole Nazi movement has given a demonstration of the capacity of the Germans for vast and ruthless organization. It is important to remember that the machinery of organization alone would not have attracted the youth of Germany, for Germany was a network of organizations before Hitler came to power, but it was the Nazis' ability to use their organization to present pageantry on a gigantic scale in which colour and music and symbol all combined that makes the appeal to youth very powerful indeed. Every boys' camp had its elaborate fire ritual; the great assemblies in the Berlin Stadium, often held at night, were directed to create the maximum emotional appeal; every Nazi funeral had its pagan rites and throughout the land in village as well as city, banners, processions and ceremonies kept alive the belief that the individual Nazi was a member of a great fellowship bound by faith and symbol. Then all turned to Munich as to Mecca, for there was their Holy Shrine and Blood Flag and not far away the rocky fastness of Berchtesgaden where their Prophet sought his inspiration.

Finally, there was the Nuremberg Congress, the greatest festival of the Nazi year. The extent to which this festival became the great powerhouse of the Nazi dynamic was often not adequately recognized by those who saw in it only a huge and vulgar demonstration and the occasion of lengthy Nazi tirades. I often think that the diplomats of the Western powers were extremely slow to seize an opportunity for making some valuable discoveries. It is true that the senior diplomats when they attended were carefully guarded and saw and heard mainly what it was designed that they should see and hear. Many of them were very reluctant to go to Nuremberg, and in talking the Congress over with the late Sir Nevile Henderson in 1937, I was amazed at how little he seemed to realize the significance of much that was going on behind the scenes. Even in the discussion of the pageantry of this vulgar Volkfest he underestimated the dynamic influence it was having on youth in all parts not only of Germany but of Europe and even further afield. During this week it was possible to talk to Nazis from all parts of the world and whenever I evaded the particular SS men who were detailed and trained to look after foreign guests, I found there was much to be seen and heard which was both illuminating and alarming. The great enthusiasm which the Congress called forth made the youth and indeed the older men talk easily because the confidence they gained from being part of so great a fellowship led them to boast freely of what Nazism would achieve throughout the world. Once I found myself in an office on the first floor of the Grand Hotel from which all the hospitality was organized. The office was one of the hotel bedrooms with connecting doors leading through to about ten other such office bedrooms. I was kept waiting some time in this office and was interested to note the walls were lined with a great library of file boxes containing information about the foreign guests of Nuremberg. A young woman secretary was quite willing to talk and to explain the excellence and care of the Nazi administration and I discovered that some of these files consisted of lists of ordinary diplomatic guests and contained suitable notes on them for the SS hospitality group to study; other lists were miscellaneous and not important and I was glad to find I belonged to this category; but the largest group were important guests such as foreign Nazis and they seemed to have pages written about their countries and the plans for their training at Nuremberg and on an extended tour in Germany afterwards. I have often reflected since, that these files no doubt contained full information of all the future quislings. But, now, about some of my visits to these Congresses:

Many years ago I had visited Nuremberg and I remember arriving there with a friend on a lovely spring evening. Climbing the hill on which the castle stands, we looked down on one of the most beautiful old towns of Germany. The ancient churches, quaint houses, picturesque bridges, the river and fruit blossom all made it a scene of great charm and peace.

In 1935 I stood on that same hill and it seemed that all hell had been let loose in this lovely German town. The Nazi flags were more like a plague of locusts than anything else I have ever seen, for not one but three or four hung from every window. Old church towers, modern hotels, railway station, telephone kiosks or iron lamp posts on graceful bridges, all flew the swastika. I realized that for the whole week it would be impossible to look anywhere for miles around without seeing that sign of brutal domination. I doubt if so much noise has ever been concentrated in so small a space as during the Congress week in Nuremberg.

The ceaseless drone of heavy aircraft overhead, the rattle of tanks and armoured cars as they crashed down the streets. Black-shirts and Brownshirts, Hitler Jugend and Labour Corps, army and air force making nearly a million men in uniform jostling one another in the narrow streets.

The blasting notes of the loudspeakers erected on nearly every lamp post in the place were continually turned on, while the hoarse shouts of the special SS police drove the bewildered but apparently entirely elated German masses hither and thither with a ruthlessness that a British crowd would not have tolerated for five minutes, let alone five days and nights.

I fled from the main thoroughfare to seek peace in some of the attractive little side streets, but there was no peace or escape for I tried five streets in turn and down every one there came an endless procession of men in one of the many uniforms. Often these men were singing their Nazi songs, not in gay light-hearted tones of students or soldiers in this country, but in harsh staccato fashion, and all the time one was aware of the deadening tones of the 'Baderweiler March' which was being played by bands in the main squares or on the wireless. That is Hitler's favourite march and is certainly more like the noise of the beating of native tomtoms than anything else. I felt dazed by it all and escaped into a tiny Catholic hospice I had known before and sat down in the simple little lounge and ordered a glass of beer. Here surely I should escape the swastika and the noise. Far from it, for to my horror the shrine of Our Lady on the wall in the lounge had now a picture of Hitler placed above it and they shared the same lighted candle. And even as I reflected on this, I noticed the other people in the lounge were standing up – the 'Horst Wessel' was being played on the wireless in the bar next door!

What a week followed. One morning I found myself being hurtled along in a bus at 6 a.m. with other guests in order to take our places on the grandstand in the great Zeppelin parade ground to see the military display – a most real battle and the grand march past of the armed forces of Germany. They started at 7 a.m. and were still marching past at 2.30 p.m. and we had had no rest and not a chance of a drop of water to drink. However, for some of the foreign guests it was worth waiting to the end of that mammoth procession for the sheer fun of seeing the navy contingent do the goose step. One associates this step with Prussian troops in leather leggings, but naval officers in their frock coats doing the goose step were unbelievably comic.

Two things interested me very much about the Germans' reactions to the various contingents. The first was their own inability to take the navy seriously. They stood rigidly to attention for most of the army march past and it seemed they were extremely proud of it and deeply impressed with the show of strength, but the remarks about the navy were illuminating. 'How charming they are. Do look. Did you ever see anything so sweet as the sailors.' Or 'Heavens, they are doing the goose step. How wonderful!' Of course it is difficult to realize that the great majority of the Germans have never seen the sea. Another point interested me about the young SS guides who looked after us. These men were attached to the various foreign delegations and all of them knew the language of the country whose guests they shepherded with great skill, and of course their propaganda was word perfect and took into account the country from which the guests came. I always asked them what they thought was the most important thing about the Congress, and which as their guest I must see at all costs whatever else I missed. I never got other than three answers and these answers told me a great deal about the men who gave them. The really pathological or stupid would say 'The Führer – if you see the Führer nothing else matters – he is Germany.' The aggressive militaristic type, by far the majority of SS men, would say 'The army march past – it is the most important of all and you will see that the Germany the world thought was defeated has now arisen to show she is powerful and undefeated.' The few who still clung on to the earlier ideals of some of the Nazis said, 'Miss everything else, but see the Labour Corps. Many nations have talked of finding ways of using all that is best in army life for the pursuit of peace; Germany is showing the world how this can be done. Never before have men been so trained to consider the land and the peaceful pursuit of farming as an essential part of national life. Germany is always accused of venerating the sword. We have a land army to show you that Nazis hold the plough and spade in just as great honour.'

On other days we found ourselves present at strange mystic rites concerned with the so-called 'Blood Flag'. This was the flag which had been held by a young Nazi struck down in the early days of the Party's struggle for power and it has since become a kind of holy symbol and the centre of Nazi ritual. It was used at all the ceremonies for the consecration of new banners, which were touched by this Blood Flag. There were several ceremonies in commemoration of dead Nazis. At one we had to stand to attention while Lutze read out slowly the names of four hundred dead Nazis. At another a vast concourse of SS and SA filled the Zeppelin parade ground with a wide pathway left between their ranks. Suddenly there was silence – and it proved the only real silence of that week and it seemed interminable because it was fraught with tense emotion. Hitler followed by Himmler and Lutze solemnly and slowly walked the entire length of the arena along this broad path and approached a fire burning in a kind of shrine. They stood there for a moment and walked slowly back.

The Germans are undoubtedly skilled in the art of pageantry, particularly of a semi-military type, and on a huge scale all that week, music, colour, lighting and every known device was used to make the scene impressive and to make the atmosphere tense. I entirely agree with another guest who wrote: 'It was at times a struggle to remain rational in a horde so surcharged with tense emotionalism.' There was only one scene that had any beauty in it and that was because the darkness blurred over the ugly symbols and we were left mainly with an impression of colour and movement which was most effective. By night we had all been taken to the grandstand and we were aware that in the arena a hundred thousand Brownshirts stood in closely packed ranks, while the grandstands which went all the way round this vast arena had giant flagstaffs erected every few yards. Suddenly someone touched an electric button and huge searchlights concealed somewhere behind the grandstands shot great pillars of light up to seven thousand feet and these met at that height, giving the effect of a kind of cathedral of light. At the same moment all the giant Nazi standards were unfurled and by the subdued light of the searchlights we saw little of the swastika and mainly the huge red flags between these pillars of light. Then as music played, way in the distance we saw what in that lighting looked exactly like rivers of red streaming down the pathways between all the grandstands and flowing into the midst of the vast brown ranks in the arena itself. They were of course the banners being carried by Gauleiters walking twenty abreast, but again the lighting only revealed them as a stream of red. Undoubtedly the scene was deeply impressive and one had only to look at the faces of the Hitler Jugend assembled in great numbers on some of the stands to see how they were caught up in the whole affair.

But, of course, most of our time was spent in what must surely be the biggest hall in the world, while Nazi orators – quite certainly the coarsest and ugliest in the world – blasted forth unending speeches and hysterical crowds drank in their poison. I was interested to discover that Goebbels was by far the easiest to listen to and for this very reason perhaps the most dangerous. His voice did not wear us out as the harsh voices of the others did, and the tortuous and sinister workings of his mind had their interest.

Then there was the Labour Day, and I agreed with the better type of young Nazi that this was most impressive. A hundred and sixty thousand men marched past with their spades and having filled the arena there was a service which could only be called 'religious', in which they dedicated themselves and their toil to the Third Reich and above all to its Leader. The form of the dedication was in a litany and the men knew all the responses by heart.

At midnight I found myself wedged in a dense crowd in the centre of the town. We stood there for hours, choking with the fumes, while thousands upon thousands of SA men passed by carrying torches burning sulphur of some kind and all the time the beating of the drums and the throb of engines and tanks and lorries in the distance.

The second time I visited Nuremberg I found myself billeted in a hotel with a number of other British guests. I never learnt the names of most of them, nor do I know who they were, except that a few of them were members of the British Fascist movement. All were intensely enthusiastic about all they saw and I felt at once that I was in the wrong company and that if I stayed I might either give the impression I shared their enthusiasm or I should exhaust myself quarrelling with them in the few hours we were free from attending Congress demonstrations. So I decided after twenty-four hours of this company that I could not remain in the same hotel as this strange mixture of criminal and pathological types and the next morning I called to see the SS reception officers. 'Look here,' I said, 'I am sorry to trouble you, but every nation has its outcasts and cranks and you seem to have got a number of these among the British delegates in my hotel, and I refuse to remain under the same roof. I find your Congress pretty exhausting anyhow, but I cannot spend my nights arguing with British renegades.' A rather cynical but very understanding smile passed over his face. 'I am sorry you are there,' he said, 'we meant you to be in another hotel in Nuremberg, but now they are all full for a few days and the only alternative is that you go into rooms in a simple working-man's home in some of the new flats on the outskirts of the city.' I was very pleased with this suggestion, but tried to conceal what might seem too great eagerness because it was just the kind of opportunity I wanted. So that afternoon SS guards fetched my luggage and motored me to this flat where I was the guest of a delightful working-class family. I found it most interesting to drink coffee with them at night and to discuss the Congress. Their comments were at times extremely shrewd and it was abundantly clear, as indeed it was wherever I did have the chance of talking to labourers, that they had two concerns only, namely would Hitler solve the unemployment problem and would he keep them out of war? Many believed at any rate in the early days that he would do these things and upon this belief hung their undoubted allegiance.

As guests at Nuremberg we had all been given tickets for such speeches and demonstrations and processions as the Nazi officials thought of propaganda value. Staying with this family I found they had different tickets and on inquiry I found out where these could be bought. I went off to one of these agents and without revealing that I was English I bought tickets for some of the things we were not invited to.

These tickets took me among another crowd and away from the foreign guests, and at times I found myself in strange and interesting places. I want to tell of one experience because it seemed to me by far and away the most important thing that happened at Nuremberg and I believe my premonitions that night have been fully justified and that in fact the repercussions may yet be felt for years ahead in the far corners of the earth.

It was dark and I was wandering along a side street when I became aware that lorry after lorry was passing by filled with young boys, most I should judge between the ages of sixteen and twenty. They did not appear to be Germans and then I saw written on the back or side of each lorry the name of a country or state or town from which presumably the boys in the lorry came. Imagine my surprise. Cape Town, Norway, Mexico, India, Australia, Arabia, Holland, New York, Paris, Egypt, San Francisco, West Africa and Chile. The procession seemed as though it would never end and I was so interested that I wandered into a little hotel with windows open overlooking the street. There were two SS men drinking beer at a table in the window, so I joined them and explained I was a guest of the Congress and that I would like to ask them some questions so that I might understand better what was happening. 'Who, for instance, are all these young boys?'

'Oh, they come from all over the world to the Nuremberg Youth Camp. Some of them are Germans who live in these countries, some are half-Germans and some are natives of these countries – young Dutchmen or Americans or Frenchmen or Egyptians who are interested in our movement and are our guests. You see, the Führer is anxious that his youth should make friends with the youth all over the world.'

And still the lorries rattled on. For nearly three hours I watched these boys from the ends of the earth going through to the specially prepared youth camp where they would mix with carefully selected Hitler Jugend – often very attractive and all afire with enthusiasm for the Party and their own part in it. The camp no doubt was run by some of the most sinister and skilful propagandists in the movement. They were subjected to the emotional appeal of this vast pageant of youth and the strange impressive pagan ritual of Nazi camps; they were visited by the Führer and swept into the scenes of hysterical devotion that his visits called forth. After the Congress they were to travel in Germany to youth hostels and camps where, during fireside talks, the poison of Nazi doctrine would be handed out to them in smaller doses and where no doubt they were trained to organize in their own countries. The vast majority of them could hardly help going back to the four corners of the globe with a sense of mission and determination almost unsurpassed in the annals of 'religious' propaganda.

I was profoundly moved by this because it was one thing to see the German youth being poisoned; that was bad enough, and it was one thing to see the ordinary German members of the Congress caught up in hysterical devotion; but here was something more dangerous for the future of the world than anything else, not only in the Congress, but in the whole of the Nazi machinery.

Late that night, I sat by the open window in my workman's flat, for it was sultry, and thought about what I had witnessed, for I knew it was of historic significance and very evil. And yet how was this menace to be met? None of the ordinary diplomatic channels had means for dealing with what was virtually the spread of a false religion. For all that, this thing had political significance, these boys have no doubt played an important part in political development since the war started. Many of them will have acted as agents and welcomed the Nazis as they have trampled down country after country in Europe. How many are there from farther afield still infected with the poison and who will still seek ways and means of fulfilling their evil mission? Surely the Nazis prepared for war with diabolical skill because in the first place they made these youthful disciples in practically all the countries in the world, and in the second place their selection of older guests, many of whom were also being trained as future agents, was psychologically clever. Among these were men who had never succeeded, never held any power in their own countries, and who responded when told that they were important and that they could become leaders.

I asked a middle-aged banker from Holland who was wearing a Nazi badge why he was a Nazi. 'I understand,' I said, 'how many Germans get caught up in this movement for various reasons, but your country has not passed through years of economic chaos and unemployment and your country has never been defeated in war.'

'I am a Nazi,' he said, 'because this Party has made me feel for the first time in my life that there is something big enough to live for and that I have a part to play and also belong to a world fellowship of others with this same purpose.'

There spoke a future quisling and he was present in great numbers at the Congress and being given 'special treatment' just as the boys of sixteen years old from his country were being prepared to back him up.

It is right to blame these older traitors who bought their power at the cost of the lives of their fellow countrymen, but one could hardly blame the youth from distant lands who had had their expenses paid, for being deeply impressed and quite uncritical of much that they saw in Germany.

In the world from which they came there may not have been the desolation that was in Germany, but in their countries too many of the young men were uncertain about jobs and even less sure of any fundamental standards, moral or spiritual. Their right to play any real part in the life of their country was, if not challenged, often ignored, and certainly this demand that they should prepare themselves for an important role must have been difficult to resist. Unaware of the dark sides of Nazi teaching and practice they were justified in being impressed with the health and happiness and apparent freedom of the young Germans among whom they camped.

CHAPTER II

HITLER

As long as history is written, so long will men seek to interpret the phenomenon of Hitler. That ugly ill-shapen Austrian painter with the raucous voice, how came it that he became the leader of the German nation and that he was able to bring war to Europe and destruction to Germany?

I am not going to prophesy what the verdict of history will be, nor am I going to discuss at length the various points of view that have been expressed, as books on Germany pour forth from the press.

As I give my personal impression, it is clear that I am more in sympathy with some of the current views than others, but nothing I have yet read seems to me to offer adequate solution of the enigma and certainly I can only hint at what I believe to be the source of his power and his ability to control a great nation.

In simple terms I would say that Hitler seems to me to be one of the greatest mediums the world has known. This means that I really believe that he had the power of identifying himself with certain elements in almost the entire German nation at the time of the Nazi revolution. So that to speak of Hitler as someone apart from Germany – a strange, evil genius who somehow got control and directed the course of German history is quite false. I do not feel that Hitler has much individual existence apart from this kind of symbolic representation of elements in the German nation at a particular time in its history. Now let me hasten to say that this does not mean that I consider the German nation is evil. That there were mentally pathological elements in Germany is obvious enough, and that under the strain of economic chaos these elements became more marked is also true. But it appears that Hitler gained power by identifying himself not only with the evil and sick types, but with the legitimate needs and yearnings of vast numbers of normal Germans and in particular with young Germans. Once he had gained full power and had built a huge organization to express the revolution, Hitler surrendered more and more to the evil elements and allowed control to pass into the hands of criminals – men who represented nothing but brute force. Hitler himself betrayed all the more legitimate hopes and desires of the nation and gave full rein to the evil and pathological groups he symbolized and by which he was now surrounded.

A number of incidents made me realize this power of identification.

The Nuremberg Party Congress gave excellent opportunity for seeing some of the more extravagant expressions of what Hitler meant to people gathered there.

On a number of occasions I escaped from the grandstand or special seats in the great hall reserved for foreign guests and mingled freely with the ordinary German members of the Congress. At one of the early congresses I was sitting surrounded by thousands of SA men and as Hitler spoke I was most interested at the shouts and more often the muttered exclamations of the men around me, who were mainly workmen or lower middle-class types. 'He speaks for me, he speaks for me.' 'Ach Gott, he knows how I feel.' Many of them seemed lost to the world around them and were probably unaware of what they were saying. One man in particular struck me as he leant forward with his head in his hands, and with a sort of convulsive sob said: 'Gott sei Dank, he understands.' Later that week I got into conversation with a member of the Labour Corps who had marched all the way from Danzig and was only three days at the Congress before starting to march back again. It was a hot day and the Labour Corps had taken three hours to march past the Führer. 'You have come a long way for that march past. Was it worth it?' I asked. 'Worth it?' he said, 'I'd march from the other end of the world to have the chance of that one moment of passing by the Führer.' Later he went on to explain that Hitler alone understood what unemployment meant and that now there would be none.

Back in Berlin I was standing in a huge crowd outside the Chancellery where thousands of people were shouting for Hitler to appear on the balcony. My attention was attracted by the face of a young man who was leading the cries. His arms were outstretched and his face white as he worked himself into a perfect frenzy shouting: '*Führer, Führer, sei doch nicht böse – komm doch, komm, wir sind trostlos ohne dich.*' ('Leader, Leader, be not angry, come, O come to us, we are comfortless without you.') And when the Führer came there was ecstasy in his face such as I have never seen and should never expect to see outside an asylum. As I hurried away to go back to the hotel, I heard uncontrolled sobbing beside me and saw it was a middle-aged woman in a bath chair: 'Now you can take me away, I will die happily – I have seen the face of the Führer – Germany will live.'

Some weeks later I was standing in a crowd in Unter den Linden, for it was expected that the Führer would be passing along. I was talking to a young woman of nineteen who ran a poultry farm, and I said to her: 'What difference, if any, does National Socialism make to you? I expect whatever government is in power, you just carry on with your poultry farm?' She looked at me for a moment and then said: 'Hitler is not a government, he is our leader, and only if you can understand what worship is will you know that now my whole life is different.' It is obvious that most of these people I am describing were pathological, whatever the cause of it may have been. They were like drowning men and women who saw in Hitler a chance of salvation, due I think to the fact that somehow he conveyed to them that he understood their suffering and hardship and that he would save them from themselves because he had made them feel they were not alone. They belonged to Germany and their destiny was bound up with the German race and there was new life ahead for it. But if Hitler had only represented these types and the out-and-out gangsters, he would never have achieved the power that he did. Some of the types whose stories I have recounted, I mean the men and women who, while indifferent or even opposed to a great many things Hitler did and said, nevertheless felt that he represented one particular aspect of their longings and desires, and therefore in a more profound sense than they were aware of, they were bound up with him and lent him their support. First of all we must remember the widespread attitude of defeatism in the nation itself. I doubt if enough importance is attached to the Germans' profound distress at their defeat in 1918. This was always obvious among the middle-aged, but for some years after the war many of the younger generation were not so much affected by this as by the more positive desire to work with the youth of other nations and to help build up a new Germany. As neither of these dreams came true, I saw growing in Germany an increasing exaggeration of a sense of injustice about the Treaty of Versailles and a longing, at first inarticulate, to see Germany rise again and shake off the gloom of defeat and despair. In writing *Mein Kampf*, Hitler showed the first signs of being sensitive to widespread and varied discontents in the life of Germany. Only so can we understand how intelligent men of all classes could say, 'Of course it is impossible as a book and most of his own ideas in it are nonsense, nevertheless there are some important truths in it showing he understands what many in Germany are feeling.' Later, with increasing force and consummate skill, Hitler gave vent to these resentments and yearnings and lashed them into passionate determination so that gentle and cultured old ladies, bright-eyed youngsters of ten, proud German officers and otherwise sober and sensible businessmen together with unemployed and disillusioned students, all began to repeat the slogans and to believe them more and more deeply. They often prefaced their beliefs with some such words as: 'Of course, we dislike a lot of this Nazi business and don't agree with much that Hitler says, but we must not forget that he alone has awakened Germany to the realization that she is a mighty nation and has a part to play and that she must throw off the mood of despair and repudiate the war guilt lie.' These men and women little realized that their partial allegiance was in fact a guarantee that Hitler would get and hold control: they became the supporters of the very movement that would enslave them, and the significant fact is that even when later they found themselves in bitter conflict with much that Hitlerism forced upon them, they nevertheless still repeated their slogans, thus revealing that their bond with Hitler was on an entirely irrational plane.

A number of incidents reflect this partial allegiance, for example, the army officer who was going to devote his life to undoing the false teaching of National Socialism and yet felt 'an eternal sense of gratitude that Hitler had brought the army back to honour and a place in the life of the nation'. Then there was his wife who felt so grateful that the dread of unemployment for her son had gone and that he would now not only be employed, but would have an honourable and gentlemanly calling as an officer in the German army. Or the old conservative who loathed Hitler and his vulgar Nazi movement, but felt that perhaps Germany was meant to learn a lesson of humiliation, and that instead of someone of his class leading Germany back to a proper and important place among the nations, this strange unseemly man of low origin turned out to be God's chosen vessel. 'For,' he added, 'we are persuaded that God has a place for this great nation and the world had denied us that place until Hitler rose and demanded it and in this demand he has the whole German race behind him in deep gratitude.' Or take a very different type of man, a former miner who had been a keen Trades Unionist but who was now a leader in the Labour Corps. I knew he was a devout and practising Catholic, so one day, after some discussions in England, I challenged him: 'Herr Schmidt, what happens when your Catholic conscience comes into conflict with your Nazi conscience about the treatment of the Jews?'

He looked at me swiftly and said: 'There will be no conflict, you don't understand. I hate the treatment of the Jews: I think it is a bad side of the movement and I will have nothing to do with it. I did not join the Party to do that sort of thing. I joined the Party because I thought and still think that Hitler did the greatest Christian work for twenty-five years. I saw seven million men rotting in the streets – often I was there too, and no one, not even the churches, seemed to care that it was a wicked thing that children of God should be thus left to rot. If individuals cared, they could do nothing. Then Hitler came and he took all those men off the streets and gave them health and security and work at least for the time being. Wasn't that a Christian act? Was it an act a Catholic could ignore? So it was because I am a Catholic that I said "I will join this party and I will do all I can to help a movement which refuses to let the young manhood of this nation be wasted." It is true that the movement does other things; some are good, some, I agree, are bad, but we must work that the bad things stop and the good things increase. You cannot achieve that unless you are inside the Party. Do you, if you're a conservative or a socialist in your country, have to agree with all your party does? Surely you are a member because on the whole you think your party helps the most.'

There was much I could have said, but as I tried to argue I realized logic could never touch his point of view. As we walked slowly through a wood, we came out on to the lovely lawns that stretched out in front of one of the most beautiful Elizabethan mansions in England. The sun was setting, and involuntarily we both stopped talking and stood still as we gazed at the beauty of the garden, the peacefulness of a lake in the distance, and the splendour of the house. Then he began again: 'Don't talk to me of conflict,' he said, 'here you live in a different world. But you,' he added almost appealingly, 'you know Germany, you know I tell the truth when I speak of the suffering of the working classes since the war, you saw what the fall of the mark meant. No, I cannot refuse to help because I am a Catholic. Hitler has given new hope and new life to millions of my fellow men who were near despair. That is enough for me. I have no conflict.'

Then we lapsed into silence and did not speak before we

entered the house and each went our way to dress for dinner, but I shall never forget the last few moments of that talk, the way he said 'I have no conflict'. For he knew, and I knew, that was a lie. His conflict was deep and bitter, but he had committed himself to enthusiastic support of Hitler and I knew that no argument I could bring forward could touch him.

Remember Hitler's appeal to the disillusioned and frustrated intellectual – the unemployed student, for many of my stories have made that clear – and a similar cry from the student: 'For God's sake don't raise any conflict for me – I have chosen Hitler – leave me with my choice.'

There were also all the little men – the men who had never held any power and who saw in this movement the chance of authority if they would burn incense at Hitler's altar. The party organization is full of men of that kind who have bought power by their allegiance and hold on to it tenaciously.

Finally, there was the genuine belief of many that the alternative was communism. This was probably true, and an enormous number of people feared it, some for political reasons, but more I think because it was identified with a very deep and traditional fear of Russia. Only those who have lived long in Germany and especially in eastern Germany recognize how deep is this fear of Russia in the heart of the average German: but even when recognized, I have never been able to get at the roots of it.

I hope this shows what I mean by the strength of the support that Hitler got from these different groups who gave their partial allegiance. This for me does dispose of the theory that Hitler is a great leader who planned and produced a revolution in Germany and became its director. And I would suggest that there was a profound crisis in German life, not only in the economic and political spheres but more profoundly in the moral and spiritual life of the people, and that at a moment of great need, Hitler gave voice to a cry that came from the heart of the nation. I do not for a moment suggest that what I have said really explains the fullness of his power, but it does suggest that it came from his ability to touch all sorts and conditions of people at the point of their deepest need.

This throws some light on the fact that non-Germans, and indeed those Germans whose needs he never touched, are completely baffled that he wields any power at all, for neither in person, nor in speech, has he any of the characteristics of a powerful personality and leader.

To illustrate this: I once met two Englishmen in Berlin. They loathed Hitler and all his works and shared this bewilderment that anyone should be moved by such a hideous little man. 'For surely there is nothing remotely attractive in his whole make-up.' Then these men went on to tell me that only once had they questioned this view. They had both been present at the official memorial service for George V, which was held in the little English chapel in Berlin. Sitting on one side of the chancel was Sir Eric Phipps, and on the other side, also alone, Adolf Hitler. 'Now,' said my friend, 'the padre came in and bowed first to Sir Eric Phipps, and there was nothing impressive in that. Then he crossed the chancel and bowed to Hitler. All I can tell you is that Adolf Hitler stood up and bowed and sat down but, believe me or not, that was much the most impressive moment of the whole ceremony. Somehow we forgot Adolf and we felt we were drawn into the presence of Germany, and Germany mourning, and afterwards I learned that we were not alone in having been thus impressed.' This story interested me. Here were two men who were amazed that anyone could ever be moved by Hitler and they were in fact definitely hostile to him, and yet on the first occasion that he identified himself with something they were conscious of, they immediately felt his power. I do not think my friends accepted this theory, but they had none of their own to offer.

A digression, for a moment, to tell of another strange impression I had about Hitler. It is the reverse side of this picture in which I have tried to express some of the reasons for his power when he acts representatively. It is his complete lack, not only of power, but even of life, when he is in repose. I have sat sometimes for two to three hours during the Nuremberg Congress and watched Hitler sitting on the platform while other Nazis were making speeches. I had an almost overwhelming impression that he wasn't there, that it was just a uniform stuffed as a Guy Fawkes might be, and I longed to stick a pin into him to see if he noticed it. Now don't mistake me: it wasn't that he looked like a dead man, because a corpse is something that has had life, but Hitler looked exactly like a dummy. There was no feeling whatever of life about him even when he smiled or looked up at the speaker standing at the rostrum and I felt someone must have pulled a string to make him look up. He often wore a strange, almost shy and slightly surprised look – a typically silly marionette look, and when it suddenly disappeared from his face, it was as though the man with the string had realized he'd left the smile there too long. Sometimes I had the same impression when he stood in his car being driven round the vast arena in the stadium, though more often on these occasions he had a faraway look as though transfixed and quite unaware of anything nearby. But when he was taking the salute or the march past, for instance of the Labour Corps or the Hitler Jugend, he seemed as intensely alive at the end of three hours as at the beginning. On the other hand, as soon as he really got going on his speeches there was tremendous vitality. Even then I felt, perhaps partly because I was prejudiced by my own theory of his personality, that he drew power and inspiration from his audience. There seems considerable evidence for the statement that unless Hitler has his speech written out, his closest associates never knew what he would say, and it seems probable that he himself was uncertain. The beginning of his speeches was invariably dull and it was only as he felt the stimulus of the audience that he gained momentum and finally got lost in the torrent of his own words and visions. I say visions, because it was not only the audience that gave him inspiration, for at times he seemed to be drawing his power from some distant land of fantasy into which his confused spirit had led him. It was as though having identified himself with Germany's distress and above all with his belief that Germany was encircled and persecuted, he then escaped into an entirely unreal world in which he became the great saviour of his people. At such times he talked of 'my Germany' or 'my German youth', and the astonishing thing to me was not so much the abnormality of this man with his illusions, but his ability to carry the audience with him so that with hysterical fervour they acclaimed all he said, however obscure or extravagant he might become. Thus they each reacted on the other, for as his tortured mind dwelt on the thought of himself as saviour, he saw before him vast crowds acclaiming him as such.

It is often discussed whether Hitler's supreme object is deception. Some maintain he has a cold, calculating mind and knows perfectly well where he means to get and has superb technique for deceiving his audience. On the other hand, astute observers such as Madame Tabouis and Dr Jung consider him to be a man without any preconceived plan.

I agree with the latter point of view and would go so far as to say that the single most powerful, and therefore most dangerous thing about Hitler, is his absolute belief in what he says at the moment he says it.

I simply fail to understand anyone who doubts this if they have heard him speak – though not on the wireless. Sincerity is obviously too good a word – it is much more a case of the obsessions of a madman. He seems to me to live entirely in the present and to have no capacity whatever for linking up what he is saying at the time with anything he has said in the recent past, or anything he is likely to say in the near future. He is completely obsessed with what he is unfolding at the moment and as much convinced of its truth as a madman I once met in an asylum who was convinced he was the Prince of Wales, but I gathered might easily decide he was someone else next week.

The big difference, of course, lies in the fact that none of us believed the madman, whereas millions of Germans and many outside were prepared to accept the most bewildering contradictions and seemed to have been infected with the Führer's own power of forgetting the past.

I remember one day at a house party in England, a group of us who had been to Germany together were discussing these glaring inconsistencies. One member of the party was a well-known psychologist and he listened to us for some time and then said very quietly: 'You wouldn't expect a crowd to be consistent, would you?' and then went on puffing his pipe and said no more till we gathered round him and said: 'Now don't stop there for goodness' sake, tell us precisely, or as nearly as you can, what you mean by that.' What followed was most interesting. I can only remember a few points, which further illustrate the things that I have been saying about my own personal impressions of Hitler, though I don't think the psychologist would necessarily agree with my conclusions or at any rate the terms in which I express them. He said it was wrong to think of Hitler as a reasonable or honourable person, because the standards of a group and of an individual vary considerably. Hitler expresses the thought of the group and must be judged as you would judge a crowd.

This should be applied to his promises also, and remember that a crowd is notoriously fickle and unreliable. He went on to explain that collective action is always different from individual action and in being potentially far below or far above the moral capacity of the individual. A crowd whether German or otherwise will stoop to doing things that it would seem impossible to believe most of the individuals in the crowd would ever do but it may also achieve greater things than any one of the individuals who make it up could achieve.

Hitler was somehow aware of both these points and was dimly conscious of what was in the minds of the crowd. 'This means,' said the psychologist, 'Hitler is really of no interest as a personal power. He is a power not because of his individuality, but because of his capacity to become the mouthpiece of the nation. This gives him terrific influence. He is not an ordinary person, but he is like the mystic or prophet, he can inspire because he is aware of thoughts which when he voices them are acclaimed and recognized by many as their own.'

This conversation linked up in my mind with what Jung had said of the comparison between Hitler and Mussolini. 'These are two types of strong men in primitive society; one is the chief who is physically powerful and is surrounded by stronger men than his competitors; the other is the medicine man who is not strong in himself but is strong by reason of the power which the people project into him. Mussolini is the former and Hitler the latter.'

This exactly corresponds with the impression I had in comparing Mussolini and Hitler moving among their people. Mussolini struts about with chin thrust out and you feel his chief quality is an aggressive assertion of superiority to all around him. He is the dictator, they the slaves. Nothing of the kind is true of Hitler. In the early days when I frequently saw him mingle with the crowd, the thing that struck me most was that as soon as he got near a group he lost identity and there was no trace whatever of arrogance or separation from those who followed him. Although I have laid stress on the mediumistic qualities of Hitler, it would be a false simplification and quite untrue to the facts to interpret this as meaning he was only a sounding board or mouthpiece for the crowd. It is obvious that Hitler is a man capable of sudden decisions of great moment, though these decisions were always based more on intuition than argument.

He seemed to have two main sources of inspiration. The first, this ability to give expression to deep distress and longing for a way out which in so many forms was characteristic of the German nation, and in the second place he drew on the fantasy and illusions of his own mind, which gave him a sense that he spoke not only in the name of the German people, but also with Divine authority in answer to the mission he felt himself called to fulfil. At one moment communing with the spirits that guided him at Berchtesgaden and the next among the crowds who confirmed him in his self-delusions, he felt he had no need to justify himself to God or man.

Fed from these sources, he would at times emerge into the world of practical affairs and intervene with considerable skill. I often think that the suddenness of his decisions was due to two things. In the first place his own recognition that he must leave the land of visions and take action which would confirm his own belief in himself, and in the second that his ability to live in an unreal world made him simplify any situation, however complex it might be. His mind fixed on his objective as on an obsession. He simply did not recognize the need for any preliminary step, for he saw no obstacle nor indeed did he visualize any consequences – thus unconcerned by circumstances or consequences, he always moved ahead of friend or foe. It is obvious enough that he often succeeded by this method, as in moving into the Rhineland. He was able to point out to his military advisers that all their fears and difficulties were unfounded. It was of course disastrous that this dangerous man should have at his beck and call a growing and powerful army on the one side, and on the other as highly organized a collection of thugs as the world has never known, always ready to give immediate and brutal interpretation to his intuitions.

It was obvious enough even to the more moderate Nazis, that if the Führer persisted in being so obsessed with his objectives and continued to ignore circumstance and consequence, there must be war in the end to stop him in his mad pursuit. But warning voices were unheeded and as time went on Hitler was more and more surrounded by gangsters who were eager to carry out his decisions with ruthless power and efficiency.

This was well illustrated by the story of Hitler in his Chancellery fondling a map of Austria and crying again and again 'Austria is mine. Oh! Is it true Austria is mine?' while his cynical lieutenants laughed and drank beer and his brutal agents were making the fair land of Austria a nightmare of blood and murder.

I am well aware that whatever is said of Hitler, there remains much that is illusive and all these suggestions fall short of a really adequate explanation of the man himself, but in closing, I should like to repeat that I believe history will declare Hitler himself to have been important mainly as reflecting or symbolizing a crisis in Germany and that the historian with insight will see this crisis to have been moral and spiritual as well as economic and political. Perhaps it would be better to say that the economic and political confusion and chaos was the setting in which a much deeper moral and spiritual crisis caused a revolution and that in this revolution the significance of Hitler lay in the fact that millions turned to him as to a saviour. As the revolution crystallized in its own worst elements, so Hitler became more and more the tool of the forces around him and as every shred of good influence went from these, he became the instrument of profoundly evil forces which he had called into being and could no longer control.

Death will come to Hitler, but the exact nature of the crisis in Germany, and above all the relation of that crisis to the rest of Europe and to the end of humanism, are problems of supreme importance not only to the historian, but immediately to all who would plan for the future in Europe. I believe that in the study of these things Hitler will ultimately find his place; and it will be mainly as a symbol.

SUMMER 1942 – A UNIVERSITY HALL FOR WOMAN STUDENTS

It was a lovely summer evening in June 1942. The students who were going down from the university had arranged a farewell dinner and coffee party and as the weather was warm we carried the coffee into the garden. While they settled down into deck chairs or on to cushions and handed round cigarettes, I looked at the group and realized that this particular generation of women students was in many ways outstanding. So much had happened during their time at the university and they had not only responded well to all the new and vivid experiences they had undergone, but owing to one or two natural leaders among them they had shown unusual powers of reflecting on the things they and their generation had experienced.

If they had missed the carefree and irresponsible days through which most students pass, they had gained greatly by seeing their training against the background of immediate responsibility as citizens in a front line area. Even their personal relationships had taken on a different character – light-hearted flirtations were fun in peacetime, but you had to know much more clearly where you stood if your friend was a fighter pilot, or had been missing from Dunkirk for three weeks, or might be leaving for the Middle East next week.

Generalizations about any generation are unconvincing, but I would be prepared to say that the attitude of mind in the university in the years 1937–9 was less happy and more unsatisfactory than at any time for the past twenty years and of course this atmosphere reflected the tension and uncertainty of the world at large. For students who entered the university during these years learnt from their seniors that however well they might do, there was no certainty that they would find posts when they went down. This was disheartening, for however much a student is absorbed by college life, her thoughts turn constantly to the future for which she is training. This is particularly true of those who come from simple homes – perhaps the first in a family to get to a university and therefore someone in whom high hopes are centred. But what if there were no future? For some unemployment would be a disaster, for their parents were poor and they themselves had borrowed money in order to train. But more fundamentally this insecurity caused resentment, that society should be so ordered, or rather disordered, that trained people eager to serve were not wanted. For the first time in my experience I recognized a growing restlessness which was by no means due only to economic uncertainty, but rather sprang from an unexpressed but profound demand that life should not be thwarted – a demand which in the case of many German students had ended in a passionate outburst against spiritual and intellectual frustration as well as material insecurity.

Then the war came to a generation of students who, in the words of one of them, 'had been taught to believe in the League of Nations since they were in their cradles'. Their fathers, many of whom had fought in the last war, had constantly told their children that 'war achieved nothing'. Now they found that life for them was to be moral combat with the youth of other countries.

It was no wonder that during the first six months of the war there was a certain unreality about the attitude of many of these students. Those to whom the call to active service seemed imperative had already gone to fight, but among the others some seemed to feel that 'being reserved' meant that they could assume that they had little part to play in the conflict. Had they not been reserved to prepare for posts in a post-war world? Certainly it was that world which interested them and there was something exaggerated about their absorption in post-war plans and problems.

Then Dunkirk and the collapse of France and their fantasy was shattered.

There would be no post-war world unless they helped to win the war, and from that time on, the more thoughtful of them only remained at the university with a sense of tension. 'If the government wants us to continue to train as doctors, teachers, etc., then we must stick to it, but we are not entirely happy that by chance we are called to serve in a way that costs us so little compared with our contemporaries.'

Then heavy and continuous air raids began and with great courage and efficiency they turned to play their part. The relief was immediate, for now they could continue to train while at the same time holding responsibility in a front line. The first University Women's Training Corps was formed, and four hundred women under student leadership gave up their spare time to train in many ways so that they might render service to the city in which their university stood. The story of their service is worthy to rank with the best in the long account of gallantry and enterprise on the home front.

No wonder as I looked at the group of students on that summer evening, I recognized how much they had gained in the momentous months they had spent at the university.

For a time we spoke of the past few years, but soon the discussion turned to the future and they talked not only of the jobs they were going to, but of the world in which they would live and in particular the post-war world.

Shall we be able to keep in touch with Russian students, or will Russia isolate herself again; what about the re-education of the German youth; how can France regain her unity and what opportunities will there be for the youth of this country to go abroad and help in countries made desolate by war?

Then one of them said, 'I know all that is important and I would like to be able to help in Europe, but what about the youth in this country, what does the future hold for them?'

For some time we talked of the plans for educational reform

and for the use of leisure and our discussion ranged over subjects as varied as school-leaving age, nursery schools, public versus
secondary schools, etc. Then a student who had remained silent
broke into the discussion by saying, 'We have been talking most
of the time of details and organization and machinery. Supposing
all these grand schemes do come off, will they in fact meet the
needs of youth?'

'Tell us what you mean,' we said.

'I was thinking,' she said turning to me, 'of some of the stories
we've heard of German youth before the Nazis came to power.
Didn't you say that however well the Nazis had organized they
would never have called forth that dynamic energy and passionate devotion of youth unless they had somehow given answers,
however false, to the more fundamental spiritual needs of youth.
Are our needs the same and are these plans concerned with
meeting these needs? If not, I cannot see that there is much point
in better education if it is only going to make us more aware of
needs that cannot be fulfilled.'

At this point the whole group came to life in a new way and
during the next hour practically every student took some part in
the discussion. On some points there was clear agreement.

It was essential that as a generation left school or university, it
should know it was wanted. 'If in wartime the Ministry of Labour
is on our tracks six months before we leave the university, surely
in peacetime we shall not be faced with long unemployment,' said
a science student.

Secondly, we agreed that youth must find not only that there is
a job – which means the chance of survival – but that they have
some part to play in fulfilling a purpose, which means that they
can look into the future with confidence. 'I should imagine,' said
the same student, 'that these two things are a minimum if we are
to believe that there is any meaning in the world in which we live
and in one sense I agree with the German students who said that
these things should fulfil spiritual as well as material needs.

'If on the other hand we discover that, through the working of forces over which we have no control, our lives become not only insecure but of no significance to the organization of society, and the building of a post-war community, then we are bound to be indifferent and even hostile to any suggestion that there is a wider purpose in which we as individuals play a part. Under circumstances of that kind especially after all the talk there has been of youth leadership and education, don't you think we might easily fall into the kind of desolation the German youth experienced, and possibly be willing to be led by any prophet who made graven images for us of political or economic systems to which we could attach ourselves with the same kind of religious enthusiasm?'

'To answer that question properly,' I said, 'I shall have to go into the reasons why I think that in planning for the future of youth in this country, a study of the form and philosophy of the Nazi Youth movement is relevant, and it will take me some time to do that.'

'Please do,' replied the senior student, 'because it is a subject which interests us very much and after all the stories you have told us of the Nazi Youth we should be grateful if you would relate it to some of the problems we are facing in this country.' So cigarettes were passed round again and the group settled down to listen.

'In the first place to answer the question whether there is any danger that, given a period of crisis, something like a British version of the Nazi Party might rise here. I think that is most unlikely. In fact it is precisely because the outward form of the Nazi revolution with its rigid collectivism, its semi-military pageantry and above all its fanatical belief in force, expressing itself in organized brutality, is so alien to us that I think we may be deceived into thinking there is no danger. By this I mean that, recognizing that these things would not call forth the fanatical allegiance of youth in this country, we may fail to realize the significance of the spiritual bankruptcy and real destitution underlying it all, for that is something which is evident in the whole of Western civilization, though in more insidious forms and subtle dress. The real tragedy of the Nazi betrayal not only of Germany, but of Europe, is that it claimed to have given a radical answer to some of the most fundamental problems of our age. It is of the utmost importance that we should understand the problems they were trying to solve and then analyze closely the fallacious and heretical character of their answers. They proclaimed a life-giving principle for their race and nation which by its very nature should have been recognized immediately both inside and outside Germany as having no universal validity, and as bound to lead to the destruction and death of other nations, as well as the German nation itself in the end.

'It is commonly recognized that Hitler gained support because he assured the youth of his country not only that there would be jobs for them but that they had an important part to play in the great struggle for the resurrection of the nation from defeat and despair.

'It is less often recognized that in addition to these two things he made them feel they belonged to something much greater than the organization they were in and that their destiny was linked with a kind of mystical destiny of the Fatherland. Now it is this last point which is so important and which constitutes what I have called the essentially "religious" side of the Nazi movement. I have tried to show in these stories of Nazi Youth that it was based not only on their faith, but on an experience within the fellowship and ceremony of the Party. This made them feel they were given new life and energy because they were caught up in some life-giving principle that transcended as well as transformed their immediate tasks and gave their own little existence a cosmic significance and eternal destiny. The Hitler Jugend themselves never talked or even thought in these terms, but it is well that we should recognize the source of their immense sense of freedom and power. The fact that their experience was based on an entirely false doctrine – a doctrine of death and destruction rather than of life and freedom, was soon obvious to those who observed the nature of that doctrine, but let us remember that the German Youth by the million have gone to their death quite unaware of their own betrayal.

'As I see it, this raises a fundamental question for those who are concerned with the education and service of youth in this country. How far will the organizations and indeed ideals they set up be instinct with life and significance because they are the expression of a faith in some Absolute with all the attraction and dramatic quality that is inherent in such a faith? We should all agree that this faith may issue in very different expressions in society whether in political or social construction, and that all such organizations, if they are to have a dynamic character, will only be a partial and temporary expression of a faith which is eternal and absolute. Further, this fellowship whether of youth or of society enriched by the integration of youth will gain its final significance because it is part of a wider fellowship that extends beyond the bounds of this life. It is membership of this that gives a sense of release from living entirely within the narrow confines of individual life and calls forth dynamic and creative energy. It is of course important to remember that the quality and even the validity of this experience born of faith and worship will be judged by the nature of its interpretation and expression.'

'But just a moment,' said a student, 'surely then what you say does make the question of a national youth movement impossible? You could never find agreement about the faith and religion which should inspire it because many people who are deeply concerned about the service of youth and education do not accept the Christian religion.'

'I am glad you have raised that question,' I said, 'because it does raise a very important point. It is for this as well as for other reasons that I am opposed to the creation of a national youth movement, which being national could scarcely have adequate aims. I would go as far as to say that there is real danger in seeking to make youth self-conscious as a group and fully aware of its needs, especially its more fundamental needs, unless you know how you are going to meet these. It would seem to me much sounder that there should be state backing and support for a variety of youth movements with their own specific aims and organizations.'

A sigh of relief came from the group and a very intelligent

medical student gave expression to this by saying, 'How thankful I am to hear you say that, because not only do I dislike the idea of a national youth movement, but I know I speak for many others when I say we are tired of some of the talk of the service of youth. In the end the British reaction to this form of collectivism might well be a revolt of youth. Surely it is wrong to talk of youth as though you could give the term precise definition as describing a separate group within the community that should be encouraged to give its contribution to society through specially provided and often artificial channels. What we want is that within the whole organization of society, whether in church or state or profession, youth should be given a chance to shoulder responsibility and thus become part of the very structure of society and not an adjunct.'

It was obvious that the entire group of students was in emphatic agreement with this point of view and one of them added, 'There surely is a danger that all sorts of committees will go on discussing youth as though it were a new phenomenon, when really what we are asking is the same steady incorporation into the service of the state in peacetime that we have been given in the whole structure of the war effort.'

'Yes,' replied the senior student, 'it is not that we don't think there is room and great value in various youth organizations, especially for the adolescent, as long as they do not become a substitute for seeing to it that youth is represented within the councils of the nation as they are now within the Forces. I don't only mean the House of Commons,' she added amid laughter, 'but on the TUC and the Church Assembly.'

'I entirely agree,' I replied, 'but mind you, it will also be your responsibility to avoid two dangers. In the first place to refuse to invest any political, economic, or social organization of society with a pseudo-religious significance in which you put your whole faith. On the other hand to avoid having a religion or faith which fails to make an attempt, or if need be many attempts, to order society, whether nationally or internationally, on a pattern that is a true, if only a partial, expression of the faith and fellowship you profess to accept. I am convinced that in seeking to avoid these dangers you will do well to continue to study both the character and forms of the Nazi revolution.

'The external manifestation of the false faith of the Nazis has been a world war, and we shall not understand why unless we also understand the deeper phenomenon of National Socialism. Only if we consider the complex material and spiritual necessities in the interior life of Germany shall we see what is involved in the task of the re-education of German Youth and in seeing this we may learn a great deal about these very necessities in the life of the Western civilization of which we are a part.

'To a generation without faith, the Nazis gave a brutal philosophy and millions of lives have been sacrificed to free the world of this false answer to a real need, but let us not fail to understand that it was caused by real need. We are now faced with the greater task of bringing healing to the nations, including our own, I am convinced this cannot be done without a faith in God adequate to the tremendous task of reconstruction.'

The discussion drew to a close and as it did so a squadron of Spitfires swept across the evening sky with their wings lit up by the setting sun. We were silent for a moment, then as the party broke up a student added, 'Well at a time when everything seemed lost, youth was given the chance to save the country – and a few of them did. The odds may be as great for reconstruction after the war, but I hope we are given as good a chance as those pilots in 1940 were given.'

AFTERWORD

On 5 August 1947, the following notice appeared in *The Times*:

> The King has granted Cumberland Lodge, Windsor Great Park, as a residence for St Katharine's Foundation. This grant has been accepted with deep gratitude on behalf of the Council of St Katharine's Foundation by the Earl of Halifax (Chairman), Dr Tissington Tatlow (Deputy Chairman) and Miss Amy Buller.
>
> The Council recognises that an ideal home has been provided for their experiment and they are greatly encouraged by this indication of the interest and understanding of the King and Queen in the work which the Council wishes to undertake.

If the foundation was born in 1947, it was conceived in the mind of Amy Buller many years earlier. The idea of a place to promote discussion and critical thinking among young people developed from her experiences of conferences held at Swanwick in Derbyshire, when she worked for the Student Christian Movement, and from conversations with close friends over her concerns about the formation of young people's minds in Germany. These friends, as Kurt Barling explained in his foreword, included William Temple. Indeed, had Temple not died in post as Archbishop of Canterbury in 1944 it is likely that his name would have appeared in that list in *The Times*. Both Buller and Temple shared a concern that what happened in Germany could happen elsewhere, and that providing a safe space for young people to discuss difficult issues was vital as a preventative measure.

What made the difference in turning an idea into reality was the involvement of King George VI and Queen Elizabeth. As also mentioned in the foreword, Amy Buller's connection with the Royal Family came about when the Bishop of Lichfield, Edward Woods, recommended *Darkness over Germany* to the King and Queen. As a result, Amy Buller was invited to Buckingham Palace in March 1944 to meet Queen Elizabeth and discuss her thoughts and ideas. Amy Buller later described this meeting as 'my miracle' because it led, three years later, to King George VI's generous gift of the use of Cumberland Lodge for the St Catharine's Foundation, as it was originally known.*

According to Elizabeth Elphinstone, a niece of Queen Elizabeth who was involved in setting up the foundation, the King had the idea of offering Amy Buller the use of Cumberland Lodge in the summer of 1947 following the death of its resident, Lord FitzAlan. She described how, looking out of a window in Royal Lodge in Windsor Great Park towards nearby Cumberland Lodge, the King said: 'Now I think that's the house you ought to have for your experiment. It's not the sort of house anyone is likely to want to live in as a private house anymore. I think it might suit very well.'†

The King's intuition was accurate. The combination of an elegant, historic country house and beautiful parkland has proved ideal for the sort of residential meetings and discussions that Amy Buller believed fostered civilized society. Had the foundation been located elsewhere – as was quite possible when a venue was being sought – then it is hard to imagine that it would be anything like the institution it is today, if indeed it survived at all.

By finding a home at Cumberland Lodge, Amy Buller also found an exceptionally supportive neighbour in Queen Elizabeth

---

*The name was initially going to be St Katharine's Foundation, as in the notice in *The Times*, but was changed to St Catharine's Foundation so as not to confuse it with another organisation with royal patronage, the Royal Foundation of St Katharine.
†Helen Hudson, *Cumberland Lodge: A House Through History*, (Chichester: Phillimore, 1989), p.149.

(later Queen Elizabeth The Queen Mother). Living less than a mile away in Royal Lodge, Queen Elizabeth became closely involved in St Catharine's as its Patron from 1947 until her death in 2002. She was succeeded in this role by her daughter, Queen Elizabeth II. Her other daughter, Princess Margaret, also played a part, serving as the foundation's Visitor (or overseer) from 1984 also until her death in 2002. This royal connection has had a profound influence in shaping the institution, and continues to give it a distinctive ethos: a place for cutting-edge thinking and discussion, combined with a sense of public service, stability and continuity.

The theologian Ulrich Simon, who was a Professor at King's College London, provides an insight into early royal involvement with the foundation when he describes how, as a curate, he was sitting on a bench in Windsor Great Park:

> My meditations were interrupted: a man, tall and serious, accompanied by a lady, short and vivacious. This was the Queen of England, accompanied by Sir Stafford Cripps. They stopped by my bench and asked after my affairs. My clerical dress gave me credibility, and I ventured to ask them about their business. It turned out to be a scheme that later produced Cumberland Lodge, as a meeting place for all sorts of matters affecting public life, moral issues, and cultural progress.[*]

With Amy Buller as Warden, Queen Elizabeth as Patron, Sir Walter Moberly (former Vice-Chancellor of Manchester University) as Principal, and a powerful Council chaired by the former Foreign Secretary, Lord Halifax, the new foundation was exceptionally well connected. From its earliest days the foundation has been able to involve leading public and intellectual figures in its work. Sir Stafford Cripps was most probably Chancellor of the Exchequer when Ulrich Simon encountered him with the Queen,

---

[*]Ibid., p. 148.

and among those who came to the Lodge in the 1950s to interact with visiting students were the towering figures of philosopher Karl Popper, theologian Paul Tillich, poet T.S. Eliot, and painter Stanley Spencer.

Not surprisingly, given Amy Buller and her colleagues' connections (there was strong Church of England representation on the Council), some of the first student groups to visit in the late 1940s were from Christian organisations: the World Student Christian Federation and Student Christian Movement. Then, during the 1950s as the foundation's work expanded, its focus shifted towards university departments, and predominantly those from the constituent colleges of the University of London. Some of the earliest university groups to visit the Lodge came from Imperial College, University College London, the Institute of Education, Birkbeck College, King's College London, Bedford College, and the London School of Economics. Some of these groups, such as the Maxwell Society from King's College London, have been coming regularly ever since. Students groups of this kind continue to visit most weekends throughout the year. What they do varies according to their area of study, but to ensure their programme is in keeping with the Lodge's founding vision and ethos they are invited to include a 'St Catharine's Session' in which they are asked to discuss a topical ethical or societal issue.

While it has a particularly close association with the University of London (and the Berkshire edition of Pevsner's *The Buildings of England* incorrectly describes it as part of the university), Cumberland Lodge has always drawn students from further afield. In 1950, for example, visiting groups came from University College Southampton and Nottingham University. Today, departments from about twenty-six universities visit the Lodge on a regular basis.

As well as working with individual university departments, the foundation has always drawn people together from different institutions. Some of the first students to visit the Lodge were from a range of universities who came for private study and discussion groups on topics such as 'The Nature of Man' and 'Philosophy and History'. Among those attending the latter, in 1950, was a young Oxford philosophy don, Iris Murdoch – one of many prominent people who came to the Lodge as a young adult. Other famous alumni from this period include the philosopher Alastair McIntyre, the physicist Peter Higgs (who came to discuss the ethical responsibilities of the scientist with a group including Charles Darwin's grandson) and, slightly later, the biologist Richard Dawkins who took part in a student reading party on logic and mysticism.

The writer and academic David Lodge visited the Lodge on several occasions in the 1950s when studying English at University College London. In his autobiography, *Quite a Good Time to be Born*, he gives a flavour of what a student visit was like in the foundation's early days:

> Twice a year a group of up to thirty students from different years in the English Department and perhaps half a dozen staff would go down to Windsor by coach for a weekend of reading and discussions around a theme. We paid a subsidised rate for the privilege – and a privilege it was to chat and eat with our teachers in such surroundings. The food I remember was fairly dire, but the table settings were elegant and the furnishings and décor quite luxurious, with deep upholstered armchairs and sofas in the vast drawing room. The grounds and the park itself invited conversational strolls in good weather.*

In many respects – apart from the quality of the food – this is similar to the student experience at Cumberland Lodge today.

Over time, a wider range of groups became associated with the Lodge. The involvement of Lord Denning, first as Chair of Trustees from 1961 to 1969 and then as Visitor from 1969 to

---

*David Lodge, *Quite a Good Time to be Born: A Memoir 1935–1975*, (London: Harvill Secker, 2015), pp. 159–160.

1984, perhaps accounts for the close relationship that has developed with the Inns of Court which, since the 1960s, have brought law students training to be barristers to Cumberland Lodge for study retreats. On one occasion, when students were role-playing a court case, *Regina v Goldilocks*, Regina herself was present to witness proceedings.

A similarly close association has developed with the medical profession, and in most months groups of trainee GPs come to the Lodge as part of their continuing professional development. No doubt the expansion into professional training was partly driven to bring in new sources of income, but it was – and is – seen as part of the Lodge's ethos of working with young adults who will go on to have public roles.

◇ ◇ ◇

It is hard to say what Amy Buller, who died in 1974, would make of Cumberland Lodge today. Among the changes she would notice is the foundation's name. It is no longer known as St Catharine's (or its later name, the King George VI and Queen Elizabeth Foundation of St Catharine) but simply as Cumberland Lodge – an indication of the importance the buildings and location plays in the life of the institution.

The facilities have certainly improved since the days when Amy Buller was Warden. This is due largely to a change in the foundation's business model following serious financial difficulties in the 1970s. Spearheaded by the economist Lord Vaizey, a trustee who became Principal to lead the process (but who sadly died in post), the Lodge was upgraded into a high-class conference centre to attract outside users and generate a new source of income. This put the Lodge on a sound financial footing with the conference trade subsidising its charitable work with students, who now enjoy luxurious accommodation and excellent food and service.

What has also changed significantly since Amy Buller's time is the volume and the balance between the foundation's three main areas of activity: student study retreats, its own conferences, and its hospitality to visiting organisations. Cumberland Lodge has never worked exclusively with students. As thoughtful people came together to address post-war issues, some of the earliest groups the Lodge welcomed in the late 1940s were from the World Council of Churches, the BBC, the Colonial Service, the Christian Frontier Council, UNESCO and the British Council. However, the need to generate a conference trade to ensure the foundation's survival has led to a considerable expansion of organisations using the Lodge as a conference venue. Nowadays around a hundred organisations come to the Lodge each year bringing about 12,000 people, of whom 3,000 are students. This is very different to the situation until the 1970s when those visiting were predominantly students, who were coming in much smaller numbers.

A noticeable feature of the Lodge's conference trade is its stability. Over 80 per cent of the organisations that come to the Lodge do so on a regular basis. The frequent return of groups from academia, public and charity sectors, and business have enabled close relationships to develop with organisations and individuals. This has fed into the foundation's educational work, as many involved as trustees or in other capacities first made contact with the Lodge as a conference delegate or speaker. Amy Buller's remarkable skill as a networker appears to have permeated the institution.

From its early years, the foundation has also organised its own conferences. What is different from Amy Buller's day, however, is that this activity has become the flagship of the foundation's educational work, tackling important ethical and societal issues, and providing opportunities for students and others to interact with leading academics and senior public figures. The expansion of this area of work took place during the 1980s when Tim Slack was Principal. Emphasis was placed on bringing together people from different disciplines and sectors, and the Lodge rapidly gained a strong reputation for this work. This includes an annual police conference, which continues to bring together senior police leaders and emerging leaders, criminologists, lawyers, parliamentarians and others to focus on issues relating to policing and society. The Lodge's links with the medical profession have also led to regular conferences on public health issues, most recently with the involvement of the Chief Medical Officer for England.

In recent years the foundation has sought to engage with students in new ways, particularly postgraduate students – reflecting the significant growth in the number of people studying at the master's and doctoral level. Recent developments include an annual conference for doctoral students to help them prepare for life 'beyond the PhD', and the Cumberland Colloquia scheme to help early career researchers gain experience in running conferences by working alongside Cumberland Lodge staff. The Amy Buller PhD Scholarship enables an outstanding young scholar to study for a doctorate at Royal Holloway, University of London in an area relevant to the Lodge's interests and to help run student study retreats and take part in the Lodge's own conference programme. And the Cumberland Lodge Scholarship scheme enables twelve doctoral students to be involved in the Lodge's activities for two years. For the first time, the foundation is working with students for an extended period to provide a more in-depth and immersive experience and, hopefully, to build a network of lasting relationships built on the Lodge's ethos.

In these various ways, Cumberland Lodge has developed into a unique educational institution that is fully independent, yet with strong and enduring links with universities across the UK. Many of these relationships were forged initially by Amy Buller and her colleagues. Promoting critical thinking and discussion among young people remains at the heart of its work, as does involving them with leading academics and public figures. In these respects, Amy Buller would certainly recognise Cumberland Lodge today.

What she would also notice is the most recent development, which is to refocus the foundation's work on its founding vision. As Kurt Barling has already discussed, recent events and social trends have led commentators to draw parallels with what happened in Europe in the 1930s. How close these parallels are is a moot point, but nevertheless Amy Buller's analysis of how a society – and particularly its young people – can be influenced in troubled times, is highly relevant, and why Cumberland Lodge is revisiting its founder's vision. As the current Chair of Trustees, Sir Stephen Wall, has stated:

> Our obligation as a charity is to be true to our founding objectives. Amy Buller saw how, in pre-war Germany, a divisive and immoral ideology had somehow captured the hearts and minds of Germans, including young and idealistic Germans. Cumberland Lodge was set up to help ensure that it did not happen again. Today, we are undergoing huge changes in society and some of the pressures young people face are insidious. So the staff and trustees have thought hard about how we can make what we do more relevant to today's challenges, so that we can provide a safe and calm space where difficult issues can be discussed by young people and by older people with leadership roles in society – and how we can bring young and not so young together to try to find answers to some of these challenges that we face.

◇ ◇ ◇

Amy Buller still keeps a watchful eye over Cumberland Lodge from the vantage points of her two portraits in the main dining room. In the original portrait she looks severe, so a second portrait was commissioned in which her stern look is replaced by the hint of a smile. However, by all accounts the first portrait is the more accurate representation of this extraordinary woman who achieved so much through sheer force of personality and will.

Amy Buller's legacy is twofold. Her book *Darkness over Germany*, as well as being of historical interest, has found a new voice over seventy years after it was first published. Her insights into how, under certain circumstances, good people – not least idealistic young people – can be drawn into collective moral failure are timeless and transcend their original context. They are warnings from history that need to be heeded. Her other legacy is Cumberland Lodge. And just as her book and the institution were bound closely together seventy years ago so too have they become intertwined again today. This new edition of *Darkness over Germany* is a testament to this. More importantly, though, it provides a new generation with the starting point for the sort of conversations, dialogue, and critical thinking that Amy Buller championed throughout her life. If it achieves this, then it could serve no better purpose in our troubled times now, and be no better tribute to its remarkable author.

Edmund Newell
Cumberland Lodge, 2017

NOTES TO FOREWORD

1   I went to discuss my book on modern extremism, *Abu Hamza: Guilty: The Fight Against Radical Islam*, Redshank Publishing, 2014. It deals with the emergence of the jihadist cult in Europe since the 1990s.

2   E. A., Buller, op. cit., Foreword.

3   Memorably captured in the Hans Fallada novel, *Jeder Stirbt fur sich allein*, published ironically in 1947, the year Cumberland Lodge was founded.

4   The SCM remains active on British university campuses to this day.

5   William Temple was Bishop of Manchester when he met Buller but was soon promoted to Archbishop of York and eventually the leader of the Anglican Church as the Archbishop of Canterbury from 1942 until his death in 1944. He was an important sponsor in a ruling class dominated by men.

6   Europe and in particular Russia were convulsed by revolution at the end of the war and many Russians, for example, sought exile in other parts of Europe. Amy Buller organized several conferences including one attended by leading Anglicans and Russian Orthodox exiles in St. Albans in 1927 and 1928.

7   It shouldn't be forgotten that the British Crown, which retained an important role in the British Constitutional settlement, was related by blood to both the Russian Tsar and the German Kaiser, and many deposed and exiled European monarchs sought refuge in the United Kingdom.

8   Buller visited Germany every year and retained strong friendships with a range of Germans right up to the outbreak of the Second World War in 1939.

9 There were many British diplomats and members of the Establishment who came to fear that the Versailles Treaty of 1919 placed too onerous a burden on Germany and that it would foment a sentiment of injustice amongst Germans, as the German negotiators never tired in pointing out. Lord Lothian, who became another Buller sponsor, was one such British diplomat and statesman.

10 Lord Lothian was British Prime Minister Lloyd George's principal private secretary from 1916 to 1921. He was intimately involved in the process of drafting the peace settlement at Versailles in 1919, of which Lloyd George was a principal architect.

11 Amy Buller Papers Collection, St. Antony's College, Oxford, private note from July 1936.

12 William Temple (1881–1942) was the Archbishop of York from 1929–42 and then the leader of the Anglican Communion from 1942 until his death in October 1944. He was Buller's closest mentor throughout his time as an Archbishop and she would always spend time with him each year. He wrote his own book *Christianity and Social Order* in 1942. It set out his vision for the post-war world. Without a doubt these views had a profound impact on Buller's work. A. D. Lindsay, who was the vice-chancellor of Oxford University, wrote the foreword to *Darkness over Germany*.

13 Part of the first group to attend the Studienwoche Englischer Wissenschaftler at the Berlin Kaiserhof in 1935 was Professor Roxby of Liverpool University, Professor J. Baillie of Edinburgh University and Professor Tom Finnegan of Magee. In 1936 Professor Charles Manning of the LSE joined Bishop Talbot and Professor J. H. Jones from Leeds University. All the visits were undertaken 'under the patronage of Dr. A. D. Lindsay the Vice–Chancellor of Oxford University and Dr. W. Temple, Archbishop of York'.

14 Taken from a speech given by Rosenberg on 3 September 1935 at the Kaiserhof. Rosenberg was the Nazi Party's chief priest

and philosopher and became a high-ranking official in the Nazi regime, convicted of crimes against humanity and hanged at Nuremberg in 1946.

15 One story has it that in order to fox those potentially listening to their conversations, the British spoke in smaller groups and even resorted to singing 'Auld Lang Syne' loudly to cover the conversation in the background. 'Auld Lang Syne' has been sung for generations as the song to see in the New Year in British homes. It raises a rather comic spectacle in the English mind.

16 Von Hoesch was the predecessor to staunch Nazi Joachim von Ribbentrop. Seen as hostile to Hitler he died in post, many suspected under the strain of the Nazis lack of diplomatic sophistication. He resolutely failed to toe their line. He was a career diplomat who was well regarded in Britain and was constantly at odds with the Nazis once they took power. Curiously, he was the only German to be given a Royal Horse Guards and Coldstream Guards send-off when his Nazi flag–draped coffin was returned to Dresden in Germany on 14 April 1936 via the port of Dover on the British destroyer HMS *Scout*.

17 Ribbentrop was never much liked as an ambassador in London. He was not a trained diplomat and used his knowledge of the world as a commercial traveller to establish himself as an expert within the Nazi Party. He was seen as a failure by many Nazi leaders but had the favour of Hitler. It was his catastrophic advice to Hitler in 1939 – that Britain would not declare war in order to protect Poland – that persuaded Hitler to invade that country.

18 Letter to von Ribbentrop dated 29 July 1937, Amy Buller Collection, ibid.

19 Lord Lothian was a career diplomat. He died in office in 1940 whilst he was the British Ambassador to Washington. He made it his business there to tell the Americans they had a duty to support Britain in its fight against Nazism. He had been a great sponsor of the Anglo-German discussion groups that Buller championed and she sought his advice regularly

in correspondence. His country mansion at Blickling Hall
was used on several occasions to host more informal meetings
between high-ranking Nazi officials and British intellectuals
who had formed part of the Buller parties to Berlin. The last
of these was held in July 1939, just five weeks before war was
declared. Lothian was clearly a sought-after interlocutor by the
Nazi high command, and by Ribbentrop in particular when
he became ambassador to London from 1936 onwards. Von
Ribbentrop later became Hitler's Foreign Secretary.

20 Letter to Frank Pakenham from Amy Buller, 13 August 1938, St.
Antony's Collection, ibid. A similar party was to visit Blickling
Hall in July 1939.

21 Adolf Rein was the Nazi director of Hamburg University.
After the war, based on his former association with Buller, his
sister pleaded on his behalf for her help in interceding with the
occupation authorities after his dismissal. Letter to Amy Buller,
17 June 1946. Amy Buller Collection, St. Antony's, op. cit. In
2015 Hamburg bestowed a PhD on a Jewish student who had
been denied the chance to defend her 'brilliant' thesis because of
Rein's regime.

22 Buller's letter to Adolf Rein, 28 September 1938. Sent two days
before the Munich agreement was signed, bringing temporary
respite to the threat of war. St. Antony's Collection, ibid.

23 Chamberlain made his claim of 'Peace for our time' on 30
September 1938 after signing the Munich Agreement with Adolf
Hitler. This has long been seen in Britain as the moment the
Nazis were appeased and is considered a low point in British
diplomatic history.

24 Fuhrerin Scholtz-Klink, as she was called, was imprisoned after
the war and remained an unrepentant supporter of National
Socialism in writing and interviews until the 1980s. She died in
1999.

25 British historians refer to this period between the invasion of
Poland in 1939 and the Battle for France in May 1940, when

Germany launched its Blitzkrieg, as the 'phoney war', because there were no serious military actions on the Western Front.

26 In my wife's hometown of Leamington Spa in the English Midlands a memorial for the murdered of Lidice is still maintained.

27 Talk given by Amy Buller on 23 May 1942, St. Antony's Collection, ibid. Buller remained in tune with what was happening in Europe through meetings with exiles like the Dutch theologian Willem Visser 't Hooft who used his Geneva home as a base for European resistance groups and became a prominent international churchman after 1945.

28 Buller, E. A., (1943) *Darkness over Germany*, London: Longman, p.2.

29 Buller, E. A., Lecture Notes, op. cit. Buller uses the term Cabinet to refer to the key instrument of executive government in the British constitution, where the Prime Minister is *primus inter pares* in a ministerial committee called the Cabinet.

30 Ibid.

31 Sereny, G. (2000). *The German Trauma: Experiences and Reflections: 1938–1999*, London: Allen Lane.

32 James, W. op. cit., p.64.

33 In her author's preface Buller writes obliquely: 'It will be evident why I can say no more ...'

34 Appeasement is a diplomatic policy of making political or material concessions to an enemy power in order to avoid conflict. British Prime Minister Neville Chamberlain was accused of this in his policy towards Nazi Germany between 1937 and 1939.

35 Queen Elizabeth is the mother of Her Majesty Queen Elizabeth II and was the wife of King George VI of the United Kingdom who held the throne until he died in 1952. She is more popularly known today as the Queen Mother. Cited in James, W., op cit.

36 Letter from Amy Buller to Queen Elizabeth, 6 March 1944, cited in James, W., op cit., p.54

37   When I was researching Amy Buller, I had a chance conversation with a member of the British Royal family who knew Buller and remembered her as a single woman who had devoted her life to public service and remarked that women like Buller are 'not made like that any more'.

38   James, W. (1979). A short account of Amy Buller and the founding of St. Catherine's, Cumberland Lodge (unpublished manuscript courtesy of Lord David Ramsbotham), p.43.

39   Buller, E. A. (1942). Lecture Notes, op. cit.

40   It is equally true that the British working class who supported the Left took a defiant stand as early as 4 October 1936 in the Battle of Cable Street, where pitch battles were fought with Moseley's 'Blackshirts', who chose provocatively to march through the most Jewish area of East London. After multiple arrests the Metropolitan Police were accused of protecting the fascists.

41   Sebastian Haffner was a celebrated anti-Nazi German journalist who exiled himself in London during the war. He later returned to Germany in the 1950s. His book, *Germany: Jekyll and Hyde*, was published in 1940 in London during the 'phoney war' and was republished in 2005. It is a deeply personal attack on Nazi Germany and much more analytical than Buller's later offering.

42   Walter, J. (1979). A short account of Amy Buller and the founding of St. Catherine's, Cumberland Lodge, quotes Dr. Kathleen Bliss's account that 'she had had a de-conversion experience and become completely convinced that Christianity was untrue and she could not be a Christian'.

43   Buller, E. A., op. cit., p.196.

44   Buller, E. A., op. cit., Foreword.